Medicine, Health and Society

SAGE has been part of the global academic community since 1965, supporting high quality research and learning that transforms society and our understanding of individuals, groups, and cultures. SAGE is the independent, innovative, natural home for authors, editors and societies who share our commitment and passion for the social sciences.

Find out more at: **www.sagepublications.com**

Medicine, Health and Society

A Critical Sociology

Hannah Bradby

Los Angeles | London | New Delhi
Singapore | Washington DC

First published 2012

SAGE Publications Ltd
1 Oliver's Yard
55 City Road
London EC1Y 1SP

SAGE Publications Inc.
2455 Teller Road
Thousand Oaks, California 91320

SAGE Publications India Pvt Ltd
B 1/I 1 Mohan Cooperative Industrial Area
Mathura Road
New Delhi 110 044

SAGE Publications Asia-Pacific Pte Ltd
3 Church Street
#10-04 Samsung Hub
Singapore 049483

Library of Congress Control Number: 2011930658

British Library Cataloguing in Publication data

A catalogue record for this book is available from the British Library

ISBN 978-1-4129-2073-5
ISBN 978-1-4129-2074-2 (pbk)

Typeset by C&M Digitals (P) Ltd, Chennai, India

CONTENTS

ACKNOWLEDGEMENTS

Many people have encouraged and provoked this book into existence. I would like to thank Gillian Bendelow, David Bradby, Gill Green, Gillian Hundt, Helen Roberts, Stuart Robertson and Jai Seaman.

I am grateful to colleagues with whom I have developed ideas through joint writing, especially Helen Minnis, James Nazroo, Tarani Chandola and Waqar Ahmad.

Serving time as a conference convenor and journal editor has informed my sense of what constitutes the sociology of health and illness, both as a group of people and as a critical practice. I acknowledge my debt to the British Sociological Association Medical Sociology Group and the editorial board of the journal *Sociology of Health & Illness*.

PROLOGUE: SOCIOLOGY, MEDICINE AND MEDICAL SOCIOLOGY

INTRODUCTION

Do all disciplines fret over the state of their own intellectual and policy-relevant health? Is it a symptom of our hyper-reflexive and confessional times that collective anxiety has to be rehearsed over the track record, and present and projected performance of a group of scholars? Medical sociology's lengthy reflections on the state of its own practice are recognizable as part of a more general trend, whereby the certainties of bodies of knowledge and the limits of disciplinary boundaries have been undermined in the light of post-structuralist thought. As sociology examines the social construction of various forms of knowledge, in particular socio-cultural contexts, how could its practitioners avoid turning the analysis on itself? Sociology's particular interest in the social nature of human endeavour and the ideological bent and constructed nature of progress and achievement renders the discussion of disciplinary origins, limits and prospects particularly hard to grasp. But that's not a reason for not trying.

Medical sociology is a reflexive area of academic endeavour which has devoted a large number of words to considering its own origins, legitimacy, progress and potential. Since the contested moment of its inception, medical sociology has struggled for legitimacy on account of its ambiguous outsider status with regard to both sociology and medicine (Bloom, 2002: 25). In the process of establishing itself as a distinct area of theoretical and empirical research, medical sociology has fretted over its relationships with both medicine and sociology, regarding neither as taking its own claims to expertise sufficiently seriously. Horrobin likened medical sociology's situation between two unsympathetic existing disciplines to sitting at the 'interstices between the citadel of medicine and the suburb of sociology' (1985: 95). Horrobin caricatures medical sociology as in the throes of an identity crisis, beset by self-doubt and failing to emulate the imperialist tendencies of sociology's territorial expansionism. The citadel and the suburb are simultaneously medical sociology's competitors, and its parents, although the precise nature of medical sociology's conception (or misconception) is disputed as part of the discussion of its place in academic and practitioner worlds. One outcome of the identity crisis was a shift away from a sociology focused on medicine and towards a broader sociology of health, illness, healing and medicine, which describes the wider remit of current work.

MEDICAL SOCIOLOGY AND ITS RELATIONSHIP WITH SOCIOLOGY

If Horrobin was correct and medical sociology has (or had) an identity crisis, perhaps it is simply following the example of its parent discipline, sociology. Writing in the late 1950s, when sociology was an even younger discipline than it is today, C. Wright Mills diagnosed a widespread uneasiness – intellectual and moral – about its direction of development (Mills, 2000 [1959]: 19). Such uneasiness was still in evidence two decades later, with Philip Abrams (1981) asking whether British sociology was in total collapse and John Urry (1981) suggesting that sociology was an essentially parasitic discipline. In seeking to characterize the discipline, Abrams pointed to an argumentative mixture of self-doubt and self-importance, while John Urry saw all innovation as originating beyond sociology's boundaries, from philosophy and cultural studies. A certain critical discontent is an inadequate disciplinary demarcation of sociology, and certainly not one that permits an assessment of medical sociology's role therein. It has been claimed that there is no essence of sociological discourse beyond a commitment to the idea of the interdependence of individuals and social groups (Urry, 1981). Horrobin states that to speak of 'sociology' is 'nonsensical reification' and the practitioners of sociology do not represent a unified view, being as they are 'riven by dissension' (1985: 96) as to what sociology might be for. The disunity or diversity of the sociological approach has been seen as a cause of its disciplinary decline, despite its 'distinguished lineage and tradition', due to its lack of relevance to policy-making (Horowitz, 1994: 3). Sociology's lack of disciplinary coherence (Collins, 1990) is interpreted by others as a virtuous willingness to get involved with the conceptual messiness that more fastidious and prestigious disciplines disown (Beck, 1999: 123).

Sociology's lack of theoretical unity applies also to medical sociology, with its equally 'eclectic character' (Riska, 2003). Again, there is little disagreement on the diversity (or disarray), only on what, if anything, should be done about it. Elianne

Riska (2003) sees sociological research into health and medical sociology as similar to any other social activity in its culturally embedded nature, and therefore the eclectic nature of the discipline is predictable as a result of sociology's development in a variety of cultural settings. Sociology is an argumentative discipline in which no single theoretical framework holds sway, instead new ones arrive to overlap with the existing array (Abrams, 1981), giving rise to a lack of unity of analytic perspective that characterizes both sociology and medical sociology (Gerhardt, 1989: xxii).

Despite sociology's characteristic diversity of approach, it is possible to outline limited features that qualify as typically sociological. C. Wright Mills described sociology as offering insight into the historical and social connections between personal troubles and larger issues in the social structure (Mills, 2000 [1959]). The systematic study of social institutions, their constituent social roles and norms and their effect on individual behaviour and practice describes sociology as a research practice. The classical statements of sociology from the founding fathers (Marx, Weber, Durkheim, Tocqueville, Comte, Simmel) describe religion, the law and labour relations as the structures which shape people's experience of society.

This commitment to refer back to the classical statements of the founding fathers and to engage with a progressive politics, which imagines a more egalitarian, more humane society is characteristic of sociology. The overt political agenda of sociological enquiry requires, to a greater or lesser extent, that the practitioner adopt a campaigning, advocacy role in combination with the position of detached, analytic scholar. As Burawoy puts it, there is a sense of the 'passion for social justice … that drew so many of us to sociology' (2005: 26). This dual thrust towards progressive reform and the development of knowledge, brings about a tension between objectivity and advocacy (Bloom, 2002: 24) that is a central part of sociology's legacy to medical sociology.

When the foundations of sociology were being laid in the nineteenth century, medicine and healthcare were not institutionalized and not yet a statutory responsibility. In considering the experience of the 'common man' in a society undergoing rapid urbanization and industrialization, the founding fathers did not recognize the well-being of individuals as a matter of academic interest. Furthermore, they did not identify how crucial a player medicine was to become, both in conveying the benefits of the scientific revolution to the populace and in developing the commercial possibilities of medical technology. Health and healthcare were not considered to be key aspects of social integration and cohesion during the time that sociology was defining its own disciplinary territory. Health and illness were not headline issues in the developing sociological purview and, furthermore, they were considered profane in comparison with the sacred matters worthy of academic study: the law, labour and religion (Gerhardt, 1989: xiii).

This lack of reference to health and medicine from the founding fathers has led medical sociology to question whether its problematic is sufficiently connected with the classical questions of sociology. Rather than berating sociology's founders for failing to foresee how the expansion of medicine's influence would develop into a statutory and commercial–scientific powerbase, medical sociologists have sought to recover the seeds of an interest in the work of Marx, Weber and Durkheim.

Turner reminds us that sociology developed in opposition to the dominance of social Darwinism, with Marx and Engels seeking to reject the survival of the fittest as an ideological distortion and bring into focus the meaning and interpretation of the social actor (Turner, 1995 [1987]: 7). The aim of asserting the active, strategic nature of members of society did not engender an interest in the sick and disabled, with their compromised ability to act, and their (perceived or enacted) passivity. For Marx and Engels, morbidity and mortality were indicators of capitalism's effects on the class as a whole rather than a way of understanding the experience of individual bodies (Gerhardt, 1989: xv). Durkheim's work on suicide is sometimes upheld as evidence of an early interest in matters of health, but of course he was primarily interested in a demonstration that sociological forms of explanation were powerful enough to explain social facts autonomously without supplementary recourse to psychology or philosophy (Turner, 1995 [1987]: 7). Suicide was taken as an example of a social fact, indicating social cohesion or its failure, rather than being an index of mental health.

The absence of medicine from the classical legacy has hampered medical sociology's sense of legitimacy with regard to the wider field of sociology. Early theoreticians' lack of interest in medicine as an institution shaping the nature and structure of society, gives medical sociology 'an aberrant character' when compared with sociology's core fields (Cockerham, 1983: 1514; see also Ruderman, 1981). The long-standing sense of medical sociology's illegitimacy within the sociological project is refuted by Uta Gerhardt's assertion that medical sociology is actually a 'legitimate offspring, if not a vital part, of … general sociology' (1989: xxix). Similarly, Bryan Turner insists that a coherent, integrated and relevant approach to medical sociology exists which 'draws on the classical legacy of sociology' (2004: ix), despite the lack of statements from the founding fathers.

The neglect of medicine in the nineteenth century means that the birth of medical sociology is usually said to have taken place in the 1950s, when the study of social expectations that defined the sick role was conceptualized and the doctor–patient relationship studied as a social system in which colliding worlds required regulation (Parsons, 1951). Parsons' work made medical sociology academically respectable, conferring 'intellectual recognition' and 'academic credence' (Cockerham, 1995: 10) because of the links that could be made back to the thinking of Durkheim and Weber. Parsons' approach has been hugely influential in defining a theoretical medical sociology in ways that can be interpreted as negative as well as positive. Since Parsons' main interest was in deviance, his focus was on the social aspects of medical consultations, their management and performance, which, arguably, led to a subsequent neglect of the experience of being ill and the content of medical knowledge (Ruderman, 1981; Cockerham, 1983).

While Parsons' 1951 statement of the functionalist understanding of doctors and patients provoked enormous discussion within sociology and the establishment of medical sociology in the USA, subsequent contributions to the sub-discipline from structural functionalists have been rare (Scambler, 1987: 2). In the absence of their further development, Parsons' structural functionalism and systems theories gave way to labelling theory, phenomenology and ethnomethodology, which characterized the 1960s. Goffman's work, in particular, promoted interplay between sociology and medical sociology, with his 1961 analysis of total institutions in *Asylums* developing theoretical insights for those interested in institutions in general and hospitals in particular. Interactionism was criticized by the conflict theorists of the 1970s but since then, according to Cockerham (1983: 1518), no new theories have emerged to rival Parsons, Becker, Friedson and Goffman (an assessment which depends on regarding post-structural research as offering a new method rather than a new theory). Gerhardt, for instance, suggests that Foucault's ideas do not even constitute a new approach, but should rather be viewed as a form of cultural relativism which amounts to a modified version of conflict theory (Gerhardt, 1989: xxvi). Those who are more persuaded by the analytic novelty and acuity of Foucault's archaeology of knowledge in demonstrating the shifts in regimes of power, argue that sociology itself has its origins in early medical surveys. Rather than medical sociology being an applied sub-discipline of sociology, medicine is, in this view, applied sociology (Turner, 1995 [1987]: 7).

Nineteenth-century writers such as Engels and Marx did not see themselves as (only) sociologists and were, crucially, part of the reform movement that campaigned to ameliorate the conditions of the urban poor. The measurement and mapping of inequality in terms of rates of morbidity and mortality by social class, gave rise to the legacy of sociology as well as that of public health and social medicine, demography and epidemiology. This empirical work demonstrating the links between poverty, deprivation and low life expectancy that underpinned the reform movements can be claimed as medical sociology's intellectual genesis, thereby conferring an intellectual pedigree that pre-dates Parsons' work (Turner, 2004: xvi). Yet such empirical work has not always been claimed as the rightful ancestor of medical sociology: Illsley refers to 'isolated sociological contributions' to the study of health and medicine, relating them to the debate on the socio-economic condition of the working class, wherein mortality and fertility are simply indices of inequality (Illsley, 1975: 64). The rejection of the study of inequality as an

insufficiently sociological task indicates complexity as a key sociological characteristic, an issue to which we return below. A lack of research sophistication in the
study of inequality may also have been relevant to medicine's failure to develop a
systematic understanding of how social factors relate to morbidity and mortality
from the basis of the pioneering nineteenth-century work. The rapid growth of
medical bacteriology and germ theory distracted medical attention from the social
environment as a causative factor in disease (Bloom, 2002: 19). Furthermore, the
establishment of the NHS and the welfare state in the mid-twentieth century
represented what was thought to be a lasting solution to the health problems associated
with poverty that social reformers had highlighted, and may have reduced research
interest in inequalities for a time.

According to one version of medical sociology's development, it is an unclaimed
offspring: too theoretically impoverished for sociology and lacking in scientific or
technological glamour for medicine. This version has been challenged as a 'founda-
tional myth' whose primary effects are to create a canon and strategically maintain
disciplinary boundaries. For Fran Collyer, the notion that, prior to Parsons, sociology
was 'largely devoid of human reflection on the experience of life, death, healing, or
bodily health', is an 'origin myth' aimed at securing disciplinary legitimation and
enhancing the processes of professionalization (Collyer, 2010: 87). Through 'a brief
reanalysis of some of the texts' of early sociologists, Collyer demonstrates that
throughout the nineteenth century, while biomedicine was in the process of emerging
as a dominant institution, 'sociology offered a continuous critique of the narrow and
reductionist conceptions of human well-being' (2010: 92). That these interventions
from the likes of Weber and Durkheim are not reflected in what Collyer calls con-
ventional histories of medical sociology is attributed to 'the institutional power of
medicine, and prevailing discourses of health, disease and mortality' (2010: 88–9).
Collyer states that the founding fathers' interests in health and medicine have come
to be widely underestimated in the recounting of sociology's early formation. This
'mis-reading of history' was due, not only to the rising dominance of biomedicine
during the first half of the twentieth century, but also to 'the newly professionalizing
discipline of sociology' seeking to establish its own distinct canon (Collyer, 2010: 95).
So, although the 'classical founders' of sociology were actively interested in debating
matters of health, disease and mortality and offered useful theoretical frameworks,
Collyer suggests that:

> these early theories of health, disease and mortality were discounted and overlooked
> in the reframing of the sociological project after the 1920s when sociologists ceded
> ground to the authority of the new experimental sciences and biomedicine. This
> occurred as a consequence neither of a sociological consensus, nor of a political or
> professional conspiracy. Instead the new conceptual frameworks of biomedicine

became the lens through which sociologists, writing in the new genre of the student text, came to select appropriate 'founders' and 'classic works' for the discipline, define the 'essence' of sociology and its landscape, and offer an interpretation of the past. (Collyer, 2010: 102)

The rival myth of medical sociology's origins traces descent from social medicine, public health, epidemiology and sociology. While medical sociology is a largely post-Second World War phenomenon in the USA, its origins in France, Germany and Britain can be traced back to the late eighteenth-century study of social aspects of disease under the auspices of social medicine and public health (Scambler, 1987: 1). The extent to which the institutions of biomedicine and the experimental sciences have shaped sociology and medical sociology have, according to Collyer (2010), been underestimated. Her reading suggests that sociologists involved in establishing the discipline in the mid-twentieth century were:

forced to accept the newly reformulated conceptions of health and disease, and reorder their knowledge base to avoid conflict and inter-disciplinary rivalry. One of the previously unacknowledged consequences of efforts to side-step this potential conflict was the separation of theories of health, disease and mortality from the mainstream of sociology, and the emergence of distinct origin myths for each subfield. (Collyer, 2010: 102)

Whatever the combination of historical and developmental factors that account for its divergence from sociology, some commentators see medical sociology as increasingly accepted by sociology (Turner, 1995 [1987]: 8), to the extent of having established itself as an independent specialism. In this view, medical sociology has developed from being something of a pariah in orthodox sociology to having achieved a separate, distinct status, cemented by contributing substantially to the development of mainstream sociological theory and methodology (Illsley, 1975: 67). However, the fact that such assertions have been repeated periodically for the last several decades, indicates an uncertainty in their veracity.

In 1978, the state of medical sociology as a sub-discipline was described as 'one of great activity, but little theoretical or methodological unity' (Stacey and Homans, 1978: 281). Yet for Cockerham, echoing Illsley, it has been medical sociology's increasing tendency to use sociological theory to promote the explanatory power of empirical findings that has amplified its connections with general sociology (2001: 4–5). This claim is taken further by Turner's confident assertion that medical sociology is at the leading edge in contemporary social theory (Turner, 1992). Perhaps a more common view is that sociology continues to treat medical sociology with some suspicion due to its close collaboration with the institution of medicine as sponsor and gatekeeper. This suspicion has been articulated in accusations of medical sociology being atheoretical and 'merely' applied.

THEORY AND APPLICATION

The accusation of the 'theoryless empiricism' stems from the assumption that much medical sociological research comments on public policy which has been formulated by the same agency that sponsors the research (Cockerham, 1983: 1514). The theoretical inadequacy of medical sociology, as judged by social theorists, potentially indicates that its collaboration with medicine has been insufficiently critically independent. Medical sociology has been described as failing to contribute to general sociological theory in any significant manner (Johnson, 1975) and British medical sociologists' attempts to theorize the discipline have been deemed at least partially motivated by a desire to 'enhance the faltering theoretical reputation of the applied subfield among mainstream sociologists' (Wegar, 1992: 964). There are echoes here of British sociology's perceived failure to contribute adequately to the nineteenth- and twentieth-century development of the discipline as compared with American, German and French thinkers, and related debates about British sociology's intellectual adequacy (Renwick, 2012).

A comparative analysis of the main sociology and medical sociology journals has shown that the theoretical interests of published medical sociologists are more limited than their sociologist peers, and that this is more marked in British than American journals (Seale, 2008: 692). The best-known medical sociology theorists have been largely American-based, including Parsons, Goffman and Straus. The precipitate post-war establishment of the NHS perhaps meant that UK social scientists became quickly involved with research into the practicalities of a national organization that moved from laudable aspiration to policy to actuality. The enormous popular support that the NHS has from the British populace has perhaps also constrained the range of theoretical questions about models of healthcare delivery that can be asked or that can be researched.

The question of whether medical sociology is sufficiently theoretical is not a dispute that can be resolved, since the answer depends on the relative evaluation of theoretical and empirical work. For some, the (alleged) applied, empirical character of medical sociology is no bad thing. Cockerham (1983) states that medical sociology is primarily an applied subject, dependent on medicine, and that cooperation with medicine is desirable, as long as the sociological perspective and objectivity is unimpaired, since sociology's contributions have to have some basis in the reality of medical practice if they are to be accurate and relevant. This, of course, assumes that medical sociology's prime objective is to comment on and improve health services, rather than to develop theoretical models of medical aspects of the social world. Bloom (2002) hopes to retain a dual thrust at the heart of medical sociology, towards both progressive reform and the development of knowledge, thereby keeping 'a tension between objectivity and advocacy' (2002: 24). The dual thrust is evident in Straus' much cited division between a sociology in medicine, which researches problems on medicine's terms, and a sociology of medicine that interrogates medicine as a sociological problem (Straus, 1957). Freidson (1970) sees medical care as a key focus for medical sociology with the study of the coming together of knowledge, staff and patients in 'concrete settings' as crucial to evaluating medicine's social worth. For Freidson, the 'special position of the medical man is … justified by his effective per-formance of practical ameliorative tasks rather than by his contribution to abstract knowledge', and therefore the study of the practical work undertaken in hospital settings is a crucial task for medical sociologists to evaluate the prospects for future improvements (1970: 32–3).

SOCIOLOGY AND MEDICINE

How close is the relationship between medicine and the sociological study of med-icine and how close should this relationship be? Is medical sociology's relationship with medicine sufficiently critical?

A sociology of medicine clearly has to have a close relationship with medicine and no medical sociologist, however critical, wishes to see an absolute divorce from medicine, but the recommended nature of collaboration varies. Freidson (1983: 219) suggests that we should be standing right outside medicine looking in, to give a critical, dispassionate analysis, whereas Straus (1957) recommends a chameleon-like insertion into medical settings. The problem with the chameleon-sociologist is that she or he might take on medical values which should, more properly, be under critical scrutiny. The presumption that all medical work is good since it relieves human suffering is one that sociologists have been accused of accepting uncritically, leading them to avoid critical analyses that might under-mine the assumption that medicine works in the best interests of humanity (Cockerham, 1983). Furthermore, medical sociologists may bask in reflected glory, identifying strongly with the medical mission and justifying sociological work in the same terms. Gill and Twaddle suggest that this danger is exacerbated by the number of assumptions that sociology shares with medicine, such as a positivist approach that looks for technological solutions, an exclusive focus on the European experience, and a conviction that medicine is beneficial and to some degree 'sacred', the most noble of professions (1977: 382). Particularly in the US context, medicine has used some of its power to sponsor and develop medical sociology (Cockerham, 2001: 4), which fuels suspicion of a lack of critical distance. Perhaps the blinding of sociologists to the more problematic aspects of medicine was hard to avoid during the golden age of medical advance through the 1940s and 1950s, but now that biomedicine is wrestling with the complexity of multiple causation (Turner, 2004: xxvi), the long-term social costs of medical work should stand in stark contrast to the benefits.

Medical sociology is accused of suspending its critical judgement due to the need to gain access to data and the desire to be accepted as a relevant health-related discipline (Gill and Twaddle, 1977: 382). Suspending a commitment to a sociological perspective results in sociologists treating 'medical categories as unproblematic, rather than as historico-social constructions meriting analysis in their own right' (Scambler, 1987: 3). Critical suspension can be exacerbated by a tendency to be employed by the very institutions that have commissioned the research (Cockerham, 1983: 1514). A sociologist of medicine working in close collaboration with medics, potentially experiences 'role strain' and, with a worsening fiscal context for the health services, medical sociology's tendency to apply sociological insight to medically defined questions becomes more pronounced (Morgan et al., 1985) as funds for more theoretical work evaporate. Scambler (1987) sees the close collaboration of sociology with medicine as damaging, not only in terms of the questions that sociology can ask, but also in the development of sociology's analytic purchase. He points to the dominant epistemological approach of science, termed 'systematic empiricism', as hindering the development of sociological insight into relationships between social structure, processes and health (Scambler, 1987: 4). Others have described how the biomedical establishment has symbolically expropriated medical sociology, not for its specific research findings, but 'for the concepts and generalizations which help them define and express their agenda' (Wegar, 1992: 964). This tendency to incorporate sociological perspectives into the medical project has sometimes enhanced biomedicine's public image without necessarily enhancing medicine's social responsibility in the long term (Wegar, 1992).

Medical sociology, particularly in the UK, has perhaps paid a price for enjoying the close patronage of medicine in terms of a degradation of the quality of research that the discipline pursues. While medical sociology's post-war expansion to become the largest sub-discipline of sociology owes much to its close relationship with medicine, excoriating critiques of medical imperialism have, nonetheless, developed at the same time (Scambler, 1987: 2). Cockerham states that, compared with the situation in the 1970s, sociology no longer depends on physicians for its practice, having 'evolved into a mature, objective and independent field of study and work' (1995: xi) and that it has 'removed itself from a subordinate position to medicine' (Cockerham, 2001: 4). By the 1970s, Illsley (1975: 66) was announcing that sociologists have access to medical settings and can formulate their own research problems without pressure to service the interests of medicine. The shift away from a medical focus was reflected in the disciplinary nomenclature which took hold from the 1980s, referring to a sociology of (some combination of) health, illness, disease, healing and medicine, rather than simply medical sociology.

US medical sociology has been seen as better insulated from and therefore more independent of medicine, compared with Britain, because US sociology became established as an independent academic field earlier (Cockerham, 1983: 1520; Bloom, 2002: 42). In this view, medical sociology starts out being in the service of medicine, but then evolves an increasingly autonomous practice allowing a more equal collaboration. This evolutionary process is portrayed as more highly developed in the USA than in the UK, to the extent that American medical sociology has achieved a state of independence allowing it to investigate applied health situations on socio-logical terms (Cockerham, 1983: 1519). But British sociologists have nonetheless claimed a maturity of their discipline with research 'no longer dependent on the goodwill of a few innovative physicians' (Illsley, 1975: 67). Concluding a survey of influential papers published in a key journal, sociological independence from medicine is confirmed by David Armstrong:

> Despite its affinity with (and often subservience to) the dominant medical empire, the sociology of health and illness has succeeded in establishing its own roots with its own agenda that is amply demonstrated by a quarter century of publications in *Sociology of Health and Illness*. (Armstrong, 2003: 72–3)

While the sociological study of health and medicine is well established in terms of academic publications and taught courses, a testy relationship between medicine and sociology, characterized as a 'struggle for legitimacy' (Bloom, 2002: 25), persists. While Bloom considers this struggle to derive from the overlap between medicine and sociology, particularly around public health, preventative medicine and psychiatry, others see the similar concerns of sociology and medicine as offering grounds for a rapproche-ment (Nettleton, 1995). Socio-demographic shifts in the disease burden from acute to chronic and increasing life expectancy, with a concomitant change in emphasis from curing to caring and towards preventative medicine with a focus on lifestyle factors, increasingly delivered in community settings, have made routine medical practice more sociological, according to Nettleton (1995: 11). Shifts in the style, content and location of the practice of medicine are, in part, due to medicine's response to sociological critiques and challenges such that, for instance, patients' views and their socio-economic context are increasingly being considered in the process of healthcare provision (Nettleton, 1995: 12). Medicine needs a sociological approach to ensure the ongoing relevance of its practice in an evolving social world. Given the enormous preoccupa-tion with empirical results which characterizes the medical approach to illness, the distinctive sociological attention to identity and 'the inter-relationship between the individual and the broader society – their interactions, their mutual constitutiveness', together with a 'conceptual invention and creativity', is salutary (Armstrong, 2003: 72). A sociological medical practice is one which Turner considers would be holistic, progressive and humanistic (1995 [1987]: 10), thereby, presumably, avoiding the problems that his criticism identifies elsewhere. Sociology is in a position to recognize the important contribution medicine makes to our lives while remaining alert to the negatives in the political and the moral domain (Turner, 2004: xv).

The differences between sociology and medicine are, of course, as important as the common interests in defining the relationship between the two. Gerhardt reminds us of the distinct nature of medicine and sociology as practices with different virtues and vices: 'Clinical work is practice and therefore case-bound and situationally specific, whereas sociology is an analytic science and a reflection on societal matters of which medicine may make use' (Gerhardt, 1989: 351). While some aspects of medicine are indeed clinically based and conceptualize disease as a matter of individual bodies invaded by germs and disorder, sociology's view of disease as a social fact has allowed it to ask questions about social action and the character of social order (Turner, 1995 [1987]: 17). But approaches that see disease as a social fact are not confined to sociology, being shared by public health, general practice and a plethora of other disciplines. The multiplicity of disciplines investigating social and cultural aspects of health, illness and medicine raises further questions about sociology's role.

INTERDISCIPLINARITY AND MULTIDISCIPLINARITY

Sociology is not alone in considering the social and cultural dimensions of health and illness, indeed the field is becoming positively overcrowded. The large number of disciplines, sub-disciplines and inter-disciplines, including cultural studies, sociology, the sociology of health and illness, medical anthropology, the history of medicine, and discourse analysis, have, according to Deborah Lupton merged 'in the wake of the poststructuralist and postmodernist movements' (2003: 3). Since sociologies, anthropologies, histories and cultural studies of medicine, health and illness share both 'intellectual tradition and trajectory' based on similar 'trends and developments in social theory', there is very little to distinguish them from one another, according to Lupton (2003: 6). This view could be character-ized as typical of a cultural studies approach, missing, as it does, the distinctive and systematic approach to power, the relations between individual and state, between biography and history, which sociologists feel to be their distinctive contribution. Moreover, since the history of academia could be characterized by the arbitrary setting of boundaries 'separating each discipline from the others' (Kaplan, 2007: 99), the post-structuralist claim that disciplinary boundaries no longer exist is no more than a post-modernist inversion of this long-standing disciplinary policing, whereby a group of scholars claims territorial rights to comment, in this case on the lack of territorial boundaries. The balkanization of disciplinary politics has drawn comment from sociologists of health and illness, usually as part of an appeal for a more interdisciplinary approach to study.

Support for the emergence of an interdisciplinary model that gets beyond the balkanized boundaries in sociological studies of health and illness has been linked with the desire to avoid 'disciplinary dogmatism' (Macintyre, 1996: 901). Calls to translate research findings across disciplinary boundaries, thereby facilitating administrative and professional action in response to research (Clair et al., 2007), are related to an aspiration to methodological diversity and international reach. Such developments are often presented as having the potential to reinforce the existence of a coherent sub-discipline, an approach that is 'truly sociological' (Blaxter, 2000: 1140), although Macintyre's plea to avoid disciplinary dogmatism may acknowledge that greater interdisciplinary could imply the disappearance of sociology. Within the crowded field of health sciences, sociological approaches are presented as offering a breadth of method and approach that other disciplines need (Clair et al., 2007: 250).

> Sociology can be at the center of an integrative network of a broad range of practitioners rather than somewhere toward the bottom of a scientific hierarchical structure, where our ideas are seen as intellectually lacking in real, relevant and relational ways. (Clair et al., 2007: 257)

The rationale for sociology becoming the lynchpin discipline within studies of health and illness is unclear from Clair and colleagues' account. For a sense of the centrality of sociology as a distinct discipline within the broader social sciences, we could refer to Michael Buroway's assertion that the 'social sciences are not a melting pot of disciplines' (2005: 24). He nominates civil society, and hence the sociology which depends upon it, as 'the best possible terrain for the defense of humanity – a defense that would be aided by the cultivation of a critically disposed public sociology' (Burawoy, 2005: 25).

Thus, for Burawoy, sociology amounts to an active defence of humanitarian values, the absence of which lead to 'Stalin's Soviet Union, Hitler's Germany, Pinochet's Chile' (Burawoy, 2005: 24). Sociology is defined by its study of a variety of topics 'from the standpoint of civil society' (Burawoy, 2005: 24) that draws on 'a century of extensive research, elaborate theories, practical interventions, and critical thinking, multiple understandings, reaching across common boundaries, not least but not only across national boundaries, and in so doing shedding insularities of old' (Burawoy,

2005: 25). Burawoy offers sociology as a disciplinary site where humanitarian values are established and hence defended but suggests that, in doing this, we need to cut across national boundaries and become less insular. Insularity is perhaps an inevitable outcome of defending a boundary and Clive Seale sees it as attendant upon British sociologists' focus on the production and refinement of social theory leading to a 'somewhat introverted sociology' (Seale, 2008: 692). Medical sociology has a certain parochialism in its relative lack of interest in the social relations of health beyond the Anglophone world.

Burawoy's call to public sociology seeks to galvanize sociologists around a progressive social project and asserts sociology's distinctive and particular character. In the more applied field of the sociology of health and illness, the diversity encompassed by sociological approaches can be seen as an advantage, since interesting advances often play out on the interdisciplinary boundaries.

> Indeed, much of the exciting work in recent decades in relation to health is that which is at the interface of sociology and/or social geography, health economics, health psychology, social epidemiology, health policy and, of course, anthropology. The boundaries between the disciplines are blurred but nevertheless the interactive effect of disciplinary engagement can give rise to novel ways of producing, 'seeing' and interpreting data. (Nettleton, 2007: 2411–12)

Sociology's close association with medicine has perhaps led to its borrowing medicine's mission statement and a sense of the righteousness of the medical endeavour for sociological research. And the righteousness of that mission perhaps chimes in with Burowoy's sense that sociology constitutes a defence of humanitarian values in the face of medicine's untamed excesses. Medical sociology, as a close observer of medicine's own dispersal and the balkanization of its subsidiary parts, knows that a lack of unity in practice, theory or method has not impeded medicine's disciplinary professional progress.

The contested nature of health sociology's interdisciplinarity pertains to how medical sociology, sociology and medicine relate to one another and to the broader project of a sociology of health, medicine and society. Excessive attention to our own boundaries potentially reinforces an introverted academic insularity, but can also be seen as part of the critical project of our research. The challenge of avoiding disciplinary and geographic introversion, to make our research internationally relevant offers progressive possibilities, but also perhaps the end of a sociology of health and illness as a recognizable organizational entity in universities and research programmes. Perhaps it goes without saying that the possibilities of progressive social change that the sociology of health and medicine offers in examining systems of power and subjectivity in a globalized world are more important than the disciplinary allegiances of the researchers.

REFERENCES

Abrams, P. (1981) 'The collapse of British sociology?', in P. Abrams, R. Deem, J. Finch and P. Rock (eds), *Practice and Progress: British Sociology 1950–1980*. London: George Allen and Unwin. pp. 53–70.

Armstrong, D. (2003) 'The impact of papers in sociology of health and illness: a bibliographic study', *Sociology of Health & Illness*, 25, Silver Anniversary Issue: 58–74.

Beck, B. (1999) 'The future of sociology', *Sociological Inquiry*, 69(1): 121–9.

Blaxter, M. (2000) 'Editorial – Medical sociology at the start of the new millenium', *Social Science & Medicine*, 51: 1139–42.

Bloom, S. (2002) *The Word as Scalpel: A History of Medical Sociology*. Oxford: Oxford University Press.

Burawoy, M. (2005) 'Presidential address: For public sociology', *American Sociological Review*, 70(1): 4–28.

Clair, J.M., Clark, C., Hinote, B.P., Robinson, O., Caroline, A. and Wasserman, J. (2007) 'Developing, integrating, and perpetuating new ways of applying sociology to health, medicine, policy, and everyday life', *Social Science & Medicine*, 64: 248–58.

Cockerham, W.C. (1983) 'The state of medical sociology in the United States, Great Britain, West Germany and Austria: applied vs pure theory', *Social Science and Medicine*, 17(20): 1513–27.

Cockerham, W.C. (1995) *Medical Sociology*, 6th edition. Englewood Cliffs, NJ: Prentice-Hall.

Cockerham, W.C. (2001) 'Medical sociology and sociological theory', in W.C. Cockerham (ed.), *The Blackwell Companion to Medical Sociology*. Malden, MA: Blackwell. pp. 3–22.

Collins, R. (1990) 'The organizational politics of the ASA', *The American Sociologist*, 21(4): 311–15.

Collyer, F. (2010) 'Origins and canons: medicine and the history of sociology', *History of the Human Science*, 23: 86–108.

Freidson, E. (1970) *Professional Dominance: The Social Structure of Medical Care*. New Brunswick, NJ: Transaction.

Freidson, E. (1983) 'Viewpoint. Sociology and medicine: a polemic', *Sociology of Health and Illness*, 5: 208–19.

Gerhardt, U. (1989) *Ideas About Illness: An Intellectual and Political History of Medical Sociology*. Basingstoke: Macmillan.

Gill, D.G. and Twaddle, A.C. (1977) 'Medical sociology: what's in a name?', *International Social Science Journal*, XXIX(3): 369–85.

Goffman, E. (1961) *Asylums*. Harmondsworth: Penguin.

Horowitz, I. (1994) *The Decomposition of Sociology*. Oxford: Oxford University Press.

Horrobin, G. (1985) 'Medical sociology in Britain: true confessions of an empiricist', *Sociology of Health and Illness*, 7: 94–107.

Illsley, R. (1975) 'Promotion of observer status', *Social Science and Medicine*, 9: 63–7.

Johnson, M. (1975) 'Medical sociology and sociological theory', *Social Science and Medicine*, 9: 227–32.

Kaplan, H.B. (2007) 'Self-referent constructs and medical sociology: in search of an integrative framework', *Journal of Health and Social Behavior*, 48: 99–114.

Lupton, D. (2003) *Medicine as Culture*, 2nd edition. London: Sage.

Macintyre, S. (1996) 'Change of editorial structure at *Social Science & Medicine*', *Social Science & Medicine*, 43(6): 901–2.

Mills, C. Wright (2000 [1959]) *The Sociological Imagination*. Oxford: Oxford University Press.

Morgan, M., Calnan, M. and Manning, N. (1985) *Sociological Approaches to Health and Medicine*. London: Croom Helm.

Nettleton, S. (1995) *The Sociology of Health and Illness*. Cambridge: Polity.

Nettleton, S. (2007) 'Editorial: retaining the sociology in medical sociology', *Social Science & Medicine*, 65: 2409–12.

Parsons, T. (1951) *Social Systems*. New York: The Free Press.

Renwick, C. (2012) *British Sociology's Lost Biological Roots: A History of Futures Past*. Basingstoke: Palgrave Macmillan.

Riska, E. (2003) Review article: 'Developments in Scandinavian and American medical sociology', *Scandinavian Journal of Public Health*, 31: 389–94.

Ruderman, F. (1981) 'What is medical sociology?', *Journal of the American Medical Association*, 245: 927–9.

Scambler, G. (1987) 'Introduction', in G. Scambler (ed.), *Sociological Theory and Medical Sociology*. London: Tavistock. pp. 1–7.

Seale, C. (2008) 'Mapping the field of medical sociology: a comparative analysis of journals', *Sociology of Health & Illness*, 30(5): 677–95.

Stacey, M. and Homans, H. (1978) 'The sociology of health and illness: its present state, future prospects and potential for health research', *Sociology*, 12: 281–307.

Straus, R.M. (1957) 'The nature and status of medical sociology', *American Sociological Review*, 22(April): 200–204.

Turner, B. (1992) *Regulating Bodies*. London: Routledge.

Turner, B. (1995 [1987]) *Medical Power and Social Knowledge*. London: Sage.

Turner, B. (2004) *The New Medical Sociology*. New York: Norton.

Urry, J. (1981) 'Sociology as a parasite: some vices and virtues', in P. Abrams, R. Deem, J. Finch and P. Rock (eds), *Practice and Progress: British Sociology 1950–1980*. London: George Allen and Unwin. pp. 25–38.

Wegar, K. (1992) 'Sociology in American medical education since the 1960s: the rhetoric of reform', *Social Science and Medicine*, 35(8): 959–65.

1
INTRODUCING THE SOCIOLOGY OF MEDICINE, HEALTH AND SOCIETY

In the face of scientific medicine's failure to offer a technique to regulate nature, we remain confronted with the inevitability of sickness, ageing, suffering and death. The democratic welfare state, which offered such hope of health for the masses, has failed to eradicate inequalities and deliver universal social justice in a national setting, and inequity in social life appears inevitable. Sociology retains a conviction that suffering in all its complexity should be kept at the heart of human society's common concerns (Fassin and Reechtman, 2009: 153). However, the means of moving beyond just witnessing or representing the suffering of others, and yet remaining in sociological territory, sometimes seems elusive (Bradby and Hundt, 2010). While globalization and new mobilities are key to our social futures, the networked nature of trans-global suffering has proven difficult to research. Healthcare systems are organized on a national basis and constitute an important part of the imagined or actual bond between the state and the citizen. The prospects for theoretically complex, methodologically robust research addressing questions that breach national boundaries and disciplinary norms seem poor at a time when global economic recession is severely limiting the funds available for speculative and sociological research.

Auguste Comte's suggestion that sociology constitutes the 'Queen of the Sciences' (Comte, 1896) because it includes and integrates all the other sciences and relates their findings into a cohesive science of human society remains an aspirational potential. However, this depends on an ability to encompass methods and material that stretch from the aesthetics of suffering to the influence of corporations on global health, without being distracted by disciplinary politics.

This book surveys the main areas covered by the sociology of health, illness and medicine in order to assess the ongoing significance and likely future direction of the field. The main research problems that are addressed through the course of the book can be described as follows:

1   Inequalities in rates of morbidity and mortality along various dimensions of stratification, particularly socio-economic class, gender and ethnic group;
2   The embodied aspects of experiencing illness, disability and pain and the ways that the body as a cultural object problematizes biomedical models of the body;
3   The organization of healthcare in a national welfare system in which the interests of capital, patients and professionals are all operating in mutual and contradictory ways.

Sociological theory as a means of analysing the social relations of health, illness and medicine is important to the field's disciplinary claims. Chapter 2 sketches out theoretical developments from Talcott Parsons' functionalism and its early role in defining the focus of medical sociology, through the development of conflict theory, interactionism and phenomenology, to the ideas of post-modernity and post-structuralism. While studies of health, illness and medicine often have implicit rather than explicit theoretical models, social theory remains a distinguishing feature when surveying the field of health studies. The implicit nature of many theoretical concepts is apparent in the body of work on health inequalities, discussed in Chapter 3. The undeniable social injustice of mortality and morbidity rates being structured by socio-economic class has meant that theoretical interrogations of the problem have been less common than studies mapping the inequalities and interventions aimed at reducing them. The relationship between socio-economic stratification and mortality levels has been well documented in British and some other European states and comparative analysis has offered clues as to the mechanisms underlying the inequalities. The issue of global disparities in mortality rates points up the centrality of gender as a social variable and shows the necessity of its consideration in conjunction with socio-economic classifications.

Chapter 4 traces the development of feminist questions about the social relations of health and illness. While the days when gender was invisible in sociological research are long gone, there are still ways in which gendered ideology renders women's illness invisible or, paradoxically in some cases, hyper-visible. For instance, women's rates of heart disease remain under-counted due to cultural assumptions about the interpretation of their symptoms, and yet with respect to, for instance, children's health, women are highly visible in that mothers' responsibility for the health of their offspring is presumed. The emergence of a field known as men's health offers interesting parallels to the development of feminist approaches to women's health in terms of identifying the vulnerabilities of a group defined by sex and/or gender. The limits of feminism, in terms of accounting for men's health and for global, gendered health problems, point to other dimensions of stratification. Chapter 5 gives an account of how ethnicity and racism have developed as part of the public health agenda in the USA and the UK, and the limitations that have emerged from everyday and scientific conceptions of difference and diversity. Studying the stratification of health outcomes by class, gender and ethnicity has been central to the development of a social model of health – a multi-disciplinary process in which sociology has played a key role – and which has presented a sustained challenge to a reductionist view of health as an absence of disease.

Chapter 6 considers another major aspect of sociology's critique of medical conceptions of health, with an account of the body and embodiment. Considering the body as a cultural object that is socially negotiated shows the ways in which medicine misses crucial aspects of illness and of suffering. Medical models of the body, its constitution in internal organs, its enhancement and capture in technological terms, can all be understood as part of bio-power – the statutory management of bodies through the technology of public health. The subjective and lived experience of pain, disability and the negotiation of medical treatment have had to be approached or recovered by using alternative methods, such as narrative, poetics and visual methods.

Chapter 7 gets to grips with the context in which medicine is practised in terms of professional, statutory and commercial structures and their interplay with patients' and professionals' values. The dynamics of the mutual and competing interests of corporation, state and professional bodies have been studied to the extent that sociologists have described the rise (and fall) of the medical profession in specific cultural settings, but it has not proved possible to make more general theses. In the final chapter, we revisit the main research problems that the book has covered and speculate regarding the future directions of the sociology of health and medicine.

As an aid to the reader, the Glossary gives the reader a brief definition of various terms used in the text. Sociology often makes specialized use of words that feature in other professional vocabularies and/or in everyday language, and so some indication of the intended meaning can be helpful. The Glossary is not meant to give finally conclusive, authoritative or definitive statements, but rather to offer indicative definitions to support the discussion in the main text.

REFERENCES

Bradby, H. and Hundt, G. (2010) 'Introduction', in H. Bradby and G. Hundt (eds), *Global Perspectives on War, Gender and Health*. Avebury: Ashgate. pp. 1–17.

Comte, A. (1896) *The Positivist Philosophy of Auguste Comte* (trans. H. Martineau). London: George Bell & Sons.

Fassin, D. and Reechtman, R. (2009) *The Empire of Trauma: An Inquiry into the Condition of Victimhood*. Princeton, NJ: Princeton University Press.

2

SOCIAL THEORY AND THE SOCIOLOGY OF HEALTH AND MEDICINE

INTRODUCTION

Given the broad and eclectic nature of the sociology of health and medicine, any account needs to attend to the substantive research topics as well as the theoretical frameworks that have underpinned or justified the approach to research. As noted in the Prologue, theoretical frameworks derived from sociology (an inherently fragmented discipline [Johnson et al., 1984]) predominate in the sociology of health and medicine. Furthermore, the problem-solving orientation and hybrid disciplinary nature of much research relevant to medical sociology, with its strong empirical tradition, means that a theoretical position is not always explicitly described in published research. Researchers have often taken a very pragmatic approach to theory, picking elements that serve specific purposes. Despite its sometimes implicit and frequently fragmentary nature, social theory is nonetheless a key attribute of the sociology of health and medicine, and seen as distinguishing it from other social science approaches. This chapter sketches out the theoretical developments of the discipline from functionalism to realism, via interactionism, while subsequent chapters concentrate on substantive findings around particular research problems as outlined in Chapter 1.

PARSONS AND FUNCTIONALISM

The obvious place to start a survey of medical sociology is, of course, the beginning. And yet, as indicated in the Prologue, the beginnings of medical sociology are contested and there is dispute as to who were the key figures. Do we start with the mid-nineteenth-century reformers who recognized the statistical link between social position and rates of morbidity and mortality? Do we follow Foucault's suggestion and tie the origins of sociology to those of modern medicine and the emergence of anatomical, sociological and demographic bodies as objects of interest? Whether or not he is regarded as the founding father, there's no denying the significance of Talcott Parsons' work for the subsequent development of medical sociology as a body of research recognized by other disciplines. Parsons offered medical sociology an 'academic respectability by providing its inaugural theoretical orientation' in the shape of structural functionalism, calling attention to its potential as an area of sociological inquiry (Cockerham, 2007: 293). Parsons recognized the doctor–patient relationship as a social system built upon Emile Durkheim's interest in the societal norms, structures and processes which were beyond individuals and whose effect is social cohesion. Durkheim (1858–1917) viewed the fundamental social problem to be the limitlessness of human desires in the face of finite resources. He envisaged the resolution of this problem through the imposition of a framework of expectation that permits only attainable aspirations. When the framework fails to limit people's desires in line with the means to respond to them, Durkheim (1952 [1897]) termed the resultant discontented normlessness 'anomie'.

Talcott Parsons (1902–1979), influenced by Emile Durkheim, Max Weber and others, was interested in the maintenance of value consensus and its translation into a stable social order. Like Durkheim, the role of people's internalized self-control in maintaining a functional social order, was of particular interest. Parsons was committed to grand theory to unify a social scientific understanding of society's working under a single framework, which has come to be known as structural functionalism. Parsons' interests were wide ranging, taking in education, race relations and psychoanalysis, and his high-profile academic career as a faculty member of Harvard University, meant that his work attracted critical comment in his own lifetime, some of which he responded to.

Like Durkheim's explanations of suicide in terms of social facts, Parsons sought to analyse individual behaviour in the context of large-scale social systems and the link between the two was 'pattern variables' which structure any system of interaction. His interest in ill health was in terms of its influence on the wider functioning of society: high levels of illness and low levels of health being dysfunctional for society, preventing people from fulfilling their social roles (Parsons, 1951: 430). A certain level of good health in the population was, in Parsons' view, a key social resource for the efficient functioning of society, with medicine working to maintain this favourable level of health. The onset of illness was of interest to Parsons because it prevented the fulfilment of social roles, such as paid employment and parental duties, and he also conceptualized disease as motivated in some measure. The motivation to withdraw from social roles and to be cared for as a sick person is, in this model, countered by the medical practitioner. Where a person's ill health requires a relinquishing of normal social roles, he or she is expected to visit a doctor and this encounter involves a reciprocal set of obligations and privileges. The incapacitated person is offered a niche, termed 'the sick role', where usual expectations are lifted and he or she is permitted time off to recover. The sick role offers the privilege of bed rest and the suspension of domestic and employment duties, on condition that professional help is sought out and full cooperation is ceded to the physician. In return, the physician is reciprocally obliged to act in the patient's best interests and to offer technically competent care in an objective fashion. Writing in the USA, Parsons underlined that the patient's welfare, rather than personal or commercial gains through the profit motive, must inform the physician's actions towards the patient (Parsons, 1951: 435). Where doctors achieve the required affect, neutrality and technical competence in the skilful application of medical knowledge to their patients' problems, they are granted the freedom to behave as autonomous professionals, and have privileged access to patients' bodies in ways that would be taboo under other circumstances.

Parsons described an ideal type, delineating institutionalized roles of doctor and patient that were reciprocal, consensual and functioned to reduce the social costs of deviant illness behaviour, such as hypochondria and malingering. The doctor's official sanctioning of a state of illness discourages illegitimate claims to the privileges of the sick role and means that doctors and the medical diagnoses they make regulate access to sickness benefit, sick leave and treatment. Parsons saw the reciprocal obligation on the patient to make an effort to recover as the means whereby people were returned to the performance of their normal social roles as rapidly as possible, thereby reducing the harm done to the social consensus by illness. Blaxter (2004: 94) describes Parsons' theoretical proposition as: 'if the function of institutions is to maintain social stability, then these are the rules which are necessarily followed in the case of medicine'.

Parsons' interest in deviance was part of a wider preoccupation in the sociology of the time. Gerhardt sees the widespread nature of the interest in deviance as a legacy of the Second World War, during which boundaries of 'normal' and 'deviant' became blurred in civilian, as well as military populations. In the aftermath of the war, it became clear that the roots of Nazi thought which justified the extermination of various 'deviant' groups, were far more widespread than had been thought (Gerhardt, 1989: xvii). Gerhardt emphasizes the dual nature of Parsons' sick role, which encompassed not only the deviancy model focusing on the 'positive-achievement' motivated aspects, but also the incapacity model capturing the 'negative-achievement' aspects of illness (1989: 15).

CRITICISM OF PARSONS' IDEALIZED TYPE

As already noted, Parsons is credited with offering a theorized sociological approach to understanding the medical treatment of illness as a social encounter. The sick role has provoked theoretical and empirical further investigation and, as a result, has been much subject to criticism. The idealized typing of doctor and patient roles has attracted criticism for being too simplified to be a useful model of real healthcare encounters. Far from the consensual negotiated doctor–patient encounter of the ideal type, a patient's entry into the sick role can be a process that is both complex and fraught, and that is mediated by specific features of the illness and of the patient. The severity, the familiarity and the likelihood of recovery from the illness may influence how easily the patient is admitted to the sick role. Parsons' model envisages the sick role as a temporary one, and whether it is primarily seen as a state of deviancy or of incapacity, there is a presumption that occupancy of the role will be resolved by recovery from illness and a resumption of normal social duties. Of course, this timely relinquishing of the sick role may not happen when the illness is chronic rather than acute. There is an assumption in the model that the nature of the illness brought to the doctor is irrelevant since the professional's affect neutrality ensures the same treatment for all conditions. However, some conditions are highly stigmatized, to the extent that at certain times doctors have been unwilling to treat, for instance, people with HIV or those who have overdosed with illegal drugs. Thus, features of the patient's illness or incapacity are relevant to the ease of their entry to the sick role, as too are characteristics of the patient. Stereotyped ideas mean that some types of people find it harder to get their symptoms taken seriously than others. For example, Black people with sickle cell disease have found it difficult to obtain good palliative care when the condition's crises occur, in the face of twin racist assumptions, namely Black people's supposed poor tolerance of pain and exaggerated risk of opiate addiction. Whether stigma applies to the individual because of their gender or racialized group, or to the condition, because of its (assumed) method of transmission or self-infliction, there is enormous variation in how people and their symptoms are treated when they encounter physicians.

Another important criticism of Parsons' idealized sick role is the presumption of its universality. Parsons was not interested in illness as a bodily state, but focused rather on the regulation of the social roles involved, and there is an implicit assumption that with the onset of symptoms, people will adopt a passive, compliant role as a patient. A minority of people who experience symptoms seek a consultation with a doctor, with the majority self-medicating, consulting with others (family members, pharmacists, internet sites) or taking no action at all beyond waiting for the problem to resolve itself.

Parsons' model is asymmetric in terms of rights and obligations and it is conceived as working consensually, with patients complying willingly with their physicians' orders and submitting to their regimes of care. Conflict theorists saw this as an inappropriate characterization, since rather than being consensual, the tenor of the doctor–patient relationship can be highly conflictual. The inequality of power and the lack of common interest between doctor and patient means that patients' efforts to get professional help with illness is more akin to a struggle than a consensual playing out of mutually agreed roles.

Beyond the workings of the idealized sick role, Scambler notes two additional, general problems with Parsons' structural functionalism. First, he suggests Parsonian structural functionalism is described at such a level of generality that it defies testing or revision (Scambler, 2002: 15). Second, he points out that 'agency goes missing' in that individuals are conceptualized as 'over-socialized' (2002: 16). Some of these criticisms are explicable in terms of what Camic (1989) sees as a key goal of Parson's work – that is to defend sociology as an intellectual enterprise at a time when its future was in doubt. With a sociological analysis of the logic of 'The Structure of Social Action' (Parsons, 1937) in the social and intellectual context of the 1930s, Camic shows that Parsons was writing an extended manifesto to defend sociology's disciplinary expertise. In making this defence, Camic sees the strength of Parsons' book as a charter laying claim to the science of the socio-cultural realm for sociology, but this is also the root of some of the problems when extracting his conceptions of social action, social structure and social order to apply elsewhere (Camic, 1989: 94–5).

Why, despite these criticisms, does Parsons' idea of the sick role continue to attract the attention of medical sociologists seeking to re-evaluate his legacy for the sub-discipline (for example, Williams, 2005)? Parsons' insight is more than simply a starting point for others' criticism and investigation, since he manages to combine a rare range of approaches to illness within his model. Gerhardt (1979) underlines how Parsons' insights range from psychodynamic features of illness and healthcare, to inequalities in power and the regulation of deviance, thereby offering a structural view of the incapacitated person in the wider apparatus of society, without losing sight of the individual sick body interacting with a professional. Furthermore, while Parsons does not anticipate the intense interest in patients' life-worlds that characterizes much later research, his grasp of the system of healthcare was acute (Scambler, 2002: 16).

As important as the strengths of Parsons' ideal type have been, it is its weaknesses that have effectively provoked further research, thereby shaping the developing character of medical sociology. A number of the criticisms of the sick role described above can be grouped together under the general problem of Parsons' model being insufficiently critical of medicine (see Prologue). Parsons problematizes the patient's behaviour during illness and considers the physician's role in regulating that behaviour. The good conduct of the professionals and the utility of their work for both individual patients and for society remains under-interrogated, while the presumption of consensus in the relationship leaves the power inequality between doctor and patient equally uninvestigated.

Structural functionalism was swept away as the leading theoretical paradigm in the 1960s and 1970s. Functionalism emphasizes equilibrium and consensus, and although Parsons saw this consensus as fragile, functionalist explanations favour the ongoing dominance of the most powerful interests in society, and relegate individuals, especially marginalized ones, to a passive role. Structural functionalism left little place for theorizing individuals and was unable to explain how social change might occur. Symbolic interactionism, developing in reaction to structural functionalism, sought to explain social life as arising from the interaction of agents making independent interpretations of a situation, thereby giving individual perception and agency a more important role. Approaches that were more explicitly critical of medical power also gained prominence – theories which emphasized conflict and political economy, and that set about emancipating analyses of health and medicine from a biomedical model to lay bare the workings of power in routine medical settings. These theories of conflict and political economy are discussed in the next section, before returning to interactionism and phenomenology.

THEORIES OF CONFLICT AND POLITICAL ECONOMY

While Talcott Parsons' (1951) work on the sick role gave medical sociology a place in mainstream sociology, it was the work of Eliot Freidson (1952–2005) that gave medical sociology its critical dimension. *Profession of Medicine* published in 1970 defined the boundaries of medical sociology, suggesting how sociological perspectives on the practice and profession of medicine as well as on health and illness could be examined. By introducing a conflict perspective to the study of medicine and taking patients' perspectives seriously, the claims of the then powerful medical profession were interrogated. Freidson advocated a distinctive kind of medical sociology that applied structural perspectives to medical institutions and yet remained 'detached from medicine's own viewpoints and assumptions' (Conrad, 2007: 142).

Whereas structural functionalism views social hierarchy as a necessary, functional feature of a complex society wherein a universal value consensus ensures stability and social order, conflict theorists view competition between groups for scarce resources as the characteristic nature of social relationships. Social structures mean that access to resources is inherently unequal and those who benefit from the inequality will seek to maintain the hierarchy, and so conflict theorists anticipate that social change will occur through revolution rather than evolution. Blaxter (2004: 95) points out that conflict theory focuses attention on sources of ill health in the economic environment and on the competition of rival interests in the healthcare sector, and hence are preoccupied with the relationship between medicine and society. She suggests that this preoccupation has distracted research interest from the broader issue of the relationship between health and society. Political economy approaches to health have the class struggle for resources at the centre of analysis, and the influence of the approach has informed understandings of other social divisions as similarly conflict-driven. Conflict theory has shaped feminist medical sociological analyses of the sexist treatment of women by physicians and the disadvantaged position of women within the medical profession. Analysis of the medical division of labour and iniquitous patients' outcomes in racialized groups interrogates another system of privilege and power. While analyses that include class, gender and racism in a single analytic framework are an ideal, the tendency to collapse all systems of inequality back to a class-based understanding of power and inequality derives from the influence of the political economy approach to health.

A political economy approach emphasizes that under capitalism a person's relationship to the means of production is central to understanding not only their position in the hierarchy, but also their prospects of wealth and health. Research by Fredrich Engels (1820–1895) showed that the aetiology and distribution of the main diseases (communicable and incommunicable) are directly associated with the means of production (Engels, 1971 [1845]). This early social class mapping of disease incidence, pointed up the centrality of socio-economic structures to understanding people's living conditions, including their experience of illness, and indicated that individual medical intervention could not, of itself, hope to eradicate disease. The central insight of the political economy approach is to understand disease as socially produced and not, as the medical model would suggest, a result of the random occurrence of infection and environmental and congenital misfortune to luckless individuals.

Political economists of health describe how capitalism's relentless pursuit of profit is regularly in direct contradiction to workers' health and how medicine is entangled in the capitalist system through its statutory roles and its relationships with a range of industries. Under highly developed (or late) capitalism, where all dimensions of life are dominated by the unregulated market, the welfare state and national health service is left with the unenviable and, by definition, impossible job of solving the health problems created by the pursuit of profit. In view of the failure of state socialism in the former Soviet Union and its modification towards capitalist forms of trade in China, there seems to be no serious alternative economic system to rival capitalism (Waitzkin, 2000). Thus, any system of healthcare apparently serves to maintain the workforce for ongoing employment in a capitalist system. Physicians have been criticized on grounds of the professional dominance (for which they have campaigned) within the division of healthcare and the statutory responsibility that they hold to keep the workforce healthy for the smooth-running of the economy. However, the political economy view suggests it is unfair to hold the medical profession responsible for medicine's complicity in the capitalist oppression of workers. Physicians are merely the lackeys of capitalism, rather than the main authors of disaster. In this view, health is simply another arena in which capital can operate in pursuit of profit and the multiplicity of ways in which this can be done is breath-taking; from the big business of servicing clinical settings with personnel and equipment for cleaning and catering to pharmacogenetic products at the fore-front of big science.

Marxist ideas developed as a critical commentary on the expansion of industrial capitalism's project to transform raw materials into commodities with stable use-value that was changing the face of Northern European cities in the nineteenth century. Manchester, the city to which Engels moved to work in his father's company factory, like other British industrial centres, was being transformed with a sudden explosion of its population and little in the way of sanitary infrastructure. Hence the squalid conditions of the working classes, which stood in dramatic con-trast to the burgeoning wealth of industrialists. Marx referred to Engels' work to demonstrate the way in which capitalism ruined workers' health in its pursuit of profit. The damage done by industrial hazards and the risks which the owners of capital ran with their human and financial assets is understood to be an inherent part of the destructive nature of capitalist accumulation rather than an avoidable side-effect. Marx divided the population according to its position with regard to the ownership or otherwise of the means of production. Under this scheme, the great majority of the population of an industrializing nation were viewed as 'working class', and, like natural resources such as iron ore, they were exploited by the small minority who did not have to sell their labour because they owned and controlled society's productive assets, that is the factory, farmland or foundry. Those who cham-pioned public health reform, such as Engels, and Chadwick (1800–1890), who sur-veyed living conditions and marked their association with rates of mortality and morbidity, had benefited from family fortunes accumulated through the industrial revolution. In this respect, they were not disinterested parties in the development of capitalism, and argued in favour of reform in terms of the interests of the middle and upper classes being served by improving the health of the poorest: preventing malnutrition and disease among the working classes to ensure a more productive workforce. While Marx referred to the exploited alienated worker who 'mortifies his flesh and ruins his mind' (Marx, 1975: 326), his analysis was aimed at explaining the motor of world history and predicting changes in the stratified order of society, rather than the definition or solution of public health problems.

INEQUALITIES AND SOCIAL STRATIFICATION

That a person's position within the social hierarchy, as defined by labour market position and property relations, affects their life chances has been a central socio-logical insight, with theories of social stratification seeking to delineate the dimensions of this relationship and refine ways of modelling it. The observation that one's experience of illness and chances of premature death are related to one's position in the socio-economic hierarchy is central to the study of health inequalities (and explored further in Chapter 3). Marx saw a social class as a group of individuals who shared similar conditions and circumstances which might have an environmental impact on health, but also as a collectivity that shared a similar history and identified its common interests to some extent. An identification of group interests facilitates a class-consciousness which may lead to collective negotiation and hence action to ameliorate class interests.

The Marxist classification of people into workers and owners, while highlighting important historical changes arising from the industrial revolution, is too crude to be useful for the ongoing study of health inequalities. A materialist emphasis persists in the ongoing interest in class-based health inequalities, but it has been modified by a Weberian insistence that forms of status other than economic superiority should be considered in the measurement of social status. The main index of social stratification used by the UK's national statistics office is the 'National Statistics – Socioeconomic Classification' (NS-SEC) which considers the characteristics of a person's employment as well as their position in the labour market. This index seeks to capture whether or not the job is routine, skilled or professional and the extent to which it involves power over other employees, and in these respects is an improvement on its predecessor, the 'Registrar General Social Class classification', which relied on individual referees' rankings given to particular occupations of their 'general standing'. Despite the somewhat subjective nature of the Registrar General classification, throughout the twentieth century it nonetheless consistently demonstrated the inverse relationship between high social class and low rates of morbidity and premature mortality that Engels and Chadwick had identified in the nineteenth century. Alternative indices of socio-economic class, such as the Erikson-Goldthorpe scheme and the Cambridge scale of occupations, rely on different weightings for aspects of social, occupational and economic life. The ongoing research into the relationship between socio-economic differentials and health outcomes has not settled the issue of the extent to which aspects of income or of lifestyle associated with absolute or with relative poverty are responsible (see Chapter 3).

Recent controversies have centred on how relative poverty, that is, having basic requirements for food, clothing and shelter met but living near the bottom rung of a wealthy society characterized by inequality, potentially damages health through psycho-social influences on the immune system. The persistence of inequalities in mortality and morbidity, even as life expectancy in wealthy nations has consistently risen, suggests that competition for scarce resources is a better model of human society than the value-consensus cooperation imagined by structural functionalism. In a competitive environment, a key resource is the possibility of an extended and disease-free life. Measurement of inequality in mortality rates has been shown to be sensitive to the degree to which equality of opportunity characterizes a society: social democracies with redistributive central taxation and high quality provision of social services have smaller disparities in mortality rates between rich and poor compared with countries without policies of reallocating social resources through education, health and social care services. The importance of equality of opportunity and social cohesion for the well-being of individuals seems to go beyond an individual's interest in the functioning of social institutions such as hospitals and schools and has been described in terms of social capital.

Turner (2004: 13) defines social capital as the social investments of individuals in society in terms of membership in groups, networks and institutions, which serves to measure the extent of reciprocity in a society and the degree of trust. A high level of income inequality reduces social trust between citizens and thereby degrades the social environment and, hence, individuals' health. The mechanisms that cause high social capital to be translated into good measures of individual health are controversial, with various models of the appropriate role of state and citizen in contention. A materialist view suggests that high levels of income inequality relate to poor health outcomes because of consistent under-investment in infrastructure (including schools, libraries, hospitals, parks, housing) that sustains the population's well-being. An individualist psycho-social interpretation contends that the trust and cohesion that typifies an equitable society provokes a good psychological response from individuals which translates into good health (Kawachi and Kennedy, 1997).

Marxist theories have been subject to ongoing and exhaustive criticism with regard to their ability to analyse high modernity and its accompanying form of disorganized capitalism. The failure of state socialist models of the redistribution of wealth and the provision of healthcare in the former USSR has been seen as undermining the validity of a political economy analysis. However, the legacy of Marxist thinking can be seen in novel philosophical developments, such as critical realism (see Scambler's [2002] comments regarding Bhaskar's work). With regard to understanding health inequalities, political economy perspectives continue to be influential. Capitalist economic development has obviously changed dramatically from Marx's day, to become a global and highly fragmented system extracting surplus value from the production of knowledge and information and through the service industry, producing no tangible product. It seems indisputable that social class alone is no longer an adequate measure to understand the social divisions in a globalized world of unregulated capitalism. Income inequality and occupational category have to be understood in the context of integration and social cohesion, which can be seen as representing a combination of Weber's insights with those of Marx (Turner, 2004: 28).

However, it can be argued that capitalism has restructured to such an extent that the validity of any Marxist analysis is called into question. The centrality of commodity production to Marx's analysis of capitalism requires that the theory be considerably modified to analyse the production of services and products without obvious use-value but which are nonetheless traded. The neo-conservative economic revolutions of the 1970s altered the groupings of political solidarity such that people are increasingly difficult to define according to their class, occupation, family or geographic origins. Unregulated capitalism has created demand for goods such as mobile phones and designer sunglasses, whose value is defined not by their use function, but by their novelty, their designer tag as a mark of their provenance and the apparent authenticity of that tag. Consumer choice has taken on a huge importance, as people increasingly become defined by how they spend their money. This tendency has been accompanied by an individualization and reflexivity whereby the body and the self have become central projects to which money and time is devoted (see Chapter 6). This has important implications for health and illness as a fit, healthy and aesthetically attractive body has itself become commodified, both as something to be attained with the appropriate expenditure on personal trainers, clothes, plastic surgery, beauty therapy, etc., and simultaneously as something that has been marketed, exploited and sold as a commodity in itself. The emergence of the reflexive individual as a central social actor, in parallel with great upheavals in manufacturing, employment, class structure and the marketplace, has been accompanied by the reconfiguration of the relationship between the individual and society, to which we return at the end of this chapter.

INTERACTIONISM

As with the rise of political economy approaches, interactionism developed as a means of interrogating vested interests. Gerhardt relates the development of interactionist approaches to sociology as part of the political scene of the 1960s, whereby old orthodoxies were abandoned in the search for 'a more humane sociology' (1989: 75). While interactionism is recognizable as a widespread practice in sociology, it is not a coherent theoretical position in the same sense as the structural function-alism against which early interactionists were reacting. Developed from the work of George Herbert Mead (1865–1931), the central proposition of interactionism is that the self is a social product, dependent on interactions with and responses from other people. As creative and thinking beings, people can choose their own behaviour to a great extent. The interactionist production of the self is highly dependent on lan-guage as a means of gauging the reactions of others and reflecting upon the meaning of this interaction. Charles Cooley (1864–1929) devised a theory of the 'Looking Glass Self' (1964) that said people see themselves as they believe they are viewed by others. The socially constructed self is limited by the responses of others and the reflexive nature of the self means that people can manage their interactions so as to select preferred responses and manage the meanings of social encounters. Annandale (1998: 22) pinpoints the contradiction inherent in any interactionist encounter: how the individual both modifies and is modified by the social relations of health and illness in which she or he participates. This theoretical paradox is central to any interactionist encounter where that encounter constitutes both the location where human agency occurs but also the main impediment to its growth. While the tension of apprehending human agency within a structural context is not confined to inter-actionism, a focus on constraints on patient agency in medical encounters in inter-actionist research has shown how little power patients often wield. Much qualitative medical sociological research has promoted the patient's point of view in the patient–carer interaction, with a particular interest in exploring the turn-taking, negotiation and blocking that occurs during the course of medical work, and the means whereby professionals' priorities are asserted.

Gerhardt distinguishes two forms of interactionist model in medical sociology: crisis and negotiation models (1989: 89). The crisis model is associated with label-ling theory as exemplified by the anti-psychiatry movement which sees medicine as a dominant profession in the process of ascribing and validating a status such as 'mentally ill' (Scambler, 2002: 17). Gerhardt's negotiation model sees the inter-action between healthcare professional and patient as more open in the process of creating meaning: while professionals may dominate in defining the meaning of an interaction, the possibility of a consensual negotiated definition is at least mooted (1989: 90).

Goffman (1922–1982) offered a dramaturgical analysis of rule-governed encoun-ters between healthcare professionals and patients, and the ways that these perform-ances played out in a constrained but not entirely scripted fashion (Scambler, 2002: 18). While Goffman's work cannot easily be subsumed under a single theoretical perspective, influential aspects are close to Gerhardt's view of a negotiated version of interactionism. Interactionism is commonly criticized for having little to say with regard to social structures and as better able to analyse agency than structure: there is more capacity to analyse the life-world than the covert constraints of the structural features of systems.

PHENOMENOLOGY

Phenomenology offers another means of apprehending the social world, and therefore the world of illness, by interrogating how social reality is maintained. Harold Garfinkel (1917–2011) developed theories about how we constitute the everyday knowledge on which we rely into the practice of ethnomethodology, which concentrates on how we create and share social order but does not seek to validate these methods of production against an external benchmark. Garfinkel paid particular attention to what happens when the everyday routines of life which constitute reality are disrupted, noting that people's strong attachment to the rules that govern daily routine lead to a designation of rule-breakers as deviants. The analysis of talk between health professional and patient to ascertain how meaning is negotiated, resisted and achieved through interaction and speech has been an important contribution to medical sociology. Maurice Merleau-Ponty (1908–1961) has been a key phenomenologist for medical sociology because of his attempt to conceptualize soul and body as irreducibly fused, which has been taken up by those seeking to theorize our 'being-in-the-world' through the body's habitual relationship with the wider world.

Gerhardt (1989: 196) points out that the phenomenological view only conceptualizes illness as trouble, which, arguably, elicits one of two possible responses. First, the ill person can neutralize their environment and reduce their participation to avoid 'deviant' encounters with others or, second, the trouble can be diagnosed and dealt with by an expert. This view allows for consideration of how the clinical encounter is achieved, but does not offer space for consideration of how medical dominance happens, nor how it might be resisted. More generally, and in common with interactionism, phenomenology stands accused of paying insufficient attention to power, to hierarchy and, crucially, to diagnosing how current social structures might be overthrown or otherwise transformed.

MODERNITY AND POST-MODERNITY

The theoretical frameworks outlined so far can all be associated with enlightenment thinking, a philosophical movement which emphasized the systematic application of reason as a means of understanding the world. The age of enlightenment has been defined in contradiction to the tradition, superstition and tyranny characterizing the preceding dark ages. Progress through the rational application of reason and the rise of the self-determining individual have been central motifs, crucial in the transformation from pre-industrial to industrial society and from the pre-modern to the modern era. The structural functionalists, political economists, interactionists and phenomenologists were all seeking to understand modernity and the changed relationship between individual and society that the rise of industrial capitalism wrought. Modernity can be recognized by an idea of the world as open to transformation by human intervention, an industrial mode of production and a market economy encompassed by a nation-state together with an ethos of mass democracy (Giddens and Pierson, 1998: 94).

A question that has exercised sociologists is whether recent shifts in these features mark a break with modernity or a continuous development of its character, in other words 'late modernity or post-modernity?' The globalizing of commodity and money markets, of human migration streams, the end of the cold war and the emergence of new forms of community and status group have prompted some to suggest that we are in a post-modern age, while others have preferred the terms hyper-, high-, late- or super-modernity. While modernity has been characterized by its search for and trust in big truths, assumed to be of universal relevance, post-modernity is recognizable by its insistence on the deconstruction and querying of truth and an assumption that any socially accepted truth has been constructed in order to serve an interest group of some description. Enlightenment approaches to understanding the world assumed that appropriate levels of knowledge and understanding would be progressive in facilitating material well-being as well as a confidence in the nature of the world. By contrast, late or post-modernity is characterized by an intensification of reflexivity through which the individual and institutions examine and reform their own practice which, in the absence of fixed certainties, intensifies uncertainty.

Taking post-modernity as a label for what follows, modernity indicates that the critical deconstructive approach is a reaction to the failures of modernity. The mass killings associated with the Second World War and perpetrated by both sides (in particular at Auschwitz and at Nagasaki) were key moments in which modern values of progress and self-determination were seen to justify genocide. Theorizing the form and prospects for the development of modernity (or its disjunct) has been the territory of critical and literary theorists as well as sociologists. The theorist most closely associated with a post-modern approach in medical sociology, Michel Foucault (1926–1984), described himself as an archaeologist of knowledge and rejected the term post-modernist. Despite disagreement over whether we are currently in a new form of capitalism or a development of the old form, there is consensus that classical notions of a single framework of truth, reason, identity and objectivity have given way to a complex, unstable, contingent, multiplicity of interpretations of what constitutes truth, identity and history, in which very little is taken for granted and nothing can be assumed to be universal.

SOCIAL CONSTRUCTIONISM

Social constructionism is arguably the most pervasive and influential legacy of post-modern theory. A constructionist view holds that knowledge or practice that is normal and taken for granted can be understood as a result of the particular power relations pertaining in that historical and social context. Understanding disciplinary knowledge as socially constructed in the context of a particular regime of authority has been the basis of a powerful critique of medicine, as exemplified by the work of Foucault. Foucault provided a means of analysing the medicalization of society by seeing the exercise of medical power as operating via diffuse and diverse local factors, rather than through a central or unified power structure. Foucault's work shows that power and knowledge ('savoir') are key to understanding medical institutions and how the moral character of disease catego-ries operates in quotidian settings. Foucault's interest in medicalization was part of a wider survey of 'the institutions of normative coercion' including the law and religion as well as medicine (Turner, 1992). Foucault's analysis of institutional discipline over individual behaviour through medical systems of surveillance, placed medical sociology as less marginal to the concerns of a broader sociological project.

Of course, the work of sociology itself can also be understood as a construction, or interpretation of signs and symbols, against which there is no external measure of intrinsic, fixed validity. The deconstruction of the truths of sociology has been taken up enthusiastically by feminist scholars analysing binary divisions between male–female and masculine–feminine as a powerful construction that defines a class of women apart from men. The binary social construction of gender creates an expectation of false opposition, such that men are assumed to have more in com-mon with other men than with women, and features that are associated with mas-culinity cannot then be associated with women and the feminine. Feminism has built on this insight across all areas of sociology, including medical sociology, such that gender has become an almost routine dimension of sociological enquiry (see Chapter 4). Taken-for-granted norms around sexuality, race, disability and age have been successfully and convincingly exploded by taking a social constructionist approach to understanding marginalized groups as constructed through highly partial value judgements being promoted as neutral, often with the support of medical authority.

POST-STRUCTURALISM AND STRUCTURALISM

This deconstructionist effort, sometimes called post-structuralism, constitutes a reaction to the widespread influence of twentieth-century structuralist thought, as initiated by the work of Ferdinand de Saussure (1857–1913) in linguistics and developed in the analysis of cultural systems by anthropologist Claude Lévi-Strauss (1908–2009). Saussure's work envisaged a linguistic system as a series of different sounds combined with a series of different ideas in which it was held that an independent signifier was superior to that which it signified. Lévi-Strauss saw universal laws as governing the symbolic elements of culture such that diverse practices, from food preparation to myth-making, could be related to the same cultural structures. Structuralism views social meaning as a product of signification, a universal process which makes up a stable, self-contained system that constrains discourse and hence the individual's potential for social action. A structuralist approach emphasizes the distinction between biological signs and their meaning within a medical system, giving rise to research into the process of diagnosis whereby people come to be defined as ill and take on the patient role. Deconstructionism developed by those now referred to as post-structuralists (Michel Foucault, Louis Althusser, Jacques Lacan, Julia Kristeva) was a response to the problems of structuralist thought as having an essentialist ahistorical view. Thus, the realities of, for instance, truth and beauty are assumed in structuralist terms to be apprehended through stable, signifying systems that correspond with systems of human thought. Post-structuralism overturns a structuralist view of humans as sacred, metaphysical beings wherein lie meaning and value, to replace it with culturally and symbolically constructed subjects in which meaning is constructed by difference and the signifier and signified are not united in a single meaning system and so need to be studied separately. Post-structuralists rejected the idea that universal rules organize social phenomena and introduced the possibility that users of language were motivated in particular directions.

Social constructionism has a powerful ability to undo assumptions which has had a liberating effect on specific interest groups, for instance by showing the situatedness of racist or sexist ideology and demonstrating the racialized or gendered interest groups that such ideas serve. The work of Foucault, and those who have developed his ideas, has sought to explicate the social construction of bodies (Turner, 1992; Shilling, 1993) and emotions (James and Gabe, 1996) with an approach that emphasizes the role of power and knowledge in shaping the body's evaluation. Scientific medicine, like any other knowledge system, is seen as an ideologically inflected product of the society in which it arises and, as such, in a radical version of constructionism, has no inherent merit over and above any other knowledge system. Foucault identified two trends in his investigation of medical practice: medicine of the species which classifies, diagnoses and treats states of disease; and the medicine of social spaces which seeks to prevent disease. The medicine of the species defined the human body as an object of study and intervention, while the medicine of social spaces defined public health as subject to surveillance and regulation by civil and medical authorities. Feminist theoretical approaches in medical sociology have drawn on post-structuralism to critique the medical regulation of women's bodies, emotions and diseases and to show how this has systematically served male interests.

CRITICISM OF CONSTRUCTIONISM

The political and ethical nature of social constructionism has been heavily criticized, to the extent that one authority has declared the failure of post-modern theory, at least within medical sociology (Cockerham, 2007). If all forms of knowledge are equally plausible interpretations of the signs and symbols around us, how can we discriminate between oppressive forms of knowledge and progressive, egalitarian and humane understandings of the human condition? The intrinsic value of the knowledge itself for explicating our daily realities and its potential for creating a better, more just world are both, apparently, impossible to evaluate in a social constructionist view. A radical constructionist view would hold that the only reality with which we can work is that which is legible because of our cultural interpretations, thereby denying the significance or even the existence of a biological base. This view draws on evidence from areas where diagnoses are contested and pathologies ambiguous, such as depression or Repetitive Stress Injury (RSI), and so risks underestimating the real advances of modern scientific medicine and ignoring the global burden of contagious disease, which is most likely to be alleviated with biomedical methods. A radical constructionist view is ethnocentric in the sense that it is only tenable in a wealthy, democratic Western setting where poverty and disease do not (mostly) structure daily life.

Like structural functionalism, constructivism can hold an over-socialized view of the individual, leaving no scope for agency and the modification of context by actors. A more defensible view is a presumption that an external reality exists, but that our interpretation of, for instance, illness is powerfully affected by the cultural values we hold and therefore the meanings that we read into that illness for our own identities and the wider social order. This 'weaker' social constructionism might be justified by the philosophical position of critical realists such as Bhaskar (1979) who distinguish between the real world and the descriptions that we make of it. Critical realists argue that social constructionism fails to account for agency and structure and offers an over-socialized view of individuals, overplaying the constraints of structure. Critical realists conceptualize agency and structure as fundamentally distinct but interdependent factors that need to be studied to ascertain their distinct contribution to social practice. A key point for critical realists is to defend the idea that social systems are open to process and change and that people have the critical capacity to affect them (Archer, 1995). As a new theoretical formulation, critical realism has yet to make much impact within medical sociology. Nonetheless, the prefix 'realism', implying a perspective that claims objects, events and beings exist in the world externally to us and independent of our experience and conception, has become routine.

The huge interest in the sociology of the body and of narrative is perhaps a reaction to some of the extremes of social constructionism. Sociology of the body seeks to understand health and illness as an embodied, lived process that is embedded in the world, without denying the importance of the social and cultural aspects of the experience. The study of narrative in the sociology of illness has sought to connect the interpretation of bodily suffering to a human lifespan. Both narrative and the body can be seen as trying to re-humanize the study of illness, which, in seeking to deconstruct the humanist assumptions of the centrality of persons to meaning, has, perhaps, lost sight of humanity altogether. In a world that is constantly subject to deconstruction, the re-telling and reconstructing of personal and familial narratives and the assertion of this as an inalienably human activity is perhaps a restorative or even redemptive reaction.

CONCLUSION

Ultimately, the interest of the theoretical positions outlined in this chapter lies in their ability to offer critical perspectives on the relationship between people's experience of illness, seeking healthcare and their place in wider social structures. The biggest factors in seeking to understand these social processes hitherto have been the inequalities in social position and the institution of medicine. Despite enormous changes since medical sociology emerged as a distinct area of sociology, in terms of the configuration of social and economic hierarchies and the statutory and commercial roles played by medicine, in many ways its core interests remain unchanged. Ever since Parsons' time, sociologists have sought to understand the regulation of health and illness in terms of the individual and the wider social order.

Questions of balance between developing theoretical frameworks and pursuing empirical enquiry (raised in the Prologue) crystallized in the accusation that medical sociology is atheoretical and empiricist. Such a challenge, issued from a comparative perspective, should not, perhaps, provoke an absolute response. Strident assertions that 'Medical sociology has become a theoretical discipline' (Cockerham, 2001: 19) and 'The notion that medical sociology is atheoretical is wrong' (Cockerham and Scambler, 2010: 21) suggest an over-sensitivity about medical sociology's image in the academic world. While medical sociology indubitably debates and tests theoretical ideas, compared with some branches of sociology, it retains, by definition, an interest in questions that relate to policy, practice and lived experience. The interest in practice and policy has kept medical sociology abreast of the world of science and technology and of government, in terms of imagining possible futures and the ways in which they might alter our humanity with both social and individual terms of reference. Medical sociology's merit should lie in understanding the excitement of scientific and technological innovation without being dazzled by its salutary potential and keeping sight of its implications in terms of social justice.

REFERENCES

Annandale, E. (1998) *The Sociology of Health and Medicine: A Critical Introduction.* Cambridge: Polity.

Archer, M. (1995) *Realist Social Theory: The Morphogenetic Approach.* Cambridge: Cambridge University Press.

Bhaskar, R. (1979) *The Possibility of Naturalism.* London: Routledge.

Blaxter, M. (2004) *Health.* Cambridge: Polity.

Camic, C. (1989) 'Structure after 50 years: the anatomy of a charter', *American Journal of Sociology*, 95(1): 38–107.

Cockerham, W.C. (2001) 'Medical sociology and sociological theory', in W.C. Cockerham (ed.), *The Blackwell Companion to Medical Sociology.* Malden, MA: Blackwell Publishing. pp. 3–22.

Cockerham, W.C. (2007) 'A note on the fate of postmodern theory and its failure to meet the basic requirements for success', *Medical Sociology, Social Theory and Health*, 5: 285–96.

Cockerham, W.C. and Scambler, G. (2010) 'Medical sociology and sociological theory', in W.C. Cockerham (ed.), *The New Blackwell Companion to Medical Sociology.* Malden, MA: Blackwell Publishing. pp. 3–26.

Conrad, P. (2007) 'Eliot Freidson's revolution in medical sociology', *Health*, 11: 141–4.

Cooley, C. (1964) *Human Nature and the Social Order.* New York: Schocken.

Durkheim, E. (1952 [1897]) *Suicide: A Study in Sociology* (trans. J.A. Spaulding and G. Simpson). London: Routledge and Kegan Paul.

Engels, F. (1971 [1845]) *The Condition of the Working Class in England* (trans. W.O. Henderson and W.H. Chaloner). Oxford: Blackwell Publishing.

Freidson, E. (1970) *Profession of Medicine.* Chicago: University of Chicago Press.

Gerhardt, U. (1979) 'The Parsonian paradigm and the identity of medical sociology', *The Sociological Review*, 27(2): 229–51.

Gerhardt, U. (1989) *Ideas about Illness: An Intellectual and Political History of Medical Sociology.* Basingstoke: Macmillan.

Giddens, A. and Pierson, C. (1998) *Conversations with Anthony Giddens: Making Sense of Modernity.* Stanford, CA: Stanford University Press.

James, V. and Gabe, J. (eds) (1996) *Health and the Sociology of Emotions.* Oxford: Blackwell Publishing.

Johnson, T., Dandeker, C. and Ashworth, C. (1984) *The Structure of Social Theory*. Basingstoke: Macmillan.

Kawachi, I. and Kennedy, B.P. (1997) 'Health and social cohesion: why care about income inequality?', *British Medical Journal*, 314(7086): 1037–40.

Marx, K. (1975) *Karl Marx: Early Writings*. London: Penguin.

Parsons, T. (1937) *The Structure of Social Action*. New York: The Free Press.

Parsons, T. (1951) *The Social System*. New York: The Free Press.

Scambler, G. (2002) *Health and Social Change: A Critical Theory*. Buckingham: Open University Press.

Shilling, C. (1993) *The Body and Social Theory*. London: Sage.

Turner, B. (1992) *Regulating Bodies*. London: Routledge.

Turner, B. (2004) *The New Medical Sociology*. New York: Norton.

Waitzkin, H. (2000) *The Second Sickness: Contradictions of Capitalist Health Care*. Lanham, MD: Rowman and Littlefield.

Williams, S.J. (2005) 'Parsons revisited: from the sick role to ...?', *Health*, 9(2): 123–44.

3
HEALTH INEQUALITIES

While sociology's claim on Marx and Engels as founding fathers and its interest in social structures and the production and maintenance of social hierarchy are indisputable, the sociology of health and medicine, like its parent discipline, lacks a unity of analytic perspective (Gerhardt, 1989: xxii). Surveys often list the theoretical perspectives that can be shown to underpin or justify medical sociology's main approaches to research and the current book makes no claims to originality in this respect (see Chapter 2). The difficulty of using theoretical paradigms as the framework for an exploration of medical sociology is that the applied nature of much of the research reduces the prominence of the theoretical position adopted relative to other aspects of the work, such as practical applications of the findings. There are, of course, exceptional scholars, who develop theoretical and empirical work in tandem, but in the main, even where published research nods towards a theoretical framework, it is the social problem under investigation and pragmatic issues of access and method that determine the character of research to a greater extent than the researcher's theoretical assumptions.

While social constructionism has taught us to treat with suspicion any claims that knowledge is neutral and ideology-free, the focus on the nature of the research problem and the solution to social problems, especially where defined by medicine, has led to medical sociology's characterization as atheoretical and even empiricist. In lieu of a theoretical position, much sociological work around illness and death is motivated by a pursuit of social justice, and in particular the goal of equity of opportunity in healthcare and in health outcome. (A slightly less demanding goal is equality or equality of opportunity in healthcare and health outcome – see page 43 for a discussion of equity versus equality.) Where classes of people systematically suffer excess morbidity or mortality or where they receive a poorer health service, a desire to promote social equity is regularly given (and accepted) as sufficient justification of the description and analysis of the problem. This chapter considers the theory of inequality in morbidity and mortality, their conceptualization and measurement, before describing the patterns of inequality, explanations for their cause and approaches to reducing inequalities.

THEORY AND INEQUALITY

The documentation and description of health inequalities between socio-economic classes and between groups defined by gender, age, disability, sexuality and ethnicity, among other characteristics, has become a major area of research and one which is populated by a range of academic and practitioner specialisms including public health, demography, general practice, epidemiology, child health and social aspects of geography, statistics and policy, as well as sociology. Collaboration with disciplines that place greater emphasis on methodological than on theoretical innovation has contributed to the apparently dispensable requirement to explore theoretical dimensions of the problem of health inequalities. An influential text on the topic opens as follows: 'This book examines a simple fact: that at the end of the 20th century inequalities in health are extremely wide and are still widening in Britain' (Shaw et al., 1999: 1). The injustice of a group of people systematically enjoying more years of healthy life than another group due to a difference in class background requires no further definition as a social problem demanding attention. But, of course, for sociology, the topic of health inequalities constitutes a debate rather than a 'simple fact' and a debate that, at least for sociologists, is 'both empirical and theoretical' (Nettleton, 1995: 161). There are technical questions about the means of measuring both health and social circumstances that are empirical in nature, whereas the issue of how to explain the association between measures of health and measures of social position turns on theory.

For some sociologists, the considerable body of work documenting and interpreting health inequalities is notable for its lack of theoretical insight. Mortality and morbidity rates (subject to so much analysis for association with socio-economic variables) can be cast as simple indices of inequality, contributing little of conceptual merit to the broader field of assessing the socio-economic condition of the working class (Illsley, 1975: 64). Empiricism – whereby scientific knowledge is based only on testable statements – is often linked with positivist thinking that asserts that the only authentic form of knowledge is that which can be affirmed through scientific methods. Scambler distinguishes between three types of what he terms '(neo-) positivist' investigations designed, conducted and/or used by medical sociologists: accounting, explaining/predicting and advising (2002: 9). Accounting refers to the health surveys of formal and informal healthcare activities and ideas that have mapped out the landscape of medical sociology. Explaining and predicting are activities at a somewhat more abstract level, and, while constant or invariant patterns of events do not often obtain in the social world, 'demi-regularities' are more common. Scambler cites women's higher levels of self-reported morbidity compared to men's and Tudor Hart's (1971) inverse care law as contrastive demi-regularities typical of medical sociology (Scambler, 2002: 11). Such demi-regularities are said to provide evidence that certain relatively enduring and potentially identifiable mechanisms have been in play, but of course the identification of the demi-regularity does not amount to the identification of the mechanism itself. The commissioning of research to support the formation or implementation of statutory policy is styled 'advising' by Scambler and seen as excessively instrumental and system-driven (2002: 11). The insights garnered by the identification of demi-regularities are dubbed 'largely fortuitous' (Scamber, 2002: 12) and various flaws with the empiricist pre-suppositions of positivism apparently render it unsuitable as a basis for developing serious critical sociological thinking.

INEQUITY AND INEQUALITY

Another approach to making sense of the preoccupation with inequality in health, points out that the term 'inequality' has taken on a specific meaning in the context of the study of health and society. Observations of inequality in health are more than simply mapping a set of naturally occurring differences, given that health conditions differ between groups and individuals arising from genetic inheritance, gender, geography and chance in a potentially infinite array of combinations. Evidence with regard to social hierarchy and health shows 'a continuous gradient in health from the least to the most advantaged' such that the phrase '"inequality in health" has come to mean a special sort of difference' (Blaxter, 2004: 104), which can be recognized by the following characteristics:

- Socially determined – that is arising largely from social factors;
- Felt to be unjust – while some differences between groups are chosen or trivial, there is a sense that health inequalities are inequitable, immoral, and, importantly, potentially subject to change;
- Not inevitable – given our current technology and knowledge, these inequalities are thought to be avoidable and as further research suggests mechanisms of causation and maintenance, new reforms suggest themselves (Blaxter, 2004: 105).

Another way of expressing this would be to distinguish between 'inequalities in health' and 'inequities in health'. While 'inequality' refers to difference between groups without comment on the source of that difference, 'inequity' refers to a normative principle of social justice which considers the differences to be unfair and unjust to the extent that they are avoidable (Siegrist and Marmot, 2006: 5). If equity in health is an ideal whereby everyone has a fair opportunity to reach their full potential health, then social gradients in health contradict this principled distribution of human life chances. A problem with drawing this precise distinction between inequity and inequality in health is that we do not yet know the extent to which inequalities between individuals or between groups are avoidable and therefore iniquitous. Until we have a better sense of the extent to which the major chronic diseases are socially determined, the lack of precision in attributing their inevitable or avoidable nature encapsulated by the term 'inequality' is an appropriate description of the dimensions of the problem (Siegrist and Marmot, 2006: 5).

Another common criticism of the health inequalities literature is the difficulty of translating research findings into measures that tackle the inequalities being described. Reducing inequalities in health outcomes between social classes is a national policy issue and, despite declared good intentions, the actual efforts towards the reduction of inequalities have been modest, with only a few countries reaching 'a stage of policy development in which serious efforts can be, and sometimes are, considered' (Mackenbach, 2006: 245). Thus, there is inadequate evidence of the application of good policy to tackle health inequalities to be able to come to a judgement on the feasibility of such a task.

MEASUREMENT OF INEQUALITY

Health inequalities by various social divisions, including class, gender, ethnic group and occupation, have been measured in a number of ways, including the assessment of: longevity or life expectancy; experience of disease; experience of symptoms; dimensions of fitness; and the functional ability to perform daily tasks. Since health is a multi-dimensional quality, in which the balance of dimensions varies according to social context, one's state of health and across the life-course, there are a huge number of means of rendering a measurement. In theory, a full assessment of health would be a composite measure, in which case the weighting of the various components becomes subject to debate: is health most appropriately measured by individual self-assessment of 'wellness', self-reporting of symptoms, the uptake of general or specialist health services or rates of sick days away from work? The demonstration of inequality in rates of morbidity, the quality of health service provision and rates of service use are beset by difficulties in defining and consistently measuring appropriate variables – for example, good quality service provision in places and at times that suit patients attract higher rates of use than poorer services at inconvenient times and in inaccessible locations, but the higher service use does not necessarily indicate poorer health. The great difficulty in measuring the many dimensions of health in a way that is comparable across populations means that univariate summary measures are very appealing.

One 'surprisingly useful' measure involves simply asking people to assess their own health, which seems to 'distinguish quite clearly the medically defined healthy or unhealthy' (Blaxter, 2004: 24). An even more widely used summary measure of health is, paradoxically, death. By contrast with measures of morbidity, wellness or service use, mortality is relatively easy to define and measure, and, since most societies record death, comparisons between populations are possible. Mortality operates as a summation of the accumulation of a population's life chances such that deprived living conditions are associated with higher mortality rates at younger ages, compared with more affluent circumstances.

The existence of measurable inequalities in mortality between occupational classes has been documented for more than 150 years, and while the mechanism for these inequalities is debated, their existence is not. However, some evidence suggests that mortality rates should be treated as a more ambiguous measure than has traditionally been the case. Mortality data in the UK rely on death certificates which include information on age, sex, locality, occupation and cause of death. Although these data are analysed as though they are objective, there is evidence of their constructed nature. For instance, middle-class deaths are routinely given a greater number of descriptions of cause compared with working-class deaths, perhaps because they are seen as requiring more explanation than the 'natural inevitability' of working-class deaths (Phillimore, 1989).

The usefulness of different summary measures of health (or its absence) vary according to the disease patterns that prevail in society: mortality and morbidity rates are useful when infectious and communicable diseases predominate. However, as longevity across the life-course increases and chronic and degenerative diseases become more important, functional definitions and measures of disability are significant for disaggregating the population (Blaxter, 2004: 25). The measure currently used most often for comparing whole populations world-wide is rate of death or life expectancy.

THE PATTERN OF HEALTH INEQUALITIES

Inequalities can be measured in relative (the ratio of the death rate in the lowest social group to the rate in the highest group) and absolute terms (the difference in years of life or of life expectancy between the two groups). A population with low absolute mortality rates may nonetheless show large relative inequalities, and measures have to be interpreted appropriately. Swedish manual workers have the lowest mortality rate across European countries where comparable data are available (Lundberg and Lahelma, 2001) and yet, because the overall mortality rate is extremely low in Sweden across all classes, it is mathematically difficult to achieve narrow relative health inequalities (Dahl et al., 2006: 211). While relative measures are important for revealing the social processes that generate inequalities, absolute measures are crucial for assessing the achievements of welfare policies, and commentators increasingly agree that both types of measure should be used (Dahl et al., 2006: 212). Evidence of strong variations in life expectancy has accumulated over the past several decades, whereby the mean difference in life expectancy between those at the top and the bottom of a society's social structure can be up to 10 years.

In the British context, life expectancy at birth is around nine years longer in the top social class compared to the bottom and this gradient is repeated across Western European nations. Comparing death rates by class in 11 countries, the probability of dying between the ages of 45 and 65 years for men in manual classes compared with non-manual classes was about the same magnitude (five to seven times) for Denmark, England, Italy, Ireland, Norway, Portugal, Spain, Sweden and Wales, with Finland and France showing ratios of 9.8 and 11.5 (Kunst et al., 1998). Such inequalities in health are said to be a 'key public health problem in advanced societies, including European countries' (Siegrist and Marmot, 2006: 1), such that social stratification of health preoccupies researchers and policy-makers alike.

Western European trends during the last decades of the twentieth century have generally shown a widening of the gap in relative terms and, at best, a stabilizing of the situation in absolute terms (Mackenbach et al., 2003). This widening of the disparity in mortality rates by social class is apparent when the most privileged class with the lowest death rate and the most deprived class with the highest death rate are compared, and it is also found when comparison is made between intervening classes with intermediate death rates. Furthermore, growing differentials are apparent for many of the major causes of death (Blaxter, 2004: 109). In Western European nations, where absolute poverty has largely been eradicated and access to healthcare has been widened as never before, how can such differentials persist?

The divergence of inequalities is clearly a problem for the poorest members of society who experience the worst health, but the social gradient in morbidity and mortality affects the whole of society. In nations where a large proportion of the population live in extreme poverty (as is the case for most of the world's population), a concomitant reduction in life expectancy is perhaps predictable. What is less intuitive is that inequality in living standards seems to translate into inequality in health, even where almost all of the population has a basic or minimally acceptable standard of living. Evidence from wealthy societies suggests that there is no discontinuity between those living in poverty and those above the poverty line, but rather the continuous gradient persists across all levels of deprivation, both absolute and relative, which requires some explanation. The Whitehall study of British civil servants has demonstrated both the better health of those at the top of the hierarchy compared to those at the bottom, and also that for each step up the occupational hierarchy, health improves (Marmot et al., 1978; Marmot, 2004). The fine level of social differentiation in health risks has been demonstrated through various types of measurement, for instance home-owners with two cars have greater life expectancy than home-owners with one car (Goldblatt, 1990). The degree of income inequality matters for health, and, specifically, the average amount of income available to each individual in a population is less strongly related to life expectancy than is the distribution of that income in the population (Wilkinson, 1986). The same average income per person more equally distributed would produce higher life expectancy across society, such that the same amount of income may benefit those who are even moderately well off less when they live in a country with a high level of income inequality, compared with those living in a country with great equality (Wilkinson, 1997). Findings that support the significance of relative affluence for health inequalities have been reproduced internationally.

Statistics showing inequality in death rates are strongly influenced by a small number of important causes of death (such as coronary heart disease), which are particularly clearly differentiated by socio-economic class. Since these conditions have become increasingly important causes of death over the last century, the steepness of the social gradient has increased (Blaxter, 2004: 111).

CAUSES OF INEQUALITIES

Much effort has gone into documenting the pattern of health inequalities, including the widening gap and the continuous social gradient of inequality. However, the moment for documentation of the phenomenon has passed and efforts are increasingly focused on how to reduce inequalities. The mechanism thought to cause documented inequalities is clearly crucial in determining what course of action to follow in strategies to tackle and prevent them. Theoretical convictions distinguish the interpretation of the inequalities data and therefore the preferred solution.

Wilkinson's assertion that, past a certain level of economic development, relative income and social status are crucial to determining health, is based on the observation that, for instance, 'Greeks have less than half the average income of Americans and yet are healthier' (2000: 10). Wilkinson points out that in comparing the 50 states within the USA, where any cultural variation is minimal, there is '(after allowing for differences in income distribution) no relationship between mortality and average state income. Yet within each state there is a clear link between income and health' (Wilkinson, 2000: 10).

Wilkinson, among others, sees the psychological effects of inequality as important and emphasizes that greater social inequality makes it more difficult for citizens to maintain social bonds and self-esteem. Without social integration, dominance becomes more important, such that deprivation in the context of inequality leads to the maintenance of social honour through aggression, with consequent poor effects on health (Wilkinson et al., 1999). Material inequality engenders social divisions, leading to anxiety, conflict and other negative emotions which have a detrimental effect on an individual's health. The psychological distress accompanying low social status in a hierarchical system is associated with a bodily state of arousal in readiness for fight or flight via a mechanism involving the endocrine and nervous systems. Where this state is maintained over the long term, through the repeated experience of shame, disrespect and insecurity, the effects are thought to be damaging in terms of an increased susceptibility to disease. One of the attractions of Wilkinson's model is that it allows research into the deleterious health effects of stress, which was important in the 1980s, to be brought into a social model of health (Blaxter, 2004: 120).

Some of the deleterious effects of inequality are doubtless mediated through health behaviours. Japan, which by the end of the 1980s topped the world for long life expectancy, had experienced a prolonged period of narrowing of income inequality as well as being a highly cohesive society, as shown by falling crime levels. Some of the positive health effects of social security, cohesion and equity may come about through reducing the tendency of damaging behaviours such as heavy drinking, drug-taking and the consequent proneness to fighting and accidents. This thesis would seem to be supported by evidence from the 1990s in post-Soviet Russia, where an increase in mortality rates for adult men of working age has been related to excessive drinking in a society with few social security mechanisms and a sudden lurch towards an inequitable distribution of wealth.

Wilkinson uses the phrase 'cash and keys society' (1996: 226) to highlight how cash permits us to participate in market-based transactions, while keys symbolize our need to protect our own gains from the envy or covetousness of others. So although our livelihoods are generally dependent on a social inter-relatedness, a harsh individualism characterizes the process of social differentiation. For Nettleton (2001: 59), the sociology of the body and embodiment provide the missing link between the tradition of research into health inequalities that has concentrated on class-based structural disparities and the greater emphasis on psycho-social processes to explain the role of relative wealth in health inequalities. How people experience their structural context, the meanings and interpretations they ascribe to it, has an impact upon their physical bodies. Nettleton sees the processes whereby reflection upon the meaning of structural position translates into health behaviours such as smoking, as a crucial means of dissolving Cartesian divisions between mind and body.

While Wilkinson's emphasis on the psychological mechanisms is far from universally supported, the concept of social cohesion and the balance between individual and social interests has been explored to account for the relative, rather than absolute form of health inequalities. Blaxter (2004: 117) highlights the direct descent of this explanatory mechanism from Durkheim's assertion that social health is related to social norms and to solidarity. Renewed interest in how 'social facts' might influence individual well-being has centred on a concept of 'cultural capital'. Research has sought to indicate how group-level attributes influence individual health status and how the social, economic and cultural attributes of networks and organizations benefit both individual social actors and groups of people. The interpretation of the precise mix of cultural and material benefits that accumulates when social cohesion among networks promotes cooperative supportive action, implied by social capital, varies greatly.

Robert Putnam's essay 'Bowling alone' (published in 1995 and re-written as a book in 2000) attracted considerable attention in its description of how Americans have become increasingly disconnected from family, friends, neighbours and democratic structures. Reductions in levels of participation in voluntary associations, family meals and organized sport reduces the possibilities for coordinated trusting cooperation for mutual benefit, which damages aspects of collective and individual life, including health. In measuring aspects of civic activity such as social support, reciprocal relations, neighbourly interdependence and participation in voluntary work, researchers attempt to operationalize the idea of cultural capital and correlate it with changing patterns of health.

The conceptual problem with these efforts to measure a health-protective quality of community participation is the assumption that social solidarity is automatically health protecting: for instance, qualitative evidence from societies that are highly gender differentiated suggests that strong social norms governing high levels of group participation can be experienced as oppressive, coercive and potentially damaging to health. Social capital has been a useful means of directing attention away from structural matters and towards social relations, but in the process the debate has perhaps neglected variations between societies in how power and resources are distributed. Blaxter (2004: 120) notes that the health-protecting effect of involvement in community groups and voluntary organizations depends on the extent to which these groups wield influence, which in turn depends on their relationship to the state. Qualitative work points to the local historical, policy and cultural specificities of how social capital operates (Swann and Morgan, 2002), such that social capital can only be considered in particular socio-political settings and generalities are likely to be misleading.

While some concepts of cultural capital concentrate on the psychological benefits of solidarity, others suggest that the mechanism connecting social equality with better health outcomes might be material. In countries with welfare regimes that offer universal access to benefits and services, alongside good employment rights, there tend to be small absolute gaps between the health of rich and poor. Financial benefits such as unemployment or maternity payments and other forms of benefit may have the effect of reducing the degree of inequality between the wealth of citizens in ways that could be modelled financially. The universal availability of many benefits in more egalitarian societies may have a significant effect in flattening out socio-economic hierarchies. Where marginalized groups engage in organized collective activity, there may be a 'socially integrative effect' (Bartley et al., 1998: 5) that is independent of levels of income or wealth.

By way of criticism, Coburn (2000) suggests that the concentration of research interest on issues around social cohesion and trust has distracted effort from examining the macro-economic causes of health inequalities, namely economic globalization and neo-liberalism. As countries allow their markets to become liberalized in a global context, income levels increase as do economic inequalities, leading to reduced social cohesion and increased health inequalities. Where inequality increases, the poorest groups may become excluded from housing, healthcare and education. Countries with stronger systems of welfare support which protect the poor from exclusion, may retain better overall health compared to countries with more neo-liberal regimes wherein citizens are expected to provide more of their own health insurance and social security.

Coburn's (2000) thesis posits strong welfare systems as protective against widening health inequalities as a result of the global liberalization of markets. This concurs with the long-standing observation that the populations of Sweden, Norway and Denmark, with a history of highly redistributive welfare systems and strongly unionized labour forces, have enjoyed good overall health, compared to other Western European nations. Welfare systems as buffers for the deleterious effects of social stratification is a familiar notion and some empirical support for this view comes from the contrast between stable health inequalities in morbidity in Sweden and Finland in the early 1990s despite deep economic recession, versus widening inequalities in morbidity and mortality elsewhere in Western Europe (Dahl et al., 2006: 214). However, some unintended consequences of welfare regimes which apparently exaggerate the scale of inequalities have been identified. Dahl and colleagues speculate that the egalitarian ethos and social structures of Nordic countries create a high level of stress and frustration for those in relative poverty, since upward social mobility and prosperity akin to those of the privileged class are expected, or at least seen as attainable, among the least privileged. Furthermore, where good welfare support maintains the income levels of the more deprived social groups, the ability to pursue health-damaging behaviours is maintained among the unemployed and/or chronically ill, which might not be possible where the economic sanctions of misfortune were more harshly felt. Thus, relative (although probably not absolute) inequalities could be supported and even exaggerated by a highly protective welfare system (Dahl et al., 2006: 214).

HEALTHCARE AND INEQUALITIES

Given medical sociology's interest in systems of healthcare, the contribution of health service use to mitigating widening health inequalities has been investigated. Compared to other aspects of the welfare state, the health services are not thought to have a major role to play in reducing health inequalities. Macintyre (1989) concludes her investigation of this question by stating that differences in health service use have no substantial influence on inequalities in health, whereas if we consider the health, education and welfare system as a whole, there is compelling evidence that the availability of services could be significant for health outcomes.

Affluence, longevity and an ethic of consumerism can all magnify our expectations of our health and of our longevity. Health has been described as a 'desirable, infinite, scarce resource', the demands for which are 'infinitely elastic' because of the medicalization of various aspects of formerly non-medical life (Turner, 2004: 295). More specifically, Mechanic states that 'medical care has always been rationed by the supply available, by its distribution, and by the public's ability to pay' (1995: 1655). If demand is infinitely elastic and rationing is based on an ability to pay, then inequalities may be widened and entrenched. Some evidence supports the notion of an ever-expanding demand for healthcare in pursuit of life-long good health. The uptake of invasive medical intervention such as drugs or surgery for problems such as infertility, the menopause, anti-social behaviour and mental illness has been dramatic. While the UK population has not taken up cosmetic surgery to the extent that Brazilians and North Americans have done, nonetheless there is a significant increase in the demand for interventions to promote the appearance of youth and vitality. Furthermore, the treatment of risk categories such as high blood pressure or raised cholesterol before the symptoms of disease per se appear, has expanded the category of people who are subject to medical services. But do we know whether the demand for such services is really infinitely expansive?

A blunt refutation of the infinite elasticity of demand for health services states that, once their problems are addressed, most people have better things to do than visit doctors and hospitals (Light and Hughes, 2002: 4). We can find support for this idea in examples whereby medicine has reduced the need for further medical services: hip replacements reduce people's day-to-day need for pain relief and help at home by curing a chronic source of impairment; ante-natal screening informs the termination of pregnancies that involve a foetus with a serious genetic abnormality; insulin reduces the burden of impairment for people with diabetes. In refuting the infinite expansion of demand for healthcare, Light and Hughes point to a prevalent popular but mistaken view of economic theory which assumes scarcity and therefore that rationing is both inevitable and ubiquitous (2002: 3). Light and Hughes criticize modern micro-economics for being 'model-driven' in that the model assumes resources and services are scarce and holds a principle of non-satiation, which states that people can never be satisfied. Light and Hughes challenge these assumptions by pointing out that, in some countries, the principle of non-satiation is violated in that adequate healthcare which has met people's needs has been provided. Indeed, for a period in American history, there was evidence of the over-supply of both doctors and hospital beds, suggesting that demand does not, of necessity, outstrip supply (Light and Hughes, 2002: 2).

GLOBAL INEQUALITY

The question of whether health (and the conditions that support good health) is inevitably in scarce supply is related to the question raised at the start of this chapter of whether inequality in society is seen as avoidable and therefore iniquitous. If inequality is avoidable, then it is also inequitable and it should be possible to design a health and welfare policy that reduces rather than exacerbates inequalities. Is there such a thing as a national health system that does not feature rationing of some type, whether through pricing structures, waiting lists or ranking priorities? Most researchers describing socio-economic inequalities in health assume that disparities in the number of healthy years lived by the rich compared to the poor could, and, importantly, should, be addressed through a policy drive towards equity (see Lahelma, 2001). The example of the Nordic countries suggests that absolute inequalities can be reduced to a far smaller degree than currently obtains in the UK and the USA. However, the extensive widening of the health gap and the obstinacy of relative inequalities in otherwise redistributive socio-economic settings suggests that social stratification inevitably translates into inequity in health. Turner's (2004) description of the commoditization of healthcare and its inevitable scarcity seems to deny the possibility of addressing health inequalities through social policy initiatives to redistribute material and cultural resources.

Looking beyond Western Europe, where much health inequalities research has been conducted, gives little hope of the possibility of achieving a more equitable distribution of health. Global health inequalities are far starker than those within Europe. It is estimated that about half of humanity live in poverty, living on less than $2 per day, and of these about 1 billion are children. Significant numbers of these children lack access to safe water, health services and shelter. UNICEF estimates that 1.4 million children die each year from inadequate access to safe drinking water and sanitation, while 2.2 million children die each year because they are not immunized (Bellamy, 2004). Water-borne infectious disease, lack of immunization and malnutrition are causes of death with which medical science is well acquainted: the solution to this global health divide, in terms of the technology of public health intervention, is relatively simple. Considering global health inequalities also reveals their strongly gendered nature (Moss, 2002). A lack of educational opportunities and access to decision-making power in many countries means that women, and the children they give birth to and care for, do not necessarily command the basic resources that they need.

The extended sociological discussion of health inequalities has not, for the most part, translated into a consideration of the global scale of the problem. The cause of health inequalities in Western Europe continues to be debated, with a range of possible mechanisms in contention. Sanitation, adequate nutrition and universal programmes of immunization in the world's poorer countries would reduce infant mortality dramatically and thereby decrease the absolute size of global health inequalities. Perhaps because the causes of the raised mortality rates in the majority world are so obvious, they are seen as a different order of research problem from the relative inequalities of rich nations.

The ongoing global deregulation of marketplaces as a means towards 'wealth creation' is a feature of the twenty-first century which is still spreading to nations which were previously highly regulated: China is the world's fastest growing economy and is predicted to outstrip even the USA on measures of both size and rate of activity. Free markets are a motor for inequality and hence inequity, whereas an ethic of equity seems to be possible only in closed societies, such as Sweden prior to the Second World War, or command economies, most of which have now opened up to some form of capitalist trading. In his retirement, Fidel Castro is reported to have said that the Cuban model has failed even in Cuba, as market forces are being gradually introduced. The rapid widening of health inequalities in Russia and Eastern Europe has been of interest as a form of natural experiment in the effects of structural change on rates of morbidity and mortality (Cockerham, 1999). The rapid emergence of a middle class in India, with the attendant chronic diseases of wealth, and the prospects for health equity with China's rapid economic development, are sites where the detailed understanding of health inequalities developed in Europe may be tested and extended. Inequalities, like other social relations, have developed a globalized character in the sense that societies' well-being and suffering are closely linked: the global North's prosperity is predicated on economic models that rely on cheap labour and raw materials from the global South. The implications of the increase in global interconnectedness can be seen in the perpetuation of global health inequalities. The serious public health problems of sub-Saharan Africa co-exist with the high rate of emigration of trained medical personnel from Africa to meet staff shortages in wealthier countries. Sociological analyses of inequality that get beyond the European setting should play a role in putting these global connections on our national public health agendas (Connell et al., 2007).

CONCLUSION

The effect of social stratification on health is a key preoccupation of medical sociology. The analysis of health and illness as products of social relations challenges a tendency to see disease as a simple matter of biology that can be adequately appraised with medical methods. As a project of modernity, medical sociology has tended to confine its investigations of social stratification to industrial and post-industrial society. The focus has been on how structures of modernity influence the experience of morbidity and mortality by class, gender, ethnicity and other social divisions. Research on health inequalities has been key to the development of medical sociology as a distinct disciplinary area. It is a literature that is set to expand, particularly with the development of statistical techniques that can model the interactions of multiple variables and so measure structural effects (Cockerham, 2007). The health inequalities literature is both a model of interdisciplinary collaboration and, to some extent, the source of medical sociology's anxiety about its own theoretical deficiencies: once a method exists for measurement, it is inevitably employed on available population data, with a consequent accumulation of data frequently outstripping our ability to reflect on their meaning and significance for tackling inequalities.

Since mapping and tackling health inequalities began in earnest after the Second World War, sociologists have increasingly recognized the globalized nature of our economic and cultural systems. Systems of consumption have little regard for national boundaries and an awareness of the wider effects of our own use of goods and services has become harder to avoid. The availability of a cheap T-shirt or an out-of-season mango has implications down the supply chain for workers elsewhere in the world. Similarly, it no longer makes sense to analyse health inequalities in wealthy 'Western' countries separately from the rest of the world. Beyond the confines of modernist society, global divisions in health tell a similar story in many respects, albeit more dramatically. The poorest countries in the world, as measured by GDP (Gross Domestic Product), show the shortest average life expectancy (Lahelma, 2010). Despite attempts to consider health inequalities as a global rather than a Western world problem (Doyal and Pennell, 1983; Waldron, 2005; Lahelma, 2010), there is a broader tendency to consider the causes of premature death in the majority world as qualitatively different from the post-industrial world's problems. However, the speed and reach of capitalist modes of development means that countries that were considered impoverished and 'developing' until recently, now show increasing rates of diseases of affluence (Yoon et al., 2006).

While clearly central to our sense of ourselves in our imagined world, the privileging of the nation-state in our analyses of health inequalities has had the effect of segregating sociological work on health inequalities from global health issues. This is paradoxical given the interest in sociological theories of globalization. An emergent sociological agenda addresses the global connectedness of health inequalities, in terms of competition for key commodities, including personnel and pharmaceutical commodities. The reduction of national health inequalities as a matter of social justice is crucial, but in the absence of work towards global health equity, it simply reinforces nation-states as boundaries that confer advantage.

REFERENCES

Bartley, M., Blane, D. and Smith, G.D. (1998) 'Introduction: beyond the Black Report', in M. Bartley, D. Blane and G.D. Smith (eds), *The Sociology of Health Inequalities.* Oxford: Blackwell Publishing. pp. 1–16.

Bellamy, C. (2004) *The State of the World's Children 2005: Childhood Under Threat.* New York: The United Nations Children's Fund, UNICEF.

Blaxter, M. (2004) *Health.* Cambridge: Polity.

Coburn, D. (2000) 'Income inequality, social cohesion and the health status of populations: the role of neo-liberalism', *Social Science and Medicine*, 51: 135–46.

Cockerham, W.C. (1999) *Health and Social Change in Russia and Eastern Europe.* London: Routledge.

Cockerham, W.C. (2007) 'A note on the fate of postmodern theory and its failure to meet the basic requirements for success in medical sociology', *Social Theory and Health*, 5: 285–96.

Connell, J., Zurn, P., Stilwell, B., Awases, M. and Braichet, J.M. (2007) 'Sub-Saharan Africa: beyond the health worker migration crisis?', *Social Science and Medicine*, 64(9): 1876–91.

Dahl, E., Fritzell, J., Lahelma, E., Martikainen, P., Kunst, A. and Mackenbach, J. (2006) 'Welfare state regimes and health inequalities', in J. Siegrist and M. Marmot (eds), *Social Inequalities in Health: New Evidence and Policy Implications.* Oxford: Oxford University Press. pp. 193–222.

Doyal, L. and Pennell, I. (1983) *The Political Economy of Health.* London: Pluto.

Gerhardt, U. (1989) *Ideas About Illness: An Intellectual and Political History of Medical Sociology.* Basingstoke: Macmillan.

Goldblatt, P. (1990) 'Mortality and alternative social classifications', in P. Goldblatt (ed.), *Longitudinal Study: Mortality and Social Organisation.* London: HMSO.

Illsley, R. (1975) 'Promotion of observer status', *Social Science and Medicine*, 9: 63–7.

Kunst, A.E., Groenhof, F., Mackenbach, J.P. et al. (1998) 'Mortality by occupational class among men 30–64 years in 11 European countries', *Social Science and Medicine*, 46: 1459–76.

Lahelma, E. (2001) 'Health and social stratification', in W.C. Cockerham (ed.), *The Blackwell Companion to Medical Sociology.* Malden, MA: Blackwell. pp. 64–93.

Lahelma, E. (2010) 'Health and social stratification', in W.C. Cockerham (ed.), *The New Blackwell Companion to Medical Sociology*. Malden, MA: Blackwell. pp. 71–96.

Light, D.W. and Hughes, D. (2002) 'A sociology perspective on rationing: power, rhetoric and situated practices', in D. Hughes and D. Light (eds), *Rationing: Constructed Realities and Professional Practices*. Oxford: Blackwell Publishing. pp. 1–19.

Lundberg, O. and Lahelma, E. (2001) 'Nordic health inequalities in the European context', in M. Kautto, J. Fritzell, B. Hvinden, J. Kvist and H. Uusitalo (eds), *Nordic Welfare States in the European Context*. London: Routledge. pp. 42–65.

Macintyre, S. (1989) 'The role of health services in relation to inequalities in health in Europe', in J. Fox (ed.), *Health in Equalities in European Countries*. Aldershot: Gower. pp. 317–32.

Mackenbach, J.P. (2006) 'Socio-economic inequalities in health in Western Europe: from description to explanation to intervention', in J. Siegrist and M. Marmot (eds), *Social Inequalities in Health: New Evidence and Policy Implications*. Oxford: Oxford University Press. pp. 223–50.

Mackenbach, J.P., Bas, V., Andersen O. et al. (2003) 'Widening socio-economic inequalities in mortality in six western European countries', *International Journal of Epidemiology*, 32: 830–7.

Marmot, M. (2004) *Status Syndrome: How Your Social Standing Directly Affects Your Health and Life Expectancy*. London: Bloomsbury.

Marmot, M.G., Adelstein, A.M., Robinson, N. and Rose, G. (1978) 'Changing social-class distribution of heart disease', *British Medical Journal*, 2(6145): 1109–12.

Mechanic, D. (1995) 'Education and debate. Dilemmas in rationing health care services: the case for implicit rationing', *British Medical Journal*, 310(6995): 1655–9.

Moss, N.E. (2002) 'Gender equity and socioeconomic inequality: a framework for the patterning of women's health', *Social Science and Medicine*, 54(5): 649–61.

Nettleton, S. (1995) *The Sociology of Health and Illness*. Cambridge: Polity.

Nettleton, S. (2001) 'The sociology of the body', in W.C. Cockerham (ed.), *The Blackwell Companion to Medical Sociology*. Malden, MA: Blackwell. pp. 43–63.

Phillimore, P. (1989) 'Shortened lives: premature death in North Tyneside'. *Bristol Papers in Applied Social Studies*, no. 12. Bristol: University of Bristol.

Putnam, R. (2000) *Bowling Alone: The Collapse and Revival of American Community*. New York: Simon and Schuster.

Scambler, G. (2002) *Health and Social Change: A Critical Theory*. Buckingham: Open University Press.

Shaw, M., Dorling, D., Gordon, D. and Davey Smith, G. (1999) *The Widening Gap: Health Inequalities and Policy in Britain*. Bristol: Policy Press.

Siegrist, J. and Marmot, M. (2006) 'Introduction', in J. Siegrist and M. Marmot (eds), *Social Inequalities in Health: New Evidence and Policy Implications*. Oxford: Oxford University Press. pp. 1–25.

Swann, C. and Morgan, A. (eds) (2002) *Social Capital for Health: Insights from Qualitative Research*. London: Health Development Agency.

Tudor Hart, J. (1971) 'The Inverse Care Law', *The Lancet*, 297: 405–12.

Turner, B. (2004) *The New Medical Sociology: Social Forms of Health and Illness*. Cambridge: Cambridge University Press.

Waldron, I. (2005) 'Gender differences in mortality – causes and variations in different societies', in P. Conrad (ed.), *The Sociology of Health and Illness: Critical Perspectives*, 7th edition. New York: Worth. pp. 38–53.

Wilkinson, R.G. (1986) 'Income and mortality', in R.G. Wilkinson (ed.), *Class and Health: Research and Longitudinal Data*. London: Tavistock.

Wilkinson, R.G. (1996) *Unhealthy Societies: The Afflictions of Inequality*. London: Routledge.

Wilkinson, R.G. (1997) 'Socioeconomic determinants of health. Health inequalities: relative or absolute material standards?', *British Medical Journal*, 314(7080): 591–5.

Wilkinson, R.G. (2000) *Mind the Gap: Hierarchies, Health and Human Evolution*. London: Weidenfeld and Nicolson.

Wilkinson, R.G., Kawachi, I. and Kennedy, B. (1999) 'Mortality, the social environment, crime and violence', in M. Bartley, D. Blane and G.D. Smith (eds), *The Sociology of Health Inequalities*. Oxford: Blackwell Publishing. pp 19–37.

Yoon, K-H., Lee, J-H., Kim, J-W., Cho, J.H., Choi, Y-H., Ko, S-H., Zimmet, P. and Son, H.-Y. (2006) 'Epidemic obesity and type 2 diabetes in Asia', *Lancet*, 368: 1681–8.

4
WOMEN, GENDER AND FEMINISM

INTRODUCTION

Sociology's early focus on key sites of institutional power such as religion, the law and the corporation meant that women as a group were neglected. This chapter considers how feminism and its development in medical sociology have addressed this deficit to describe the influence of gendered power structures on health and illness. In the aftermath of feminism, women feature as subjects of sociological research, but often with a less than sophisticated theory of gender to underpin a focus on a single gender. Early work in health inequalities tended to explain gendered inequalities in terms of inherent differences between women and men, either in biological or occupational terms, thereby compounding rather than interrogating gender as an immutable category. As will be discussed in this chapter, much research on women and, more recently, on men makes no effort to theorize gender, beyond claiming 'women's health' (or 'men's health') as a legitimate area of practice and study on the grounds of 'difference'. Without a theory of why gender inequalities arise, research that describes gender difference potentially (albeit unintentionally) confirms these differences as inherent and unavoidable.

Sociology has been a key discipline in which the feminist challenge has provoked the development of analytic tools to challenge gender stereotyping and discrimination, thereby revising our understanding of social relationships. The identification of women as a significant category for study and for social action has been informed by conflict theory and social constructionism (see Chapter 2). In both cases, women are identified as a category worthy of consideration because of their structural position in the political economy and/or the social construction of femininity that rendered their health needs and their contribution to formal and informal health work, largely invisible. The roots of the feminist challenge to society can be traced back to the nineteenth century, when those described as first-wave feminists began to agitate and campaign for women's right to own property and vote. Now, when women in Western European countries have legally protected rights in many spheres of domestic and public life, it is difficult 'to recall the time when gender relations were not regarded as a legitimate focus for sociological study' (Maynard, 1990: 269).

Sociological methods have been important in developing feminist critiques of medicine and in rendering visible women's health; nonetheless sociology as an area of study has been subject to feminist criticism of the systematic invisibility of women and women's issues. There is no single, unified feminist theory or practice, but rather, as with other theoretical positions, a variety of overlapping positions, which can be more or less strongly applied in developing theory, methodology and practice. Feminist ideas have informed an important swathe of sociological research, particularly from the 1970s onwards, and these ideas have been influential in the evolution of other forms of identity politics, including those with a focus on ethnicity, disability and sexuality. This chapter will consider the contribution of the feminist challenge to the emergence of a sociology of health and medicine and the ways in which the early invisibility of women has been modified as patterns of morbidity and mortality have been charted.

FEMINISM

In so far as it is possible to describe a feminist position, the unravelling of an unwarranted conflation of sex with gender has been a central mission. Feminism asserts that while biological differences distinguish male from female and, particularly after puberty, can be seen in morphological, hormonal and functional differences, gender roles are culturally ascribed and socially acquired. Masculinity is a trait that is theoretically independent of maleness and men learn how to perform male gender roles, just as women learn to adopt a feminine practice. While some cultures recognize a third gender which is often a feminine male role, the existence of differentiated gender roles for men and women, and for girls and boys, seems to be universal. Masculine and feminine gender roles are not only differentiated from one another, but they are also differentially conceived, with men being a norm against which women's difference is seen as a deviation. The deviance of women from the male norm is used as a justification for discrimination against women as a class.

Gendered ideology has limited the theoretical and practical inclusion of women in sociological research due to a division between the male public sphere, where activities such as politics, education, economics and policy formulation are conducted, compared

with the female private domain of the family and household, where children are conceived and reared and where production and consumption is on a domestic, small
scale. The public activities associated with men command a higher status and an
authoritative legitimacy lacking from the private, domestic matters associated with
women. This male–female binary division serves to homogenize the category of men
as public and the category of women as privately domestic, which hides from view
domestic men, public women and the scale of domestic activity that might be
contributing to public economic or political ends. The differential value associated
with men's work and the systematic devaluation of women's work benefits men in
material and symbolic ways. Thus, a central aim of feminism in deconstructing
gendered social divisions is to ameliorate women's position by releasing them from
assumptions about their inherent suitability for low paid or unpaid, low status work
and other marginalized social positions.

Sociology's initial disciplinary focus on public life in the form of the state, religion,
employment and the law ensured women's marginalization. At sociology's inception,
as now, women were under-represented in public institutions that were accorded
status, such as parliament, the church and the high courts. Feminists have argued that
sexist values explain the early sociological lack of interest in the domestic sphere,
leading to an under-representation of research into domestic labour, the lives of
families and children, and in occupations where women are over-represented such
as nursing, childcare, cleaning and prostitution. Since the 1970s, sociological research
into women's lives in domestic and public settings has flourished as feminism has
challenged sociological inquiry, among other sexist practices. The form that this challenge has taken has been the subject of intense debate among feminists, emphasizing
different political justifications and ideal outcomes for the 'Women's Liberation
Movement' ranging from liberal to radical positions.

Liberal feminists, building on the foundations of thought laid by the eighteenth-
century writer Mary Wollstencraft, have urged women to participate in those aspects
of public life from which they have historically been excluded, claiming that, as a
class, women's capacity for rational thought and sustained logic is as good as men's.
A more radical feminism dismisses the liberal version as seeking to insert women into
public life on terms defined by men, and instead promotes a fundamental challenge
to the constraints of a sexist notion of womankind. A radical feminism seeks to
redefine the social norms of womanhood beyond those set by the norm of
'mankind'. Two main alternative routes for such a redefinition have been advocated:
first, urging women to avoid reproductive roles and thereby liberate themselves from
domestic servitude and the duties of social, as well as biological reproduction; second,
and contradictorily, by making women's reproductive potential a central motif to be
celebrated by a 'woman-centred' feminism that asserts women's superior status on the
basis of her association with 'the natural'. Liberal feminism can be accused of failing

to see the entrenched masculine advantage inherent in gendered norms whereas radical feminism, in both its anti- and its pro-reproductive type, fetishizes the biological features of womankind that have been central to sexist justifications of women's inferiority to men. Conceptions of womankind as inherently more spiritual, ecological or communally minded due to child-bearing abilities, hormonal factors or her evolutionary origin myth as a gatherer rather than a hunter, have all, intentionally or otherwise, reinforced a gendered divide. Writers and activists working from the 1960s onwards, from all varieties of feminist thinking, have come to be identified as 'second-wave feminists'.

A querying of the routine division of the sexes into distinct realms, culturally, socially and economically, whereby women are consistently less valued than men, underlies the development of feminism. Feminist politics depend on a premise that collective and concerted action can change the undervaluing of women and that equality between the sexes is a legitimate social goal (Humm, 1992: 1). Feminist activism seeks to win for women the rights that men have taken for granted. Feminist theory seeks to explain how disparities between men and women have been normalized and maintained and why, even once women have been granted formal rights to equal treatment in the workplace, home and courts, gendered discrimination and inequity persists.

A particular target of feminist thought has been the unwarranted conflation of sex with gender which is used to justify sexist assumptions: the inferiority of women, or at least their unsuitability for particular social roles is read from embodied sex differences. Morphological, hormonal and functional differences between men and women's bodies are imagined as opposed and highly differentiated categories of male and female, thereby facilitating the conflation of sex with gender. The fantasy of the opposition of male and female works to keep a polarized, binary gender division intact as a cultural category (see Chapter 6). Feminism emphasizes the differentially valued readings of male and female bodies and delineates the processes that have led to the establishment, maintenance and reinforcing of gendered roles.

Sexism as a discriminatory system associated with institutionalized power is justified in contradictory terms. Feminism seeks to highlight the contradictions of sexism, with the obvious example being the ideal of the saintly wife and mother which sanctions sexual activity as part of child-bearing while proscribing wider sexual expression with the shameful and vilified figure of the whore. Thus, the acceptable expression of women's sexuality takes place within limitations, which have evolved as neo-liberal markets have sold sexual expression as a form of individual empowerment. Feminist analysis has shown the ways in which medicine, among other social institutions, has upheld the contradictions of sexism that have simultaneously made women's deviant madness and promiscuity highly visible, while rendering other health needs invisible. Medical sociology's early failure to interrogate medicine's sexism, has, in the wake of feminism, given way to an over-representation of women as research subjects in investigations of particular issues such as depression and reproductive healthcare, thereby re-inscribing polarized gendered opposition between categories of men and women. The next section considers some of the contradictory evidence around women's over-representation and invisibility in medical encounters and healthcare policy and how this is related to polarized conceptions of gender.

GENDERED VISIBILITY

Masculinity's tendency to render women and women's concerns invisible can be seen in medicine's upholding of the myth of female frailty. This myth has had the contradictory effect of disqualifying women as healers and rendering them highly qualified as patients, thereby helping to reduce women's visibility in the practice and policy of medicine (Clarke, 1983: 64). The logic of female frailty supports a gendered reading of the human body such that women could not be well because of their disadvantaged cultural position and men could not be ill because of their superior status (Annandale and Clark, 1996). The ideal of female frailty has been mediated by other dimensions of structure and identity, particularly social class and racialized group. Historically, working-class and immigrant women whose paid and unpaid labour has been key to the household economy, could not afford much in the way of feminine frailty. By contrast, their wealthier, middle-class (and usually native-born) sisters enjoyed the 'privilege' of frailty which contained its own penalty as a means of curtailing women's autonomy. Other forms of medically mediated sexism, such as the ready diagnosis of female madness and hysteria, cut across class and racialized classes. The myth of female frailty is no longer as evident as it once was in the medical treatment of women, but updated versions of sexism can be seen in the gendered application of healthcare practice and policy.

Women were largely invisible in the early discussion of the epidemiology of AIDS (Acquired Immunodeficiency Syndrome), despite the significant nature of the risk to health world-wide. Rather than being considered as potential sufferers of AIDS, women only appeared as potential vectors for the Human Immunodeficiency Virus (HIV) as sex workers (Holland et al., 1990). As they began to appear as more than just problematic virus vessels, women became the target of a public health expectation that they should take responsibility, not only for their own bodies and reputations, but also for policing men's health (Holland et al., 1990: 347). Women were presumed to be passive partners in heterosexual encounters and this was regarded as highly problematic in the public health initiative to contain HIV. Efforts to convert women's presumed passivity into assertiveness with regard to condom use, entirely overlooked men's responsibility in matters of sexuality and sexual intercourse (Browne and Minichiello, 1994: 232).

Feminist analysis of negotiations over sexual encounters between men and women has emphasized the determinate influence of inequalities in gendered power. Women's lack of social, economic and political power translates into a lack of self-determination in sexual matters. Sexist roles and behaviours present a significant sexual health risk in the context of heterosexuality (Browne and Minichiello, 1994: 248), not least where a dominant patriarchal ideology justifies rape (Jewkes et al., 2005). The significance of gendered power has, eventually, informed public health interventions around the prevention of the spread of HIV to the extent of promoting so-called 'female-controlled' preventative methods such as female condoms and microbicides. However, the extent to which these have been taken up depends on local regimes of gender relations (Mantell et al., 2005).

Another example of the paradoxical invisibility of women and the entrenched nature of sexist thinking in medicine concerns heart disease. Although significant numbers of women die from heart attacks, albeit at a later age than men, heart disease continues to be widely regarded as a men's problem (Emslie et al., 2001: 224). Where men and women present similar symptoms, men are more likely to be diagnosed with heart disease and women's symptoms are more likely to be attributed to age. This contrast can be understood as part of a gendered cultural symbolism whereby men are associated with culture and the failure of their body parts rests on explanatory metaphors around mechanical failure, whereas women's proximity to the 'natural' makes a more organic, quiet death appropriate and acceptable (Emslie et al., 2001: 227). In contradiction to earlier feminist concerns that women were culturally locked into a category of frailty, these later analyses suggest that for some disease categories it is women's vulnerability that is invisible, rather than their illness that is excessively visible. These examples show how gendered thinking remains entrenched and thus hard to detect and culturally variable. Since there is no gender-free standpoint, we must make sense of gendered thinking as a developmental process.

GENDERED POLARITY AND THEORIZING DIFFERENCE

Constructed as a binary opposition, gender is a relative concept in that feminine and masculine only make sense in relation to one another. Compared to other mammalian species, humans are fairly undifferentiated by gender: the traits that we think of as gendered such as height, weight, hairiness, depth of voice and musculature show considerable overlap when measured in populations of men and women. The supposed binary opposition of masculine and feminine is often justified in determinist terms by the biology of sex difference, although the science does not support a clear-cut differentiation. A person's sex is ascertained in medical terms by comparing gonadal, hormonal, chromosomal and psychological dimensions of gender which may contradict one another and may also be at odds with the gender identity with which the person lives day to day.

While science cannot 'measure' sex difference in a clear-cut way that would justify deterministic, sexist thinking, women's role in reproduction has been crucial in underpinning sexism. The potential for women to conceive and bear new life has been key in maintaining a binary gendered division. Women's potential to carry babies homogenizes all women as mothers, with the effect of locking women into reproductive roles that assume child-bearing to be central to everyone's lives, thereby echoing medicine's determinacy (Annandale and Clark, 1996: 29). Thinking premised on a binary division between men and women, between male and female, has the unfortunate effect of 'universalizing and valorizing' gender differences. Medical sociology's focus on the abnormalities of women's reproductive health has also meant that, at the same time as sociology criticizes biomedicine's pathologization of women, it also replicates its problematic (Annandale and Clark, 1996: 32), allowing women's health problems to stand for the broader issue of gender and health. Research that measures or describes the inferiority of women's health compared with men's health without reference to a theoretical position, can have the effect of reinforcing a categorical difference between the genders, and identifying an inherent feature of womankind as the source of their own misfortune. Researchers' concentration on medical problems confined to women, such as childbirth, breast cancer and menstruation has, ironically, reinforced women as the vulnerable and 'weaker sex'.

The invisibility of women in specific areas of diagnosis, such as heart disease, and health policy (despite gender being a routine variable in sociological analysis), is perhaps explained by the lack of theoretical development in what gender means. Feminist theory has 'often been used tacitly in research on gender and health' such that 'interpretive frameworks are implicit rather than explicit' and women's health is discussed without reference to patriarchy as a theoretical justification of women's disadvantage (Annandale, 1990: 62). 'Women's health' has developed and persists as a subject area largely without the support of theoretical justification. Books devoted to 'women's health' can describe the problems that afflict women at length, without offering a rationale for why women as a group should be studied in political or theoretical terms. Without a theory of gendered power, such as patriarchy, women are potentially understood as the authors of their own trauma and oppression. The rise of the self-help industry, based on therapeutic psychological discourse, has occupied the space left by the atheoretical description of women's health problems (Illouz, 2008 and see Chapter 6). This theory-free development of women's health as an area that requires special attention has, in turn, allowed 'men's health' to develop as an atheoretical specialism with attendant commercial provision of 'gender-specific health services' (Annandale, 2010: 99).

'Men's health' tends to focus on men's bodies as a site of disease (Oliffe, 2006), describing how men are ill (Robertson, 2006) and how they experience recovery (Robertson et al., 2010). One effect of collecting research on men's illness is to present men as a disadvantaged group whose needs have been hitherto underestimated and who are in need of an urgent public health campaign (Courtenay, 2000). The discussion of male health disadvantage is part of a competition for limited resources but risks establishing a competition over whether men or women are sicker. Such discourse tends to re-inscribe gender in determinist terms, and elide aspects of gender that are contested or that affect men and women.

This re-emphasis on the male body as worthy of close examination, albeit as a potential site of sickness, can be seen as one of the ways that feminism has been acknowledged, and this acknowledgement has allowed its claims to now be ignored. Angela McRobbie (2009) argues that post-feminism is a state in which feminism has been undone through a process of disarticulation which represents feminism as a truncated, censorious and limited version of itself, devoid of solidarity with other groups. She explores the way that the idea of a feminist collective has been subsumed into policies that offer young women the possibility of individual success, often in commercial terms and disconnected from any collective promotion of women's rights. Women's demands for more autonomy in determining their own healthcare, particularly around obstetric and gynaecological medicine, have become less prominent since the 1980s, while the men's health movement and the commercial provision of gender-specific services have grown. Feminist demands to recognize women's particular experience of healthcare have thus been acknowledged, but the response has not necessarily offered women greater autonomy. Indeed, the recognition of gender as a key dimension in illness and healthcare has paradoxically served to highlight masculinity as a potential risk to health.

Feminism has sought to undo sexist assumptions by demonstrating the socially constructed nature of gender: demonstrating that gender roles are culturally and historically variable, learned not given. Sociological models of gender as a set of roles which men and women are equally able to take on but which have no genesis in biology, have been powerful in opening up opportunities for women to demonstrate their abilities. The disadvantage of reducing gender to a set of learned roles, without a theory of gendered power, is that it ignores embodied aspects of men and women's lives. Without a theory of gender that encompasses lived bodily aspects of gender, we cannot integrate an understanding of the gendered dimension of a range of conditions, from menstruation to arthritis.

In a discussion of doctor–nurse relations, Karen Davies observes that one of the difficulties in theorizing gender is that in Western society it is a primary social category into which we automatically and unconsciously categorize any specific other with whom we must relate (Davies, 2003: 729). Thus, a social relationship with a person of indeterminate gender is culturally less tolerable than ambiguity around age, sexuality, class or disability. The combination of the social centrality of gender, underpinned by an assumption of biological difference, has made sexist thinking difficult to deconstruct, despite the widely shared feminist understanding of women's experience as socially constructed rather than built directly upon biology or the materiality of the body (Annandale and Clark, 1996: 19). The availability of safe contraception and the receding social pressure for women to marry and reproduce has supported a feminist endeavour to discredit fixed sex roles by treating men and women as entirely equivalent social actors who are differentially subject to gender prejudice. It is empirically, as well as theoretically, possible to disaggregate biological sex from social gender roles. Using social survey methods to measure dimensions of gender in men and in women, high 'masculinity' has been associated with better health for men and women, such that masculinity clearly carries rewards regardless of gender (Annandale and Hunt, 1990: 43). But this ability to think about gender as a quality or condition independent of sex is rare.

RECONCEPTUALIZING GENDER

In the early 1980s, Juanne Clarke lamented that there could be 'no adequate, systematic theory-building as of yet because of the conceptual indeterminacy in the definition and problems in the measurement of illness and gender' (1983: 77), suggesting that significant reconceptualization was required. More than a decade later and, more hopefully, feminist theory was said to be 'in the midst of significant change' (Annandale and Clark, 1996: 38).

Post-structuralism has offered one route for a reconceptualization of gender that keeps bodies, including bodily difference, in the analysis without collapsing gender onto sex and without making sex determinate. If bodies are 'only knowable through the discourses that constitute them', then they cannot be reduced to an unproblematic biological base on which gender is inscribed (Annandale and Clark, 1996: 20). Gender differences are created and understood through hierarchical opposition, such that the category 'women' is meaningful in reference to 'men'. Feminism's aim to destabilize or overturn such oppositions (Annandale and Clark, 1996: 21) offers the possibility of a novel and less fixed gendered regime.

UNDOING POLARITIES

A study of healthcare professionals in a hospital setting which describes the active performance and subjectivity of the continual creation, maintenance and contesting of gender relations in daily life (Davies, 2003: 720) shows how empirical work has a role to play in undoing the polarity of gender. The concept of the body is central to examining the doing of dominance and deference by doctors and nurses between whom, despite progressive change in the late twentieth century, gendered relations hold sway. Davies argues that bringing in the body gives access to complex multiple relations at work at the crossroads of gender, profession, hierarchy and bureaucracy, allowing analysis to identify where gender relations can be contested and change introduced (2003: 737). The role that gender plays within the complex multiple relations for users of health services is, as for doctors and nurses, non-determinate. Cathy Charles and colleagues (1998) considered the extent to which women perceived that they had options with regard to treatment for breast cancer, how they understood the risks and benefits of various options and the role they wanted for themselves and their oncologist in decision making. The paper documents how women developed their own constructions of scientific information on treatment risks, concluding that most women wanted shared decision making so that their physicians' skills and experience would contribute to making the 'right' decision and avoiding the 'wrong' one (Charles et al., 1998: 90). In this context, divisions between healthcare professionals and recipients of services seem to have emerged as more important than gender. This is notable given that breast cancer is often described as having an important effect on gendered identity.

Although embodied characteristics have been used to justify sexism, an embodied approach to gender can be part of the undoing of polarized thinking. As with other forms of reductionist prejudice, sexism constantly re-inscribes gender so that diversity and complexity become rewritten as binary contrasts. The need to get beyond this process of re-reading gender as sex has been addressed by post-structuralist thinkers.

As described in Chapter 2, post-structuralism rejects enlightenment-style grand narratives which justify particular types of knowledge as authoritative and legitimate. Instead of viewing humans as sacred objects that are inherently meaningful, a post-structuralist approach considers how subjectivity is constructed rather than how humans make the world. A post-structuralist feminism rejects the identification of an ultimate cause of oppression such as 'class' or 'patriarchy'. And, in consequence, it does not grant particular groups, such as women or the working class, any privileged understanding of the working of oppression (Annandale and Clark, 1996: 21).

Donna Harraway (1990) has argued that our current existence, with its enormous dependence on machines, has opened up a new means of reading women that can avoid the familiar dualisms of home/work, public/private, etc. The integrated and intimate role of machines in human life means that any contrast between natural and artificial, mind and body has been problematized. Instead of dualities, we are faced with a network image of permeable spaces and identities consisting in interpenetrated people and machines that can be read as 'cyborgs, hybrids, mosaics, chimeras' (Harraway, 1990: 220).

Annandale and Clark suggest cyborg imagery as a means of deconstructing duality and challenging theoretical positions which view science and technology as amounting to little more than male demonology (1996: 38). If bodies can be envisaged as networks, it becomes difficult to think, for instance, of 'problems in fertility' belonging specifically to women, rather than to parents or couples. New reproductive technologies such as in vitro fertilization (IVF), gamete intrafallopian transfer (GIFT), intracytoplasmic sperm injection (ICSI), and egg and gamete donation, all show how technology disrupts bodies' boundaries which in turn has implications for their gendered relations. When the conception and bearing of babies comes to involve technological intervention as a routine matter, what happens to pro- and anti-feminist ideas that rely on men and women's 'natural' abilities?

Actor network theory is another approach that re-casts familiar and apparently intractable dualisms by describing material relations alongside those of meaning (or semiotics) as a single entity which performs a particular function. As a form of 'relational materialism', actor network theory offers a non-dualistic account of the relation between 'society' and 'technology' and, as such, can help in understanding the intricate and mutually constitutive character of the human and the technological in the processes and relationships of sickness and healing, particularly the cultural performance of illness (Prout, 1996: 214). Cyborg imagery and actor network theory both problematize the role of intention and agency of people (and of things), which, at the very least, disrupts a simplistic model of men and women as inevitably holding opposed interests. Examples of research which considers gender as a relational property alongside other aspects of medical work are rare, but an example can illustrate its potential importance for designing healthcare interventions.

Methods of HIV prophylaxis that can be employed by women are seen as key to safeguarding women's health where behaviour is strongly constrained by patriarchy (Mantell et al., 2005). A trial in Africa showed that women who were asked to use a diaphragm as well as a condom in sexual intercourse were less likely to sustain condom use compared with women recommended to use only condoms (Padian et al., 2007). The use of condoms by women's male partners seems to have been affected by the participant's diaphragm use which, in turn, negatively effected evaluation of the diaphragm's efficacy. While this study failed to show whether diaphragm use offers additional protection against HIV due to insufficient statistical power, it did show the relational way in which men and women's behaviour unfolds in the context of a medical intervention or technology (Rosengarten et al., 2008).

Analyses of the complex contingent relations between gender and other social factors (Mol, 2002) notwithstanding, the duality of most gendered analysis persists. In part, this persistence of binary gender thinking can be understood as a legacy of the importance of quantitative analyses of health inequalities which have been so important to medical sociology's claim to disciplinary distinction. The gendering of health inequalities, which we consider next, inevitably relied on a dichotomous operationlization of gender.

HEALTH INEQUALITIES

A long-standing observation of difference, central to medical sociological under-standings of health inequalities, is that women live longer lives (Waldron 1976), but are more beset by symptoms compared with men. While this statement is an over-simplification (Macintyre et al., 1996), the apparent stability of the gendered contrast has attracted various explanations, some of which have compounded assumptions of the inherent and immutable nature of gender differences.

In a few countries with a high prevalence of mortality from infectious disease, for example Bangladesh and Zimbabwe, women have no mortality advantage over men (Waldron, 2005). However, across most countries of the world, women's life expect-ancy is longer than men's, but the extent of women's greater longevity varies markedly. In wealthy countries such as Australia, Finland, the USA and the UK where men and women expect to live into their late 70s or early 80s, women's life expectancy at birth is five to seven years greater than men's. By contrast, in the United Republic of Tanzania and Rwanda, average life expectancy is in the early 50s with women having only one to two years advantage over men (WHO, 2008). Women's longevity compared to men is generally agreed to stem from biological advantages, making them more resilient across the life-course. Social factors which disadvantage girls and women are likely to reduce their mortality advantage and increase their morbidity burden (Sen and Östlin, 2008). The sensitivity of longevity to social and economic change can be seen in longitudinal data: the ongoing war in Iraq has left men with a life expectancy 20 years lower than women, while the dramatic break-up of the former Soviet Union in the early 1990s can be traced in terms of changed gendered rates of longevity (Cockerham, 1999).

It was not until the late 1980s that medical sociology's interest in health inequali-ties became gendered. While the role of occupation-based social class had dominated research into men's health inequalities, for women the focus was on their multiple roles as mothers and wives as well as workers (Arber and Khlat, 2002). Sociological research rejected early crude explanations referring to inherent biological difference, seeking rather to differentiate and evaluate the effects of social and economic condi-tions on health. The focus was initially on whether structural factors, particularly social class and material disadvantage, were associated in a similar way with women's and men's health. Feminist approaches emphasized that women's health should be understood both in terms of their structural position within society and their family roles (Arber and Khlat, 2002).

Dramatic changes, particularly during the late twentieth century in terms of actual and expected gender roles, especially for women, mean that the patterns of gendered health inequalities are likely to be complex and variable over time and across culture. Probably the most important change has been the increasing rate of women's participation in paid employment, but this does not represent a simple convergence of men and women's experience, since women's employment differs from men's in important ways. While many jobs have opened up for women, giving them greater financial independence, women and men still usually occupy different structural locations within society, with persistent patterns of occupational sex segregation, and women having lower earnings (Rake, 2000). Women, on average, have less power, status and financial resources than men, as well as less autonomy and independence (Doyal, 1995; Arber and Khlat, 2002: 643).

The effect of different types of work – formal and informal, paid and unpaid – on health has focused on whether paid work damages or protects women's health. The evaluation of the contribution of employment and domestic responsibilities to rates of mortality and morbidity sought to avoid essentializing gender difference by interrogating (not assuming) the type of work that men and women undertake. This type of investigation offers insight into how the effect of social class on health is mediated by gender as well as how gender mediates the effects of social class.

MORBIDITY, GENDER AND THE EFFECT OF WORK

The rise in the proportion of women in the workforce has facilitated the disaggregation of the content and quantity of women's work and stress and the quantitative study of its health effects. An examination of whether or not paid employment benefitted women's health looked for variation according to the women's age, number of children and whether in full- or part-time work (Arber et al., 1985). The theory that paid employment benefits women's health was supported for women without children and for women over 40 years old with children. The theory that employment damages women's health was supported for women under 40 with full-time work and children, but higher levels of illness were less marked for women in managerial and professional jobs. For young mothers, evidence was found that full-time work was detrimental for health unless sufficient resources were made available to mitigate the strain of multiple domestic and professional roles or 'until the sexual division of labour in the home changes' (Arber et al., 1985: 375).

Arber and colleagues' carefully qualified conclusions notwithstanding, Bartley and colleagues argue that, in general, research into the effects of work on women's health has been structured so as to show that paid work benefitted women's health. Women tended to be treated as an undifferentiated category, and mental rather than physical morbidity was studied, so as to confirm an association between paid employment and better mental health among women (Bartley et al., 1992).

Disaggregation of women's work into domestic labour and paid employment confirmed that women with full- and part-time paid work were more likely to experience lower levels of physical and psychological symptoms than those who were exclusively housewives. Bartley and colleagues' work paying attention to the content and quantity of women's paid and unpaid work was part of a tradition of research in which the benefits of paid work for women's health could be precisely circumscribed (Bartley et al., 1992). With such detailed operationalization of gender and of work variables, it became possible for similarities and differences within and across gender to emerge from analysis (Hunt and Annandale, 1993: 660). This detailed survey work also showed up the methodological difficulties of using gender as a statistical variable: the deeply gendered nature of our culture means that it is difficult to 'control for gender' so as to render de-contextualized comparison of men and women appropriate. For instance, in comparing paid and unpaid work of men and women, even when in the same occupation, men and women have different work roles and aspects of that occupation may take on different significance because of different family responsibilities (Walters et al., 1997: 340). The gendered variation in domestic and occupational roles has a significant effect on health, for example the consistent finding that women have a greater risk of depression compared with men has been related to the differences in their roles and the stresses and expectations that go with them (Nazroo et al., 1998: 326). This contributes to the case that it is the content and context of gendered roles that are important in explaining women's excess morbidity, rather than some inherent feature of women as a gendered group.

Viewing gendered health inequalities in the context of other aspects of social stratification has become possible as data sets have built up over the past decades, allowing global trends to be described. Annandale (2010) describes broad tendencies with regard to contrasts in men and women's health: the reduction of women's life expectancy advantage and especially the healthy life expectancy compared to men in the West, and the widening gap between men and women's life expectancy in Eastern Europe as men seem to have been most vulnerable to the effects of rapid social change. The gender convergence of the West compared with the gender divergence of Eastern Europe can be understood in terms of health-related behaviours in structural context.

Despite feminism's associations with post-structuralism, which would suggest the rejection of grand narratives, there is nonetheless an implicit assumption that with greater gender equality in society men and women's health status will inevitably converge (Annandale, n.d.). This assumption is supported by evidence that, in countries where the gender distribution of political power and work is comparatively egalitarian, both girls and boys had lower levels of self-reported health complaints (Torsheim et al., 2006). At the sub-national level, analysis from Sweden, with its long-standing gender equality legislation, shows that some but not all indicators of gender equality have been positively associated with some positive health outcomes: although greater gender equality was associated with longer life expectancy and less sickness absence, it was more generally correlated with poorer health for both men and women (Backhans et al., 2007). The authors' interpretation of this counter-intuitive finding is that women may have become more burdened while men have lost many of their old privileges, such that further expansion by women into traditionally male roles, spheres and activities will not lead to positive health effects unless men also reconfigure their gender roles to take on domestic and familial responsibilities traditionally shouldered by women. Backhans and colleagues' work suggests the limits of a liberal feminist analysis: the expansion in the range of roles that women take on is no longer offering health benefits. Instead, a more radical gender revolution, whereby men alter their roles and activities, may be needed in order to see further public health benefits.

CONCLUSION

The feminist effort to de-couple sex and gender has been important in developing conceptual and empirical work around health inequalities, public health policy and understandings of illness causation. The success of this effort can be measured in the mainstream acceptance that gender is, in large measure, a matter of social and cultural construction. However, the reluctance of feminist theory to grapple with embodied aspects of sex difference in relation to gendered ideas, together with medical sociologists' fascination with obstetrics, gynaecology and midwifery, has left undisturbed a Victorian core of thinking that gendered illness patterns are a matter of reproductive physiology. In destabilizing ideas about the fixity of a biologically determined sex difference, models associated with post-structural thought, such as networks and cyborgs, have yet to make their mark in the record of published research. This is notable, given that metaphors of machine-enhanced humanity and networked beings are not unusual in science fiction and fantasy in various media; indeed they make up a substantial part of the mainstream entertainment industry. The potential for disrupting traditional gendered practice through human–machine interactions, to which Donna Harraway drew our attention, remains under-realized in popular culture, as in sociology. What is more evident is the re-inscribing of gendered roles onto machines, as though humanity cannot relate to a robot unless it has a gendered nature. The role of technology in our embodiment has been interrogated by sociology of the body and is explored further in Chapter 6.

The indeterminacy of definition and measurement of sociological concepts noted by Clarke in 1983 has been overcome to a great extent. The measurement of the gendered effects of changing employment patterns (occupational variation over a lifetime), household structures (cohabition and divorce) and welfare policies' mitigating effect on carers' double-shifts (subsidized childcare, paid parental leave) has developed dramatically over several decades (Arber and Khlat, 2002). But the process of developing a sophisticated theoretical conceptualization of gender that permits flexible empirical operationalization and also makes sense in the everyday gendered world is not yet finished. Only now are studies emerging that conceptualize gender in combination with other sociological variables, and admit the power of social constructionism as well as the fundamentally embodied nature of our experience of health and illness.

As the generation of researchers who witnessed the urgency of the gender politics of the 1960s and 1970s retires, it is a cohort schooled in the cynicism of the 1980s and 1990s who must avoid the complacency of post-feminism in rising to this challenge. As Angela McRobbie (2009) has made clear, the danger is of feminism's challenge being acknowledged in superficial or individualizing ways, which ignore and neutralize the imperative of the collective demand.

In developing a theory of gender that avoids polarizing binary oppositions in the study of health and illness, feminist sociology needs to be in conversation with disciplines such as development studies and anthropology, which are engaged with the study of global health matters. The starkness of the health inequalities that affect the world's poor, who are disproportionately women and children, should not become an excuse to allow gender to be collapsed back into a biologically justified notion of a female health deficit.

REFERENCES

Annandale, E. (n.d.) 'Editorial. Virtual special issue: gender and health.' Available at: www.elsevier.com/wps/find/S06_351.cws_home/JAS_editorialedit

Annandale, E. (1990) *The Sociology of Health and Medicine: A Critical Introduction.* Cambridge: Polity.

Annandale, E. (2010) 'Health status and gender', in W.C. Cockerham (ed.), *The New Blackwell Companion to Medical Sociology.* Malden, MA: Wiley-Blackwell. pp. 99–112.

Annandale, E. and Clark, J. (1996) 'What is gender? Feminist theory and the sociology of human reproduction', *Sociology of Health & Illness,* 18(1): 17–44.

Annandale, E. and Hunt, K. (1990) 'Masculinity, femininity and sex: an exploration of their relative contribution to explaining gender differences in health', *Sociology of Health & Illness,* 12(1): 24–46.

Arber, S. and Khlat, M. (2002) 'Introduction to "social and economic patterning of women's health in a changing world"', *Social Science & Medicine,* 54(5): 643–7.

Arber, S., Gilbert, G.N. and Dale, A. (1985) 'Paid employment and women's health: a benefit or a source of role strain?', *Sociology of Health & Illness,* 7(3): 375–400.

Backhans, M., Lundberg, M. and Månsdotter, A. (2007) 'Does increased gender equality lead to a convergence of health outcomes for men and women? A study of Swedish municipalities', *Social Science & Medicine*, 64(9): 1892–903.

Bartley, M., Popay, J. and Plewis, I. (1992) 'Domestic conditions, paid employment and women's experience of ill-health', *Sociology of Health & Illness*, 14(3): 313–43.

Browne, J. and Minichiello, V. (1994) 'The condom: why more people don't put it on', *Sociology of Health & Illness*, 16(2): 229–51.

Charles, C., Whelan, T., Gafni, A., Reyno, L. and Redko, C. (1998) 'Doing nothing is no choice: lay constructions of treatment decision-making among women with early-stage breast cancer', *Sociology of Health & Illness*, 20(1): 71–95.

Clarke, J.N. (1983) 'Sexism, feminism and medicalism: a decade review of literature on gender and illness', *Sociology of Health & Illness*, 5(1): 62–82.

Cockerham, W.C. (1999) *Health and Social Change in Russia and Eastern Europe*. London: Routledge.

Courtenay, W.H. (2000) 'Constructions of masculinity and their influence on men's well-being: a theory of gender and health', *Social Science & Medicine*, 50(10): 1385–401.

Davies, K. (2003) 'The body and doing gender: the relations between doctors and nurses in hospital work', *Sociology of Health & Illness*, 25(7): 720–42.

Doyal, L. (1995) *What Makes Women Sick: Gender and the Political Economy of Health*. London: Macmillan.

Emslie, C., Hunt, K. and Watt, G. (2001) 'Invisible women? The importance of gender in lay beliefs about heart problems', *Sociology of Health & Illness*, 23(2): 203–33.

Harraway, D. (1990) 'A manifesto for cyborgs: science, technology and socialist feminism in the 1980s', in L. Nicholson (ed.), *Feminism/Postmodernism*. London: Routledge.

Holland, J., Ramazanoglu, C., Scott, S., Sharpe, S. and Thomson, R. (1990) 'Sex, gender and power: young women's sexuality in the shadow of AIDS', *Sociology of Health & Illness*, 12(3): 336–50.

Humm, M. (ed.) (1992) *Feminisms: A Reader*. Hemel Hempstead: Harvester Wheatsheaf.

Hunt, K. and Annandale, E. (1993) 'Just the job? Is the relationship between health and domestic and paid work gender-specific?', *Sociology of Health & Illness*, 15(5): 632–64.

Illouz, E. (2008) *Saving the Modern Soul: Therapy, Emotions and the Culture of Self-Help*. Berkeley: University of California Press.

Jewkes, R., Penn-Kekana, L. and Rose-Junius, H. (2005) '"If they rape me, I can't blame them": reflections on gender in the social context of child rape in South Africa and Namibia', *Social Science & Medicine*, 61(8): 1809–20.

Macintyre, S., Hunt, K. and Sweeting, H. (1996) 'Gender differences in health: are things as simple as they seem?', *Social Science & Medicine*, 42: 617–24.

McRobbie, A. (2009) *The Aftermath of Feminism: Gender, Culture and Social Change*. London: Sage.

Mantell, J.E., Myer, L., Carballo-Diéguez, A., Stein, E., Ramjee, G., Morar, N.S. and Harrison, P.F. (2005) 'Microbicide acceptability research: current approaches and future directions', *Social Science & Medicine*, 60(2): 319–30.

Maynard, M. (1990) 'The re-shaping of sociology? Trends in the study of gender', *Sociology*, 24: 269–90.

Mol, A. (2002) *The Body Multiple: Ontology in Medical Practice*. Durham, NC: Duke University Press.

Nazroo, J.Y., Edwards, A.C. and Brown, G.W. (1998) 'Gender differences in the prevalence of depression: artefact, alternative disorders, biology or roles?', *Sociology of Health & Illness*, 20(3): 312–30.

Oliffe, J. (2006) 'Embodied masculinity and androgen deprivation therapy', *Sociology of Health & Illness*, 28(4): 410–32.

Padian, N.S., van der Straten, A., Ramjee, G. et al.; MIRA Team (2007) 'Diaphragm and lubricant gel for prevention of HIV acquisition in southern African women: a randomised controlled trial', *The Lancet*, 370: 251–61.

Prout, A. (1996) 'Actor-network theory, technology and medical sociology: an illustrative analysis of the metered dose inhaler', *Sociology of Health & Illness*, 18(2): 198–219.

Rake, K. (2000) *Women's Incomes over the Lifetime: A Report to the Women's Unit.* London: HMSO.

Robertson, S. (2006) '"I've been like a coiled spring this last week": embodied masculinity and health', *Sociology of Health & Illness*, 28(4): 433–56.

Robertson, S., Sheikh, K. and Moore, A. (2010) 'Embodied masculinities in the context of cardiac rehabilitation', *Sociology of Health and Illness*, 32(5): 695–710.

Rosengarten, M., Michael, M., Mykhalovskiy, E. and Imrie, J. (2008) 'The challenges of technological innovation in HIV', *The Lancet*, 372: 357–8.

Sen, G. and Östlin, P. (2008) 'Gender inequity in health: why it exists and how we can change it', special supplement of *Global Public Health*, 3 Supplement 1. Available at: www.who.int/pmnch/topics/maternal/r_maternal20080506/en/index.html

Torsheim, T., Ravens-Siebererb, U., Hetlanda, J., Välimaac, R., Danielsond, M. and Overpecke, M. (2006) 'Cross-national variation of gender differences in adolescent subjective health in Europe and North America', *Social Science & Medicine*, 62(4): 815–27.

Waldron, I. (1976) 'Why do women live longer than men?', *Social Science & Medicine*, 10(7–8): 349–62.

Waldron, I. (2005) 'Gender differences in mortality – causes and variations in different societies', in P. Conrad (ed.), *The Sociology of Health and Illness: Critical Perspectives*, 7th edition. New York: Worth. pp. 38–53.

Walters, V., French, S., Eyles, J., Lenton, R., Newbold, B. and Mayr, J. (1997) 'The effect of paid and unpaid work on nurses' well-being: the importance of gender', *Sociology of Health & Illness*, 19(3): 328–47.

World Health Organization (WHO) (2008) *World Health Statistics 2008: Global Health Indicators.* Available at: www.who.int/whosis/whostat/EN_WHS08_Table1_Mort.pdf

5
ETHNICITY, RACISM AND DIFFERENCE

INTRODUCTION

As has been examined in preceding chapters, the effect of social stratification on health and longevity is a key area of research for sociological approaches to health and illness. This chapter explores how ethnicity and racism have emerged as dimensions of stratification in the social relations of health along with class (Chapter 3) and gender (Chapter 4). The different ways in which ethnic or racial inequalities in health have been addressed in the UK and the USA are related to the conceptualizations of migration, cultural difference and hierarchies of class and race that have informed research. The cultural context of research is a key aspect of understanding what questions can and cannot be asked, let alone answered. The pitfalls of qualitative and quantitative conceptualizations of the complex contingency of racialized or ethnic groups as both structural constraint and cultural resource are considered in an attempt to unravel the contradictions of researching a dimension of identity that, as well as being cultural and structural, also captures genetic variation, both real and fantasized. While epidemiological approaches define ethnic group categories to permit comparison across populations, sociological interrogations emphasize the multiplicity of identities referred to as 'race' or 'ethnicity' and their genesis from a complex of socio-historical relationships and their ensuing outcomes. The diverse ways in which these relationships play out in specific social settings means that sociologists often emphasize the plural nature of 'racisms' and 'ethnicities' to avoid an impression that unified or stable definitions are possible. The desire to define stable comparative categories is perhaps aided by the common terminology of 'race' used in the USA and the UK, which is misleading given the contrasting socio-historical development of the terms in the two national settings, as sketched below.

BACKGROUND – UK

The UK has long received migrants, particularly in commercial and maritime centres, such that the flow of people between the British Isles and neighbouring countries – Ireland, France, the Netherlands – predates the Romans. Wars and political oppression have often driven people to Britain, in flight from fascism and anti-Semitism in the first half of the twentieth century and subsequent waves resulting from conflicts in the Balkans, Iraq and Somalia, among others. The mass migration of the 1950s when former colonial subjects were urged to migrate to the UK to make good labour shortages and rebuild Britain has been seen as a key moment in the creation of multicultural Britain. Migrants from the Indian subcontinent, East Africa and the Caribbean took up work in various occupations in public and private sectors and were crucial for the functioning of the NHS, among other organizations. During the post-war period, racism was neither proscribed nor enacted by legal means and there was a presumption that immigrants would seek to assimilate to the British way of life. Assimilation (or not) was the focus of interest for the development of a sociology of race relations using a Marxist approach to consider migrants' class interests and a Weberian perspective to assess the interpretation of the status of former colonial subjects in the British urban context.

The liner 'Empire Windrush' has come to symbolize the onset of mass migration to Britain when it arrived from Jamaica in 1948 bringing nearly 500 passengers who had responded to an offer of cheap transport to the UK for those seeking work. The 'Windrush generation' of migrants whose arrival created visible and long-standing minority ethnic groups was a significant demographic moment which eventually led to Britain having to reassess her sense of herself as the mother country to an empire and adjust to being a post-colonial, plural society. The 'failure' of immigrants and their descendants to adopt a British lifestyle, instead maintaining distinct patterns of family life, and dietary and religious practice, showed up the prevailing 'assimilationist' assumptions. The need to reassess assumptions of assimilation led to questions about the extent to which acculturation was a voluntary process, whether immigrants were exercising free choice in retaining a distinct identity and the role that racism and religious prejudice played in preventing assimilation. Multiculturalism and anti-racism emerged as contested approaches to difference and discrimination within sociology, public policy and media discourse. During this argument, 'culture' and especially 'minority culture' or 'cultural difference' became loaded terminology whereby a problematic deviation from the ethnic majority's norm could be referred to without deploying crudely racist language.

BACKGROUND – USA

In contrast to the UK's relatively recent mass immigration, the USA is a nation-state built on the idea of immigrants seeking acculturation to an American way of life. Only about 2 per cent of the US population can claim descent from the indigenous inhabitants who populated the continent prior to the arrival of Europeans. Even while acknowledging the damage done to indigenous societies, the ideal of a new world, made up of immigrants who have left behind their old allegiances and loyalties, remains powerful. However, research suggests that the melting pot in which these new social relations were formed included European and especially Protestant migrants, but excluded native Americans and African-Americans, and, more recently, Hispanics and Asians (Perlmann and Waters, 2002). The USA has long held a multi-cultural ideal, although from the outset this co-existed with institutionalized slavery which involved a set of trading relations that systematically destroyed the culture of those who were transported across the Atlantic in the middle passage and during the second middle passage across America. Even now, more than a century since slavery's abolition, its effects remain discernable in patterns of residential segregation and other aspects of inequality, such that being of African-American descent is strongly associated with under privilege. Compared to the focus on minority culture in the UK, American approaches have been more concerned with the implications of racial group for poverty and deprivation, for instance in terms of White versus non-White mortality (McCord and Freeman, 1990).

SOCIOLOGY OF RACE RELATIONS

Early sociological interest in the variation between cultural groups focused on differences in how various groups responded to pain and other symptoms (Zola, 1966). Following up earlier work (Zborowski, 1952), Irving Zola (1966) observed doctor–patient communication in medical clinics, comparing how Jewish, Italian and Irish patients responded. In comparison with 'old Americans', Italians were found to be expressive and the Irish stoic. Zola's work allowed that ethnic variation could be explained in terms of cultural (and not socio-economic) difference and has been widely cited.

Compared with other branches of sociology, medical sociology has been accused of failing to address the social changes engendered by migration. In the

1970s, research around the post-Second World War migration to the UK using sociological and anthropological methods had led to a distinct field of study known as 'race relations' (Rex and Moore, 1969; Banton, 1977; Anwar, 1979; Saifullah Khan, 1979). Medical sociology's initial neglect of the social relations of health among immigrant and minority groups left the field open to other disciplines to conceptualize and develop, with medical approaches setting the tone of research from the 1970s.

Public health and tropical medicine focused on the diseases of immigrants, especially infections that could have represented a threat to the resident British population. A focus on the potential threat of infectious disease from abroad helped to reinforce a view of immigrants as representing a danger to public health. Through the 1980s, interest in tropical infectious disease as exotic and peculiar gave way to research on more familiar disease but with a focus on cases where epidemiological presentation in the minority differed from the population norm. Epidemiological approaches have tended to compare the relative risks of different populations, to contrast the risk of developing a disease of the minority group with that of the majority. Comparisons of minority ethnic communities against a majority 'norm' in terms of morbidity, mortality or health-related behaviour have concentrated on excess morbidity, mortality or deleterious health behaviour among the minority in question (Bhopal, 2010). This has given rise to the misleading impression that the diseases that affect minorities are distinct from those from which the general population suffers.

The focus on diseases and conditions peculiar to minorities has been unfortunate in its effect of ignoring both the health issues that concerned the communities themselves and the diseases which affected the largest numbers of people in these communities (Ahmad and Bradby, 2007). Epidemiological approaches to minority ethnic health which have focused on relative risk carried two major disadvantages for the development of a sociology of ethnicity and health. First, the impression developed that minority ethnic health exists primarily as a comparative problem, rather than as a phenomenon worthy of study in its own right. Descriptions of minorities' deviation from a norm (albeit a statistical rather than a lived norm) reinforced a model of minorities' cultural and/or genetic deficit compared to the general population. Second, the focus on conditions where minority ethnic groups have a raised incidence or prevalence ignored that condition's significance for the minority group itself and also made no assessment as to the implications for the majority population. For example, despite tuberculosis rates remaining higher among some minorities compared with the majority population, this is of limited significance for public health policy since the overall prevalence rates are low and improved treatment has reduced tubercular mortality. In contrast, cancers, which account for around one-sixth of all deaths among minority ethnic groups, are neglected, as the relative prevalence rates for minorities are lower than in the ethnic majority population (Ahmad and Bradby, 2007).

An emphasis on 'relative risk', and the 'treatment' of heightened risk, can be seen as part of a broader tendency to treat minority ethnic patients as if they had special needs. It would be better to view minorities' needs as normal and the NHS structures that fail to meet them as problematic. The 1970s saw the beginning of a series of 'special initiatives' in health service provision to remedy minorities' supposed cultural deficit, which was subtly constructed as 'causing' the health problem in question. 'Asian rickets' (Dunnigan et al., 1981) was tackled through a 'Stop Rickets Now!' campaign, but proposed remedies implied that the cause of 'Asian rickets' differed from the causes of rickets in the general population (Donovan, 1984). The 'Asian mother and baby campaign' was launched in 1984 to address the epidemiological finding of poor perinatal outcomes in babies whose mothers were born in the Indian subcontinent. Yvette Rocheron (1988) discusses how, despite reformist intentions to eradicate individual racism and address health needs, the campaign nonetheless reinforced a model of Black pathology whereby Asian mothers are blamed for their babies' poor outcomes.

Cultural guidebooks appeared at this time (for example, Henley, 1979), intended to inform service providers regarding the peculiarities of minority ethnic cultures in a way that stripped those cultures of their complexity, contingency and dynamism and presented them as static, homogenous artefacts. In a cultural guide, all members of a 'culture' are implicitly assumed to share common features of diet, worship and family life. Concepts of racism and discrimination did not fit well with this formulation of ethnic minority 'special' needs. Cultural guidebooks implied that with adequate information, racism would somehow disappear. Sadly, this assumption proved false, as discriminatory professionals with greater awareness of other cultures may simply target their abuse more accurately (Bowler, 1993).

The 'deficit' that minority groups showed compared to the minority cultures was addressed through the state provision of special initiatives and by cultivating the minority ethnic voluntary sector. Rex (1991) pointed out that the development of minority ethnic voluntary organizations in the 1960s and 1970s was supported by the British state, as being an efficient, cheap means of meeting minority 'special needs'. By promoting this type of separate provision, populations' needs were firmly located in terms of cultural or linguistic difference, offering a rationale for why they could not be met by existing statutory or voluntary sectors. The definition of minority ethnic needs in terms of 'cultural difference' gave important impetus to both separate provision, supported by distinct streams of state funding, and statutory sector funded 'special initiatives'. 'Special projects' with separate funding for minorities reinforced the location of these needs in minorities' own presumed cultural deviance such that the statutory sector could absolve itself of any responsibility to change. This response to minority health needs assumed that supporting migrants' transition to assimilation into British society was a short-term project and hence there was no requirement for a wholesale reform of services to meet society's changing needs. The provision of separate services was a cheaper option than reforming mainstream services to be more accessible to all, and gave opportunities for high-profile promotion of initiatives within the community in question, in the name of improving 'community relations'.

Despite anthropological work addressing the development of patronage and networks within minority communities of migrants (Anwar, 1979; Werbner, 1990) and the gendered politics of minority ethnic groups (Jeffery, 1976; Bhachu, 1985; Shaw, 1988), the process whereby 'community leaders' were identified by statutory agencies remains under-studied. The singling out of prominent community representatives as unelected spokesmen (and less frequently spokeswomen) was a tacit process in the years after mass migration. Migrant professionals were presumably more likely than unskilled migrants to take on such roles due to their graduate qualifications and English-language skills. In this respect, physicians from former British colonies and protectorates were key figures in the development of ethnic relations and the negotiation of cultural difference within the healthcare system.

By the mid-1980s, two critiques of UK public health approaches to minority cultures' health-related practices and healthcare needs had published (Donovan, 1984; Pearson, 1986). In highlighting problems with the existing (fairly limited) literature on ethnicity and health, these papers emphasized the importance of locating minority ethnic health and care needs in the context of socio-economic disadvantage and racial discrimination, rather than assuming that problematic minority cultural practices explained health deficits. By this time, the inappropriateness of presuming that immigrants would either return to their sending society or 'become British' by abandoning a distinct culture, was becoming apparent.

The focus of research on a deficit model of minority culture meant a failure to apprehend the complex interrelations that minorities had with a wider diasporic network, which had implications for understanding day-to-day medical pluralism. Later qualitative work would show that minorities, like the ethnic majority, used alternative systems of healing alongside biomedicine. However, in the 1970s, there was a sense that where minorities were using alternative systems, these were being used instead of orthodox health services, thereby jeopardizing people's health. Evidence of the use of a taveez (Islamic prayers written on fragments of paper and worn around the neck) or herbal medicine was interpreted as a problematic refusal to assimilate, rather than a practice complementary to medical treatment. Not only did research largely ignore minority health practice except as part of a Black pathology, it also failed to see how the general culture, including that around health and illness, was developing with the arrival of migrants. For instance, traditional Chinese medical services, largely provided by immigrants, have become commonly available on the British high street. However, the main customer group for Chinese medicine is the White middle classes rather than Chinese immigrants who regard it as too expensive and unreliable compared with provision at home (Green et al., 2006).

ETHNICITY AND HEALTH INEQUALITIES

While mainstream sociology was asking how immigrant workers would fit into the occupational and class hierarchy (Rex and Moore, 1969; Castles and Kosack, 1973; Smith, 1977), medical sociology showed little interest in how health inequalities would reflect the process of immigration and the reproduction of minority ethnic groups. The Black Report included mortality by country of birth and occupational class for men of working age (Townsend and Davidson, 1982: Table 3). The age-standardized mortality ratios of immigrant males compared favourably with their British-born equivalents in the lower social classes, but less so in the higher classes (however, interpretation is difficult in classes I and II because of small numbers). Although evidence of minority ethnic disadvantage suggested that higher than average rates of mortality and morbidity should be in evidence, the report pointed to various reasons why this might not show up. The healthy migrant effect, together with the younger average age of immigrants might have been masking ill effects in terms of raised mortality rates. It was noted that hypotheses regarding ethnicity and socio-economic status could not be tested using official data at this time since country of birth was the only available proxy for ethnic group (Townsend and Davidson, 1982: 50).

Despite fewer than 300 copies initially being produced, The Black Report (DHSS, 1980) was key in the development of research into socio-economic health inequalities, but did not herald a similar surge of research into inequalities with a racialized or ethnic dimension. This may have been due to the impact of Marmot and colleagues' (1984b) study of immigrant mortality rates, which combined British census data with death certificate data to study the relationship between country of birth and mortality rates that had been noted in the Black Report. A central finding was that there was no relationship between occupational class and mortality for immigrant groups, even though there was a clear relationship for those born in the UK. It was concluded that differences in socio-economic position could not explain the higher mortality rates found in some migrant groups in the UK (Marmot et al., 1984a). These findings gave impetus to the existence of a 'healthy migrant effect' which had been suggested in other contexts, where immigrants' rates of service use were lower than the general population (Cochrane and Stopes-Roe, 1977, 1981). The healthy migrant effect suggests that trans-continental migration, particularly where motivated by the search for paid employment, would only be undertaken by relatively healthy individuals and thus rates of morbidity and associated health service use would be depressed. (More recently, the healthy migrant effect has been tested in the national register data sets of Nordic countries and, as with anything to do with ethnicity, context is key: migration from Finland to Sweden [like that from Ireland to England] is associated with an unhealthy migrant effect, whereas migration from Southern Europe to Sweden apparently shows a healthy migrant effect [Weitoft et al., 1999].)

Marmot and colleagues' paper may have set back the search for the effects of socio-economic position on minority ethnic group health, with its dismissal of social class as a valid explanation for inequalities by ethnic group: 'Social class as usually defined does not account for the high mortality of Irish immigrants. Nor do social class differences account for mortality differences among other immigrant groups' (Marmot et al., 1984a: 1457). After this statement of the irrelevance of social class for explaining mortality inequalities among migrant groups, it was perhaps not surprising that for more than a decade socio-economic position was not discussed with respect to the relationship between ethnicity and health. When analysis of immigrant mortality data was undertaken 13 years later, it again appeared to deny a socio-economic explanation for the different rates of mortality across immigrant and non-immigrant groups (Harding and Maxwell, 1997). By contrast, analysis of self-reported morbidity suggested that socio-economic factors made a major contribution to ethnic differences in health (Nazroo, 1997). Referred to as the Fourth National Survey, these results were significant in defining future work on the relationship between ethnicity and health: the survey sample was nationally representative, encompassing 5,196 people of Caribbean and of South Asian origin, who, like the 2,867-strong White comparison group, were interviewed in detail. Complex weighting made these results as representative as possible and detailed questions around health and health service use made this the first detailed national morbidity survey that could make valid comparisons across ethnic groups (Modood and Berthoud, 1997: 6).

For each of the ethnic groups included in the Fourth National Survey (White, Black Caribbean, Indian, Pakistani, Chinese), a clear relationship existed between reported general health and income (Nazroo, 2003). This relationship was not just a British phenomenon: in the USA, all cause mortality in data with a 16-year follow-up period showed a clear relationship to median income rates in the area of residence of respondents for both Black and White men. Mortality rates for Black and White men increased with decreasing income such that those in the highest income band showed a twofold difference compared with the lowest income band (Davey Smith et al., 1998). Thus, within ethnic or racial groups, health was shown to be patterned by socio-economic position such that Black American men in more privileged socio-economic positions have better health, as do similar British minority ethnic people.

Having established socio-economic patterning within groups, there is growing consensus, despite the inconsistent and limited nature of the data available, that the same patterning can be seen across groups too. A key disentangling of the relationship between ethnic group, socio-economic status and health has been the recognition that standard measures of socio-economic status, developed for the ethnic majority, do not operate in a stable fashion across other ethnic groups. The language of data analysis is obfuscatory in that data sets are routinely standardized for socio-economic status so as to permit comparisons across other variables, including ethnic group. The process of standardizing for socio-economic position rests on an assumption that all necessary variables are accounted for by the measures available, but where socio-economic status is assessed by limited proxies, this may be an inappropriate assumption (Bradby and Nazroo, 2010).

For minority ethnic groups, social class does not indicate socio-economic status as it does for the ethnic majority. This has been shown in an analysis of the Fourth National Survey, where within each class group minority ethnic people had a smaller income than White people. For the poorest minority ethnic group – Bangladeshis and Pakistanis – the differences were twofold, meaning that within a single class group, there was a difference equivalent to that between the richest and poorest class groups (Nazroo, 2001). Evidence from the USA supports the suggestion that standard measures of socio-economic status do not necessarily work across racialized groups. Within occupational groups, White people have higher incomes than Black people, and within income bands, Black people have significantly less wealth than White people (Oliver and Shapiro, 1995). These systematic racial or ethnic inequalities mean that when a single or crude proxy of socio-economic status is used to 'standardize' data, the impact of socio-economic position is not, in fact, being accounted for. Thus, when analyses are presented on 'standardized' data, it is mistakenly assumed that the effect of socio-economic position has been 'controlled for', and so any residual difference is assumed to be an ethnic or racial effect, all too often misattributed to cultural or genetic difference (Bradby and Nazroo, 2010). This type of misattribution fails to take into account the growing evidence of the deleterious effect of the experience of racism on health (Karlsen and Nazroo, 2002; Williams et al., 2003), which occurs over the course of a lifetime and so is not easy to assess in cross-sectional data.

Socio-economic status properly measured, the experience of various forms of discrimination and a variety of behavioural factors, combine to bring about patterns of inequalities that show heterogeneity within ethnic groups as well as between them. The great size of the disparities between rates of morbidity and mortality by ethnic group suggests that something powerful is being captured, notwithstanding problems interpreting the data. For instance, in the UK, although Caribbean-born men show low mortality rates overall and especially from coronary heart disease, mortality from stroke is high, as it is for Caribbean-born women. In general, non–White migrants to the UK have hitherto shown lower mortality rates from respiratory disease and cancer, but high death rates from diabetes (Harding and Maxwell, 1997). Similarly, morbidity by ethnicity shows variably increased risk of poor health compared with White groups (Erens et al., 2001). This variability is best illustrated by the disparities within South Asians, a group who have often been analysed in a single group, although Indians show better health than Pakistanis who in turn show better health than Bangladeshis (Nazroo, 2001). US data on racial groups also show a heterogeneity of outcomes, but with the general pattern being White advantage over minority groups. This pattern is illustrated by the interest in the so-called Hispanic paradox, whereby the poor socio-economic status of Hispanics is not translated into poor health outcomes, although evidence from the poor health of other impoverished minorities suggests that it should (Nazroo and Williams, 2005).

The inequalities across broad ethnic or racial groups have proved difficult to interpret in a way that is progressive and that informs health policy reform. A central dilemma for studying ethnic and racial groups is the reification of socially constructed categories which, regardless of progressive intent, may nonetheless facilitate reductionist explanations of difference. Sociologists have argued for an understanding of ethnicity that reflects the complex contingency of an identity that is in some contexts chosen or emphasized and in other settings may be imposed by co-ethnics or by outsiders. The degree of constraint which operates for different groups is related to racism as well as socio-economic status. However, keeping a complex contingent view of ethnicity is easier in abstract discussion than in empirical research where concepts must be operationalized, which means using proxies despite their crude or otherwise unsatisfactory nature.

The temptation to suspend knowledge of the limitations of data and to read meaning directly from the categories around which statistics are constructed, such as 'Bangladeshi' or 'Hispanic', seems to be irresistible. Any ethnic categorization becomes reified, and, particularly where the data purport to have been controlled for socio-economic status and are presented by gender, the cause of ethnic disadvantage is sought in what it means to be, for instance, Bangladeshi or Hispanic. Some feature of the culture or the genetics of people from Bangladesh or from a Spanish-speaking culture is sought as an explanation for a measurable health deficit. The diversity of outcomes across ethnic groups can compound the assumption that culture or genetics is to blame for minority health deficits. For instance, if Pakistanis in Britain have high rates of heart disease but Caribbeans do not, how can low socio-economic status, which cuts across the two groups, have any explanatory power? Given that Pakistani peoples' low rates of respiratory illness and lung cancer can be related to low rates of smoking, why not also find a cultural behavioural explanation for high rates of cardiovascular disease (Bradby and Nazroo, 2010)?

Given that genetic explanations are not prominent in discussions of socio-economic health inequalities, their attraction for explanations of ethnic health inequalities (for instance, Wild and McKeigue, 1997) is worth considering. Sickle cell disease, together with other haemoglobinopathies, has played a role in maintaining assumptions about genetic difference underpinning ethnic health inequalities. Sickle cell disease is a simple recessive disorder whose genetic basis has been understood since about 1910 and that occurs most commonly in people of African and Caribbean descent. In both the USA and the UK, the disease has been a focus for Black identity politics (Tapper, 1999), including campaigns for adequate screening and healthcare policy (France-Dawson, 1986). Although the trait is not confined to Black populations, sickle cell disease is widely regarded as affecting only Black people. The presumed 'blackness' of sickle cell disease has been held responsible for the lack of statutory funds forthcoming for service development (Anionwu and Atkin, 2001). The simple genetic basis of sickle cell and the evolutionary explanations for its distribution in areas where malaria is endemic provide a clear illustration of evolution in human populations. However, with respect to the total burden of disease affecting minority ethnic groups, sickle cell as a single gene mutation with an unambiguous effect on haemoglobin, is highly unusual. While campaigns around improving sickle cell services have successfully raised the profile of the disease and counteracted racist myths about people with the disease, they have also had the ironic (and unintended) effect of confirming minority ethnic disadvantage as an inherent feature of the minority itself, chiming in with older ideas of hierarchical determinist racism.

The reification of ethnic groups through the (mis)interpretation of quantitative data together with the presumption of their homogeneity is unfortunate, and apparently hard to avoid. One response has been to call for qualitative and ethnographic research to illuminate the complexity of minority culture with regard to health and illness. There is undoubtedly a need to examine culture and deprivation in context and to look for the variations within ethnic groups as well as the continuities. Qualitative work has considered dimensions of health and illness around meaning and morality in minority cultures and how these interact with the moral categories of healthcare providers. Some of this work has been problematic in its insistence on the cultural nature of particular problems such that the socio-economic context drops out of the analysis. However, qualitative research can offer a complex view of how people negotiate the constraints and resources that a minority ethnic identity offers in the context of another culture (Bradby, 1997, 2007). But, as with quantitative approaches, it seems to be difficult to avoid making essentialist interpretations of contingent, cross-sectional qualitative research findings.

Qualitative approaches notwithstanding, quantitative research on inequalities by ethnicity must translate the subtle, shifting cultural commonalities that render an ethnic group recognizable, into a measurable variable (Bradby, 2003). As soon as a variable has been constructed, it seems inevitable that it is interpreted as a naturally occurring essential characteristic that is causing any ill health that can be measured. The limitations of a proxy can be carefully acknowledged in the methods section of a published analysis, the classificatory compromises rehearsed, and yet once a statistically significant inequality exists, there is an irresistible tendency to search for a single or simply measurable cause. Perhaps this tendency arises from the close association in research on inequalities between the sociology of health and illness, and epidemiology. Epidemiology looks for cause-and-effect associations between exposures and health outcomes by comparing groups with different experiences. Migrant and minority groups are epidemiologically interesting because of the ways that their experience differs or has differed from the majority. This method's focus on difference and contrast makes it difficult to bear in mind commonalities, alternative interpretations and moral dimensions of difference. We have seen the tendency to focus on difference in terms of relative risk and that this resonates with tendencies to presume the pathology of Black and minority culture and hold it responsible for any health deficit.

In noting sociology's 'naturalist essentialism' underlying the search for a single determinant factor that explains everything, Wacquant reminds us that Weber himself commented that race theories can prove and disprove anything. Wacquant comments on the constructed nature of race categories as follows:

> The salience of race in social life and social consciousness is a historically contingent and sectorally variable outcome of ongoing classification struggles which takes place both in academia and in the larger society and polity, as interested contenders strive to impose the criterion which best fits their specific interest. (Wacquant, 1989: 16)

Natural essentialism manifests itself both in the comparative methods of epidemiology and in the desire for a single cause of inequality that can be addressed through a policy intervention. The contested nature of the meaning of ethnic and racial classifications and their complex interaction with other structural and cultural variables, including gender and socio-economic status, can be illustrated by evidence on mental health.

MENTAL HEALTH

Ethnicity is a matter of both inequality and of identity. The meaning of a specific minority status comes about as a result of the claims that the minority makes for itself and how these are received by the majority, as well as the attributions made by that majority. Ethnic identities arise through these subjective and group processes which include voluntaristic and discriminatory elements, as well as structural constraints in terms of bureaucratic processes that facilitate and impede the legitimacy of particular identities. One of the ways that these complex processes are seen is through rates of mental illness and use of mental health services. Disparities between the mental health of minorities and the general population have been of interest both for what they say about the public health of the minority itself, as well as being a means of assessing the integration and assimilation of migrants and their descendants.

The direction of the disparity between minority and majority populations in measures of mental illness has not been consistent. During the 1970s and 1980s, explanations were sought for low rates of hospital admission for psychological illness among people of South Asian origin (Cochrane and Bal, 1987, 1989) and low levels of symptoms in community surveys (Cochrane and Stopes-Roe, 1977, 1981). South Asian family structure was argued to have a protective effect for symptoms of psychological distress in an early version of 'they look after their own'. The healthy migrant effect may have accounted for some of this advantage.

Since then, a consistent picture of poor mental health as well as poor mental health services for some minorities has emerged, characterized by excess rates of illness and detention and poorer pathways to care (Commission for Healthcare Audit and Inspection, 2007). The inequalities that disadvantage ethnic minorities and which can be stark are likely to have complex causes (Sainsbury Centre for Mental Health, 2006) and the role which discrimination plays in this complexity is contentious. Excessive use of involuntary detention and persistently excessive rates of acute mental illness have been cited as demonstrating discrimination at work within the system of medical care (McKenzie and Bhui, 2007). However, others cite competing hypotheses including diverse patterns of help-seeking to suggest that the evidence that racism causes inequalities is inadequate and contradictory (Singh and Burns, 2006).

In mental health, even more than in other branches of medicine, the expression of symptoms, their meaning and interpretation, is central to the diagnostic process, as well as to some therapeutic options. An interest in highlighting differences between ethnic groups has manifested itself in investigations of the cross-cultural validity of psychiatric diagnostic practices. As differences in rates of mental health service use have been documented, a concern has arisen that cultural differences in the idioms used to express mental distress would result in contrasting symptomatic accounts, hence differential diagnoses. Kleinman's work (1987) on the culturally distinct idioms for expressing mental distress suggests that a category of illness that has developed in one cultural group will fail to identify ill people in another cultural group, since it lacks coherence in that culture. While depressive illness is generally treated as if it were a universally applicable diagnostic category, one line of critique suggests that it is actually embedded in 'Western' culture to the extent that depression amounts to a culturally specific diagnosis (Jadhav, 1996). Hence, immigrants (and possibly their descendants) suffering mental distress might not be diagnosed with depression because their particular means of expressing this distress is culturally distinct. This area of research was given impetus by epidemiological evidence of a high relative risk of suicide among young Indian-born women (Soni Raleigh et al., 1990), although this finding disappeared in subsequent analyses (McKenzie et al., 2008).

Qualitative work has found that although some standard symptoms of depression were absent in South Asians' expression of distress, the commonalities were such that cultural differences were confined to the detail of the idioms used to express distress rather than the construction of depressive illness itself (Fenton and Sadiq-Sangster, 1996; Nazroo and O'Connor, 2002). People of Pakistani origin living in the UK show considerable fluency across different symbolic domains, refuting the suggestion that culture-bound metaphors or similes might determine patterns of help-seeking and healthcare use (Mallinson and Popay, 2007). Disparities in rates of mental illness and experience of care are unlikely to be due to culturally dependent means of expressing mental distress, even where interpretation of symptoms is a key aspect of diagnosis.

CONCLUSION

The ongoing controversy over the cause of minority ethnic group excess in some rates of serious and enduring mental illness illustrates the challenge of studying health inequalities around ethnicity. Ethnicity is a variable of structure and of identity and, while the same can be said of social class and of gender, the sociological urge towards natural essentialism (Wacquant, 1989) seems to find particularly fertile ground when ethnicity is in question. While the constructed nature of gender is a focus of sociological approaches, gender is nonetheless commonly assumed to have an unambiguous biological basis and the terms gender and sex are used interchangeably (see Chapter 4). While feminist and queer theory has sought to disrupt binary readings of heterosexualized gender, the everyday and public policy meaning of gender remains distinctly un-queered. Enormous efforts have been expended on devising improved means of measuring socio-economic status which, as the name suggests, is understood to be a social and economic category (see Chapter 3) and, in sociology at least, is not conceptualized as having a genetic basis. So, while gender is distinctly biological and class is not, ethnicity has a more liminal status. Theories of cultural difference overlay older racialized ideas whereby variation in skin colour, hair type and facial morphology are assumed to reflect heritable, stable distinctions between human sub-species.

In the medical and epidemiological context, it seems almost impossible to escape an implicit assumption that genetics must underpin ethnic health inequalities, especially where they are most pronounced. While scientific racism lacks respectable proponents, molecular medicine's search for single nucleotide polymorphisms that vary by population (Rose, 2007: 169) and the licensing of drugs for racialized groups (Kahn, 2006; Temple and Stockbridge, 2007) can support racist assumptions about difference. The injustice of the recourse to biology to account for ethnic health inequalities can be countered by pointing to racism in the role of creating ill health in minority groups (Karlsen and Nazroo, 2002). Racism and socio-economic status both contribute to ethnic inequalities, with genetics playing a role in some contexts, for some conditions, but classification struggles makes any discussion of this fraught (Wacquant, 1989: 16). In the discussion of mental health inequalities by ethnicity, positions have become polarized in the light of injustice, making nuanced discussion difficult (Bradby, 2010).

The anthropologist Marshall Sahlins observed that 'Events are ordered by culture, … in that process, the culture is reordered' (1981: 8). The naturalist essentialist search for single variables that explain difference, combined with historically racialized thinking, has made it difficult to escape a simplistic approach to complex problems. In the case of mental health inequalities, this has led to embattled positions where racism, behavioural factors or socio-economic deprivation have all too often been seen as alternative causative hypotheses and painstaking documentation of complex interactions has been avoided. Since both race and mental health are subject to the classificatory struggle for meaning, that struggle is also part of the understanding of inequality. The endless tension between showing inequality by measuring it and thereby reinforcing the categories of differentiation is also part of that classificatory struggle, and unfortunately, this tension will not disappear simply by declaring one's progressive and anti-racist intent.

REFERENCES

Ahmad, W. and Bradby, H. (2007) 'Locating ethnicity and health: exploring concepts and contexts', *Sociology of Health and Illness*, 29(6): 795–810.

Anionwu, E.N. and Atkin, K. (2001) *The Politics of Sickle Cell and Thalassaemia*. Buckingham: Open University Press.

Anwar, M. (1979) *The Myth of Return*. London: Heinemann.

Banton, M. (1977) *The Idea of Race*. London: Tavistock.

Bhachu, P. (1985) *Twice Migrants – East African Settlers in Britain*. London: Tavistock.

Bhopal, R. (2010) 'Thesis: medicine and public health in a multiethnic world', *Journal of Public Health*, 31(3): 315–21.

Bowler, I. (1993) '"They're not the same as us": midwives' stereotypes of South Asian descent maternity patients', *Sociology of Health and Illness*, 15(2): 157–78.

Bradby, H. (1997) 'Health, heating and heart attacks: Glaswegian Punjabi women's thinking about everyday food', in P. Caplan (ed.), *Food Health and Identity*. London: Routledge. pp. 211–33.

Bradby, H. (2003) 'Describing ethnicity in health research', *Ethnicity and Health*, 8(1): 5–13.

Bradby, H. (2007) 'Watch out for the Aunties! Young British Asians' accounts of identity and substance use', *Sociology of Health and Illness*, 29(5): 656–72.

Bradby, H. (2010) 'Understanding and apprehending institutional racism in mental health services: compromised conceptualization', *Sociological Research Online*, 15(3): 8.

Bradby, H. and Nazroo, J. (2010) 'Health, ethnicity and race', in W.C. Cockerham (ed.), *The Blackwell Companion to Medical Sociology*. Malden, MA: Blackwell. pp. 113–29.

Castles, S. and Kosack, G. (1973) *Immigrant Workers and Class Structure in Western Europe*. Oxford: Oxford University Press.

Cochrane, R. and Bal, S.S. (1987) 'Migration and schizophrenia: an examination of five hypotheses', *Social Psychiatry*, 2: 181–91.

Cochrane, R. and Bal, S.S. (1989) 'Mental hospital admission rates of immigrants to England: a comparison of 1971 and 1981', *Social Psychiatry and Psychiatric Epidemiology*, 2: 2–11.

Cochrane, R. and Stopes-Roe, M. (1977) 'Psychological and social adjustment of Asian immigrants to Britain: a community survey', *Social Psychiatry*, 2: 195–206.

Cochrane, R. and Stopes-Roe, M. (1981) 'Psychological symptom levels in Indian immigrants to England: a comparison with native English', *Psychological Medicine*, 11(2): 319–27.

Commission for Healthcare Audit and Inspection (2007) *Count Me In. Results of the 2006 National Census of Inpatients in Mental Health and Learning Disability Services in England and Wales*. London: Commission for Healthcare Audit and Inspection. Available at: www.cqc.org.uk/_db/_documents/Count_Me_In_2006.pdf

Davey Smith, G., Neaton, J.D., Wentworth, D., Stamler, R. and Stamler, J. (1998) 'Mortality differences between black and white men in the USA: contribution of income and other risk factors among men screened for the MRFIT', *Lancet*, 351: 934–9.

Department of Health and Social Security (DHSS) (1980) *Inequalities in Health: Report of a Research Working Group*. London: DHSS.

Donovan, J. (1984) 'Ethnicity and race: a research review', *Social Science and Medicine*, 19(7): 663–70.

Dunnigan, M.G., McIntosh, W.B., Sutherland, G.R., Gardee, R., Glekin, B., Ford, J.A. and Robertson, I. (1981) 'Policy for prevention of Asian rickets in Britain: a preliminary assessment of the Glasgow Rickets Campaign', *British Medical Journal*, 282(6261): 357–60.

Erens, B., Primatesta, P. and Prior, G. (2001) *Health Survey for England 1999: The Health of Minority Ethnic Groups*. London: The Stationery Office.

Fenton, S. and Sadiq-Sangster, A. (1996) 'Culture, relativism and the expression of mental distress: South Asian women in Britain', *Sociology of Health and Illness*, 18(1): 66–85.

France-Dawson, M. (1986) 'Sickle cell disease: implications for nursing care', *Journal of Advanced Nursing*, 11(6): 729–37.

Green, G., Bradby, H., Chan, A. and Lee, M. (2006) '"We are not completely Westernised": dual medical systems and pathways to health care among Chinese migrant women in England', *Social Science and Medicine*, 62(6): 1498–509.

Harding, S. and Maxwell, R. (1997) 'Differences in the mortality of migrants', in F. Drever and M. Whitehead (eds), *Health Inequalities: Decennial Supplement Series DS no. 15*. London: The Stationery Office. pp. 108–21.

Henley, A. (1979) *Asian Patients in Hospital and at Home*. London: King Edward's Hospital Fund.

Jadhav, S. (1996) 'The cultural origins of Western depression', *International Journal of Social Psychiatry*, 42(4): 269–86.

Jeffery, P. (1976) *Migrants and Refugees: Muslim and Christian Pakistani Families in Bristol*. Cambridge: Cambridge University Press.

Kahn, J. (2006) 'Race, pharmacogenomics and marketing: putting BiDil in context', *The American Journal of Bioethics*, 6(5): W1–W5.

Karlsen, S. and Nazroo, J. (2002) 'Agency and structure: the impact of ethnic identity and racism on the health of ethnic minority people', *Sociology of Health and Illness*, 24: 1–20.

Kleinman, A. (1987) 'Anthropology and psychiatry: the role of culture in cross-cultural research on illness', *British Journal of Psychiatry*, 151: 447–54.

McCord, C. and Freeman, H.P. (1990) 'Excess mortality in Harlem', *New England Journal of Medicine*, 322(25): 173–7.

McKenzie, K. and Bhui, K. (2007) 'Better mental healthcare for minority ethnic groups – moving away from the blame game and putting patients first: commentary on institutional racism in psychiatry', *Psychiatric Bulletin*, 31: 368–9.

McKenzie, K., Bhui, K., Nanchahal, K. and Blizard, B. (2008) 'Suicide rates in people of South Asian origin in England and Wales: 1993–2003', *British Journal of Psychiatry*, 193: 406–9.

Mallinson, S. and Popay, J. (2007) 'Describing depression: ethnicity and the use of somatic imagery in accounts of mental distress', *Sociology of Health and Illness*, 29(6): 857–71.

Marmot, M.G., Adelstein, A.M. and Bulusu, L. (1984a) 'Lessons from the study of immigrant mortality', *The Lancet*, 323(8392): 1455–7.

Marmot, M.G., Adelstein, A.M., Bulusu, L. and OPCS (1984b) *Immigrant Mortality in England and Wales 1970–78: Causes of Death by Country of Birth*. London: HMSO.

Modood, T. and Berthoud, R. (1997) *Ethnic Minorities in Britain: Diversity and Disadvantage*. London: Policy Studies Institute.

Nazroo, J. (1997) *The Health of Britain's Ethnic Minorities: Findings of a National Survey*. London: Policy Studies Institute.

Nazroo, J.Y. (2001) *Ethnicity, Class and Health*. London: Policy Studies Institute.

Nazroo, J.Y. (2003) 'The structuring of ethnic inequalities in health: economic position, racial discrimination and racism', *American Journal of Public Health*, 93(2): 277–84.

Nazroo, J.Y. and O'Connor, W. (2002) 'Idioms of mental distress', in W. O'Connor and J.Y. Nazroo (eds), *Ethnic Differences in the Context and Experience of Psychiatric Illness: A Qualitative Study*. London: The Stationery Office.

Nazroo, J.Y. and Williams, D.R. (2005) 'The social determination of ethnic/racial inequalities in health', in M. Marmot and R.G. Wilkinson (eds), *Social Determinants of Health*, 2nd edition. Oxford: Oxford University Press. pp. 238–66.

Oliver, M.L. and Shapiro, T.M. (1995) *Black Wealth/White Wealth: A New Perspective in Racial Inequality*. New York: Routledge.

Pearson, M. (1986) 'The politics of ethnic minority health studies', in T. Rathwell and D. Phillips (eds), *Health, Race and Ethnicity*. London: Croom Helm.

Perlmann, J. and Waters, M.C. (2002) 'Introduction', in J. Perlmann and M.C. Waters (eds), *The New Race Question: How the Census Counts Multiracial Individuals*. New York: Russell Sage Foundation.

Rex, J. (1991) *Ethnic Identity and Ethnic Mobilisation in Britain*. Warwick: Centre for Research in Ethnic Relations.

Rex, J. and Moore, R. (1969) *Race, Community and Conflict*. Oxford: Oxford University Press (for the Institute of Race Relations).

Rocheron, Y. (1988) 'The Asian Mother and Baby Campaign: the construction of ethnic minority health needs', *Critical Social Policy*, 22: 4–23.

Rose, N. (2007) *The Politics of Life Itself: Biomedicine, Power and Subjectivity in the Twenty-First Century*. Princeton, NJ: Princeton University Press.

Sahlins, M. (1981) *Historical Metaphors and Mythical Realities*. Ann Arbour, MI: University of Michigan Press.

Saifullah Khan, V. (1979) *Minority Families in Britain*. Basingstoke: Macmillan.

Sainsbury Centre for Mental Health (2006) *Policy Paper 6: The Costs of Race Inequality*. London: Sainsbury Centre.

Shaw, A. (1988) *A Pakistani Community in Britain*. Oxford: Blackwell Publishing.

Singh, S.P. and Burns, T. (2006) 'Race and mental health: there is more to race than racism', *British Medical Journal*, 333: 648–51.

Smith, D.J. (1977) *Racial Disadvantage in Britain*. Harmondsworth: Penguin.

Soni Raleigh, V., Bulusu, L. and Balarajan, R. (1990) 'Suicides among immigrants from the Indian subcontinent', *The British Journal of Psychiatry*, 156: 46–50.

Tapper, M. (1999) *In the Blood: Sickle Cell Anemia and the Politics of Race*. Philadelphia: University of Pennsylvania Press.

Temple, R. and Stockbridge, N.L. (2007) 'BiDil for heart failure in black patients: the US Food and Drug Administration perspective', *Annals of Internal Medicine*, 146: 57–62.

Townsend, P. and Davidson, N. (1982) *Inequalities in Health: The Black Report*. Harmondsworth: Penguin.

Wacquant, L. (1989) 'The puzzle of race and class in American society and social science', *Benjamin E. Mays Monographs*, 2–1(Fall): 7–20.

Weitoft, G.R., Gullberg, A., Hjern, A. and Rosen, M. (1999) 'Mortality statistics in immigrant research: method for adjusting underestimation of mortality', *International Journal of Epidemiology*, 28: 756–63.

Werbner, P. (1990) *The Migration Process: Capital, Gifts and Offerings Among British Pakistanis*. New York: Berg.

Wild, S. and McKeigue, P. (1997) 'Cross-sectional analysis of mortality by country of birth in England and Wales', *British Medical Journal*, 314: 705–10.

Williams, D.R., Neighbours, H.W. and Jackson, J.S. (2003) 'Racial/ethnic discrimination and health: findings from community studies', *American Journal of Public Health*, 93(2): 200–8.

Zborowski, M. (1952) 'Cultural components in response to pain', *Journal of Social Issues*, 8(4): 16–30.

Zola, I. (1966) 'Culture and symptoms: an analysis of patient's presenting complaints', *American Sociological Review*, 31(5): 615–30.

6
BODIES, PAIN AND SUFFERING

INTRODUCTION

So far, this book has considered health inequalities as a theoretical and empirical problem and as a matter of social justice. Tabulated mortality figures show how poor living conditions, including low income, are associated with premature death. Variable rates of morbidity and mortality are summary measures of the embodiment of political, economic and social conditions and while they represent illness and death, they do not speak of the loss and pain of the bodies themselves. Health inequalities research has been of progressive intent, seeking to reduce the excess rates of morbidity and mortality suffered by marginalized groups. However, a representation of death or illness that elides the suffering of individual bodies, failing to bear witness to their pain, could be seen as a problematic technology of biomedical surveillance. Turner (2004: xxviii) suggests that sociology should work at two levels, both analysing social structure (and global processes) and describing individual experiences of health and illness. Such a dual focus reveals the body to be a site and a metaphor for analysing individual and social processes in tandem.

Sociology has interrogated the body over the past two decades, seeking to explain the nature of embodiment, together with the body's subjectivity and its role as site of both struggle and of meaning. The surge of interest in the body can be seen as a reaction to social theory's abandonment of matters bodily for the earlier part of the twentieth century. The body as a site of pain and suffering and as a site of wider subjectivity was an absent presence in sociology, which had surrendered bodies to the naturalist perspective that characterizes biomedicine (Shilling, 1993). The idea of the human body as a cultural object has been analytically important in developing criticism of medical dominance, while a focus on social conceptions of the body as a critique of naturalistic essentialism in medicine has developed social construction-ism as a key theoretical approach in medical sociology (Bury, 1987). Post-modern notions of the body as a text – as an effect of a discourse, prevalent as a result of Derrida's work – have been balanced by anthropological interest in the body as a narrative of social processes and social structures, representing fundamental features of society (Turner, 1992: 8).

Anthropological readings of the body demonstrate that culture, and specifically the culture of medicine, shapes the body, as well as how the body is read in medical set-tings. Turner (1996) points to the Abrahamic tradition of Judaism and Christianity, wherein the human body has been both powerfully symbolic of the profane world and a sacred vessel that is the focus of religious ritual. In noting parallels between spiritual and physical well-being in religious traditions, Turner (1996: 101) asks why the sociology of religion has largely neglected the intimate relationship between body and belief, and, relatedly, between medicine and religion. He contends that this theoretical negligence is also characteristic of medical sociology, which, with its preoccupation with institutionalized medicine, has often devoted itself to what Turner terms limited empirical issues, in which he includes doctor–patient inter-action, hospital administration, social factors in the aetiology of sickness and the role conflicts of nurses. So, in this view, medical sociology has been complicit with the limited way in which the body and its relationships with medicine and with religious belief systems have been appraised.

Mechanistic models of the body have come to be accepted as common sense across a range of quotidian discourses. Reductionist models of the human body, conceptualized as a number of interlocking mechanisms, can be seen in their wide-spread distribution beyond medicine: plumbing metaphors are used to advertise over-the-counter medication for digestion and urination problems; health behav-iours such as regular exercise and balanced diets are justified with car metaphors since good fuel and regular activity keeps an engine in working order, while the human brain is regularly described as a powerful computer. The body-as-machine has become the dominant everyday metaphor for understanding bodies in the post-industrial 'West'. How and why this particular model of the body spread has been a key question for social theory and has opened up other questions around the body in the social context. Mechanistic thinking about the human body has facilitated the development of biomedicine's various bodily modificatory interven-tions and technologies, from heart transplants to new reproductive technology, which have, in turn, reinforced mechanistic models.

Sociological theorizations of the relationship between the body, the self and soci-ety have tried to get some purchase on the ubiquity of body-as-machine metaphors. Social constructionist and phenomenological analysis of the embodiment of illness and injury in terms of pain and suffering have looked at the relationship of body and emotion in the co-production of the self as a stable, integrated social entity. This chapter charts some of the work that has problematized what constitutes the body, and the conditions that, according to some, have led to the body's disappearance from medical encounters. Sociological efforts to reassert some theoretical stability in bodily matters have had recourse to emotions, to narrative and to the social solidarity and the collective consciousness of particular types of bodies through the study of specific disability, injury and genetic disorder.

THE SOCIOLOGICAL BODY

Sociology's emphasis on the abstractions of social structure, with class, poverty and discrimination as key medical sociological explanatory variables for ill health, had, to some extent, obscured the body as a site of sociological interest. A trenchant sociological critique of health policies that focus on lifestyle change (diet, smoking, exercise) has been their tendency to individualize problems that can be more readily understood as structural in origin: by holding the individual responsible for maintaining a healthy body through exercise, diet and moderation, statutory agencies divert attention away from socio-economic causes of ill health. Thus, attention to individual bodies in medical sociology had been associated with an oppressive individualizing lifestyle approach to understanding health problems. Sociology has tended to view progressive struggle around political action and identity taking place at the level of the group defined by gender, class or occupation. Group solidarity contrasts with the individualizing tendencies of medicine and health promotion, which has been cast as bearing down upon the vulnerable individual.

The body as a natural and universal aspect of being human has meant its social and sociological aspects have frequently been subsumed under a naturalistic empiricism that presents 'natural' features of the body as fixed. Marx taught us that the competitive individualism of the nineteenth-century industrialized city, while important for the development of capitalist modes of production, was not a 'natural' immutable fact. Feminism taught us that women's bodies are not naturally predisposed for caring roles, even though pregnancy and lactation are confined to (although not universal among) womankind. Social constructionist approaches prompt us to see that in contemporary society the human body has become a project (Shilling, 1993).

What has been referred to as 'sociological naivety' regarding the physical (Turner, 1994: 27) was overturned during the 1980s as interest in the body as a sociological problem developed against a backdrop of demographic, viral and biomedical changes that made it difficult to ignore the body as a key site for understanding individuals' relationship with society. Ageing populations in the Western world, the global spread of HIV, the threat of new viral epidemics and advances in medical technology, from neuroscience to cloning, were the setting for a burgeoning interest in the body. The 'rise of the body' as a subject for academic study was part of its wider prominence as a topic for artistic and journalistic investigation, the entertainment industry and political activism (Petersen, 2007).

Sociology's 'discovery' of the body can also be seen as a corollary of the wider 'linguistic turn' of the twentieth century, whereby reality was understood to be constituted through the interplay of language and not to exist independently of the constitutive language (see Chapter 2). The linguistic turn conceptualizes everything as a text, written or constituted through language. Social constructionism, the daughter of the linguistic turn, declared grand theory and meta-narrative to be dead. Post-structural understandings of the late modern condition are anti-foundationalist, anti-deterministic, anti-essentialist and, hence, the corporeality and vitality of the body offered a place from which to assert a point of view on a world which had been destabilized by our own analyses. The contradiction of late capitalism's com-modification, fetishization and modification of the body, while that body had been declared a text by leading philosophers, may be why 'the body' as a cultural object came to prominence in academic circles. At a time when the 'enlightenment values of rationality, truth and progress were collapsing into their own categorical empti-ness', the body was 'something to grasp. It made no grand claims' (Hughes and Paterson, 1997: 327). The recognition of language as a structuring agent for the social world, also exposed the body as the physical basis of our lives and hence the key and perhaps only site for asserting meaning and claiming identity in a destabi-lized world.

DISSECTING THE BODY

The need to theorize bodies presented a challenge that medical sociology viewed itself as ideally placed to take on, both in theorizing the body and researching the implications of these theories in social settings where wellness and illness, health and disease were in negotiation. Sociology delineated a natu-ralistic view of the body, associated with the natural sciences and contrasted this with constructivist approaches by way of critique of naturalism's inadequacies. A naturalistic approach sees the body as a discrete biological entity that exists as a stable object regardless of its cultural, historical context. The naturalist under-standing of the body is closely associated with the medical study of anatomy and can be traced back to the work of Vesalius, a physician appointed as the dissector in sixteenth-century Padua. In 1543, Vesalius published *De humani corporis fabrica*, translated as 'On the structure of the human body', which is credited with founding human anatomy as an area of study and as being the moment that wrenched Northern Europeans into modernity (Bamforth, 2003: ix). Vesalius rejected the Galenic schooling in which he had been educated and published pictures of partially dissected human corpses, often in allegorical poses. Instead of interpreting the body through Galenic tradition based on ancient Greek humoral medicine, he relied on dissection and observation, creating images of skeletons digging their own graves and corpses suspended by the neck, displaying their flayed muscles. While the mixture of classical landscapes and sliced bodies is odd to the contemporary eye, the detailed observation of bodily structures showing the body as a three-dimensional vessel filled with organs revolutionized medical practice. The carefully observed and described structures of flesh, bones, neurones and organs answered a human curiosity about our inner selves which can be seen echoed centuries later in the world-wide interest in Gunther von Hagens' Körperwelten or Body Worlds exhibition.

Vesalius' work was the cornerstone for the development of modern medical practice in which the dissection of a human corpse became a rite of passage that has not yet been dislodged by the technology of virtual three-dimensional dissection. The cultural dominance of the biomedical anatomical conceptualization of the human body is suggested by its reputation as the best, that is, the most accurate representation available. Anatomical representations observed from life, including Vesalius's images, show individual bodies, with their own peculiarities. The rite of passage of the medical school dissection of a cadaver necessitates students' intimate appraisal of a real body with its own oddities. Thus, medical students learn that dissecting a fat body means searching for organs amongst adipose tissue, which is not shown in textbook anatomical representations. The widespread use of medical textbooks dating back to the start of the twentieth century, with their idealized and average representations of gendered and raced bodies, has been highly influential. The reproducibility of these images made them widely available and the naturalist medical version of the body became an incontestable truth (Boyle, 1970). Clinicians, through their contact with bodies, learn experientially about variation, but the schematized human body exists nonetheless as a dominant cultural model. More recent and controversial representation of the body in the plastinated cadavers of Gunther von Hagens' Körperwelten/Body Worlds exhibition (Walter, 2004) shows that naturalist perspectives are no longer the prerogative of professionals and have implications for what bodies mean across a range of contexts.

The Körperwelten/Body Worlds exhibition has provided material for the social constructionist understanding of bodies, by bringing together the material of real bodies, with all the potential visceral shock value implied, but placing this in naturalistic settings. By exhibiting dead human material posed in particular and explicitly social settings, such as playing basketball or chess, as well as more recognizably scientific exhibits reminiscent of the naturalist essentialism of medical anatomical truth claims, Körperwelten has blurred the boundary between scientific and lay understandings of the body. The exhibition claimed to be democratizing knowledge and visitors were described as calm in their contemplation of the plastinated corpses, showing little evidence of disgust or horror (von Lehm, 2006). The close observation of visitors' reactions to the exhibits showed a cerebral engagement whereby people related what they could see to their own biographies and bodies. The materiality of the body – its shape, form and function – clearly resonates at a popular level, given the enormous success of this exhibition (32 million visitors to date and counting, according to www.bodyworlds.com/en/exhibitions/unparalleled_success.html). Gunther von Hagens, the exhibition's originator, aspires to more than just anatomical education for these numerous visitors, stating: 'I hope for the exhibitions to be places of enlightenment and contemplation, even of philosophical and religious self recognition, and open to interpretation regardless of the background and philosophy of life of the viewer' (www.bodyworlds.com/en/gunther_von_hagens/life_in_science.html). Von Hagens suggests that the body, albeit dead and plastinated, offers a way of reflecting on existential and moral matters. The use of the body as a means, whether metaphorical or corporeal, of appraising the human condition is central to sociological approaches and, as we will see, offers echoes of Christian transcendent understandings of the body.

The explanatory power of medical models of the body is both their ongoing development in line with wider cultural influences, which include medical advances and their appeal to existential curiosity. The brouhaha surrounding von Hagens' public dissection of a corpse in 2002 was reminiscent of the dissections that provided popular entertainment in Britain before the Anatomy Act of 1832 (MacDonald, 2006). Gunther von Hagens currently holds a visiting professorship in the New York University College of Dentistry where he is designing an anatomy curriculum using plastinated specimens in place of dissection. So although von Hagens has described his exhibitions as democratizing bodily knowledge, against medicine's tendency to protect expertise, his techniques are also being co-opted for medical education. Hermeneutically, it is helpful to distinguish naturalist and constructivist views of the body, but in practice, they are difficult to disentangle in their mutual interpenetration.

Plastination is but one cultural moment where technological approaches are in development to remove the need to use cadavers in medical schools, and where constructionist and naturalist understandings of the body can be seen in intimate embrace. The Visible Human Project is an effort to create three-dimensional representations of 'normal' human bodies using transverse sections of cadavers (National Library of Medicine, 2008). The Virtual Physiological Human is a methodological and technological framework funded as a European project (Clapworthy et al., 2007), which aims to model the body in a way that will make possible the combination of patient-specific data with population-based representations. The naturalistic view of an average human body as delineated in the earliest medical textbooks is, thus, far from finished as an aid to research, education and medical practice, despite the insights into its limitations generated by a constructivist approach to the body. Furthermore, without the naturalistic view, as offered by the spectacle of a dissected, displayed body, the concept of a 'body without organs' delineating the virtual body of habits, traits and affects that accompanies every physical body (Deleuze and Guattari, 1972, 1980), would not have presented itself.

CULTURAL BODIES

Sociology's main criticism of the dominance of medical ideas about the body has been to show all the ways in which the human body is a cultural object (Turner, 1995). The constructionist view of the body has been a key means of undermining various manifestations of biological reductionism, including those around bodies. Feminist work has shown us the deeply entrenched and sometimes pernicious ways in which bodies are gendered so that women's symptoms are read differentially from men's (see Chapter 4). Medical imperialism with regard to the management of childbirth has constructed women's bodies as in need of control and intervention. The liberation and reclamation of women's bodies from medical systems has underpinned feminist analyses of childbirth, menopause, menstruation, and sexual and mental disorder. The liberation of bodies from coercive medical regulation has emerged from activist politics as well as the constructivist understanding of the emergence of medical and sociological knowledge, together with a phenomenological approach which considers the individual actor as part of a process of embodiment.

Bryan Turner tells us that 'any comprehensive sociology must be grounded in a recognition of the embodiment of social actors and of their multiplicity as populations' (1996: 37). And it is the twin sociological project of understanding individual bodies and populations as socially co-constructed which has arisen from Foucault's work. Foucault tells us that bodies are discursively constructed and the lived body is an outcome of social processes (Foucault, 1979, 1980). Foucault's description of the body's historical evolution as an object of the medical gaze and its becoming subject to medical dominance has been hugely influential in medical sociology. Foucault's central theme was the shift in the operation of power over time: in premodern times, power resided in the body of the monarch, whereas in modern times disciplinary power has shifted to the bodies of the wider population (Foucault, 1979).

Foucault conceives of the body as both an object of knowledge and a target for the exercise of power, and he explores the ways in which the body is rendered docile and productive, and therefore politically and economically useful, by the various techniques and technologies of power (Foucault, 1979). The body is a consistent theme throughout the analytic structure of Foucault's work, appearing as a focus of military discipline, monastic regulation and medical governmentality (Turner, 1997: xv). Foucault remained attentive to the ways that bodies were produced, regulated and represented in the context of disciplinary surveillance from the publication of *Discipline and Punish* in the mid 1970s to the third volume of *The History of Sexuality* a decade later (Turner, 1984). The examination of social control and deviance in a bureaucratic state, to which Foucault's analysis contributed, has come to have less significance as deregulation and uncertainty and the culture of risk have become the central motifs of our time. Nonetheless, bodies remain crucial sites for understanding sociological processes, as, for instance, the trafficking of people and their organs demonstrates the differential evaluation of discursively produced bodies.

Turner (1992) develops Foucault's analysis of the regulation and monitoring of individual bodies and populations in claiming that late modern societies have become somatic: that is the body has become the central field of political and cultural activity. Turner suggests that the history of the Western world is not so much the transformation of culture under the influence of rationality, as the transformation of the human body under a range of practices, with medicalization, secularization and rationalization being the major forces operating on the body in the social world. Turner sees the somatic society as a social system in which the body is 'the dominant means by which the tensions and crises of society are thematized; the body provides the stuff of our ideological reflections on the nature of our unpredictable time' (Turner, 1992: 4). He goes on to describe how we live in a world which is out of kilter and offers as evidence public health challenges and their associated lobbying groups, from AIDS to ageing populations to global warming. Turner claims that in our high modern state, Western society's preoccupation is no longer with production so much as with reproduction, and that in seeking to promote safe sex, free condoms and clean needles, the regulation of the interfaces between bodies has become the key goal of governance. His claim is that the 'somatic society is thus crucially, perhaps critically, structured around regulating bodies' (Turner, 1992: 13).

BIOTECHNOLOGICAL BODIES

For Foucault, the human subject in modernity is constituted by disciplinary techniques of biopower, which structure, produce and optimize the capabilities of the body, enhancing its economic utility and ensuring its political docility (Hughes and Paterson, 1997: 332). Biopower as a technology which manages bodies through the modern state's practices of public health, can be detected in new digital apprehensions of the human body. For instance, the online digitized cross-sectional images of dead human bodies in the Visible Human Project is described as a transformation that extends biopower (Waldby, 2000). The Visible Human Project is a biotechnology, arising from the raw material of two dead bodies, which is 'intended to eventually assist in the instrumentalisation of an open-ended number of bodies for therapeutic ends' which Catherine Waldby describes as producing 'surplus biovalue' (2000: 33). Such technological interventions are designed to improve understanding and treatment of disease, but are also involved in the pursuit of exchange value of biomedical commodities and 'biovalue' which Waldby claims is 'increasingly assimilated into capital value and configured according to the demands of commercial economies' (2000: 34). By considering the Visible Human Project alongside cloning and the Human Genome Project, Waldby suggests that there is something sinister in the exploitation of dead bodies as a form of data for the living.

Nikolas Rose agrees that 'our vitality has been opened up as never before for economic exploitation and the extraction of biovalue' (2007: 8), but optimistically refutes its sinister possibilities (despite also writing that he will leave any such judgement to others [Rose, 2007: 255]). The cause for this optimism is Rose's claim that the new bioeconomics alters our conception of ourselves and hence enables new interventions of a social and political character. The new possibilities for genetic and biological determinism are, in this view, held in balance by a particular somatic ethics that places a virtue on the search for profit through the management of life, such that health-damaging interventions are subject to 'the most moralistic of condemnations' (Rose, 2007: 8). Rose sees and perhaps overstates the possibilities of new biosocialities and biological citizenship arising through the knowledge of our molecular, genomic and neuro-chemical selves. Controversially, he also sees merit in the deeply divided and divisive issue of biomedicine's exploitation of biological markers of racial difference. Whether the benefits of racialized genotyping in terms of targeted pharmacogenetics outweigh the risks of reinvigorating old categories of discrimination is a judgement that will be easier to make in retrospect (Hunt and Megyesi, 2008). Since precious few of the much-anticipated benefits of pharmacogenetics have yet become available to a wide range of patients and racialized differences have been exploited as a means of circumnavigating pharmaceutical licensing regulation (Kahn, 2006), while racism persists and adjusts to new cultural forms, a sceptical response seems warranted.

The term 'genohype' was coined to refer to the discourse of exaggerated claims and hyperbole attached to the effort to map the human genome (Fleising, 2001), and could, perhaps, be usefully extended to cover a wider range of biotechnological inno-vations. Rose (2007) accuses sociological critics of being unduly pessimistic about the deterministic tendencies of innovative biomedical interventions. A level-headed assessment of the effects of the biotech advances on our socialized selves is what medical sociology seeks, but the range of innovations and their variable impact on the individual and his or her relationship with society is staggering. The cloning of Dolly the sheep, the completion of the Human Genome project, the ability to grow human tissue on animal vectors, nuchal fold prenatal screening and the arrival of Ritalin and Prozac as routine prescriptions, need to be assessed in terms of the embodied indi-vidual and of social cohesion, locally and globally. Advocates for the sociology of the body claim that this is possible through an embodied approach to society.

EMBODIMENT

The phenomenological approach to bodies has been described as providing a bridge between the naturalistic and constructivist approaches (Nettleton, 2010), in which the process of embodiment rather than the body itself becomes the focus of study: how the body is lived and experienced as an embodied actor makes choices in particular settings that in turn fashion the body to some extent. Phenomenological approaches to the body are traced back to the insight that the body, regardless of its status as diseased, disabled or otherwise, is an agent of experience, a subject (Merleau-Ponty, 1962), and hence a site of meaning and a source of knowledge about the world. The sociology of embodiment offers ways of understanding the processes of illness and disablement, as previously taken-for-granted abilities and routines are disrupted. For instance, the experience of trembling, shaking or stiff limbs associated with Parkinson's disease brings about new routines, such as dressing in shirts and trousers with pockets in which to hide hands that jerk involuntarily and, more drastically, avoiding speaking or eating in public due to the risk of dribbling and mumbling (Nijhof, 1995). People seek to manage their bodies, even when the disease or disability is apparently unmanageable through any embodied strategy. A man with HIV describes his morning routine: 'Every morning when I get up, I look at myself to see if I'm OK, see whether I have anything like Kaposi's [he laughs]. I stick out my tongue to see if I have any fungus' (Carricaburu and Pierret, 1995: 76). Another man from the same study details how, through a mixture of self-medication and periodic medical surveillance, he maintains a sense of self:

> Now I have a test every three months, because my T4 count had dropped and I'd refused to take AZT. At that time, you had to take huge doses, but I waited for the

next blood test and, thank God, it improved. It improved by itself. That's when I noticed something. It's a personal tip, but I don't know whether I should tell the doctor: when I stop taking vitamin C and magnesium, I feel a little weaker. Yeah, from the position where I am, I think vitamin C, magnesium, vitamins do work. They suit me to a T. They reassure me, make me feel safer. The test every three months is my race against the clock, a way of keeping an eye on myself. I think you take responsibility for your own body. It's a decision. The doctor can't do anything. (Carricaburu and Pierret, 1995: 78)

BODIES AND DISABILITIES

The lived experience of bodies with illness or disability is a critical site for testing ideas about the discursive construction of bodies. The view of the body as a historically contingent product of power has underpinned feminist disaggregations of sex and gender (Butler, 1993), permitting feminists 'to use post-structuralism as a point of departure for a critical theory of embodiment' (Hughes and Paterson, 1997: 332). The constructionist view of the body has been a key means of undermining various manifestations of biological reductionism, including those around bodies, where human conditions, from homosexuality to xenophobia, are read off a single determining gene (Turner and Wainwright, 2003). The possibility of a progressive deconstruction of other types of oppressed bodies, including the extent to which impairment can be re-represented and reconstructed, offers an interesting case study. Part of this interest lies in the way that the social model of disability, which has been so influential in disability politics, denies the body and its suffering a place in an identity constructed around disability.

From the 1970s onwards, the social model of disability emerged as part of activists' struggle to establish the needs of people with disabilities as legitimate, for these needs to inform the provision of statutory services, and for their rights to be protected by legislation. Disability activists employed strategies that emphasized the collective interests of 'people with disability' and promoted their self-determination. The social model of disability focuses on the discrimination experienced by those with visible disabilities and de-emphasizes individual bodies' pathology. The distinction between impairment and disability has been central to the social model of disability in its emphasis on disability arising from social, financial, physical and attitudinal barriers, rather than individuals' bodily impairment. In the effort to liberate people with disabilities from being defined by their impairment, a distinction is drawn between disability – the pathological assessment administered by medicine – and impairment – the effect of barriers to full participation in society which damage people's interests. This strategy seeks to liberate the disabled body from medicine, but in the process abandons the body to medicine altogether, seeking to analyse the process of impairment exclusively in terms of the politics of social space and entitlement to social support (Oliver, 1990). Reclaiming the body and a phenomenological approach to disability is a move that seeks to redress the limiting dualisms on which the social model of disability is predicated, while acknowledging the political impact of the model. Hughes and Paterson argue that:

> Disability is experienced in, on and through the body, just as impairment is experienced in terms of the personal and cultural narratives that help to constitute its meaning. Impairment and disability meet in the body not as the dualistic clash of inner and outer phenomena, but insofar as impairment structures perceptions about disability and disablement is part of the 'felt world'. Most importantly, the (impaired) body is not just experienced: It is also the very basis of experience. (1997: 334–5)

One aspect of the lived experience of disability can be pain. The social model of disability does not make sense of pain as a feature of disability, beyond seeing it as a manifestation of oppression. Hughes and Paterson see this inability of the social model to analyse embodied pain as an unhelpful severing of pain from politics and of bodily experience from social experience. Pain should, they argue, be understood as both sensational and meaningful. The body as a subject is 'a purely experiential ontological condition' (Hughes and Paterson, 1997: 335) such that personal embodied knowledge and abstract cultural beliefs – the shared social knowledge of pain – combine and are transformed. The vehicle of this transformation is narrative. Narrative is the process whereby the corporeal, personal and cultural collapse together into what Hughes and Paterson refer to as a 'living unity'. In this view, narrative is a conceptual means of circumventing the limitations of exclusive dualisms on which the social model of disability relies. However, constructing narrative is not necessarily a liberating process, since both form and content are culturally mediated such that certain forms of story are favoured in specific social settings, for particular bodies voicing particular experiences: in other words, not all stories are equally valued or equally heard.

BODIES AND NARRATIVE

One of the aims of the social model of disability has been liberation from what has been called the 'personal tragedy model of disability' (Oliver, 1990). This is the assumption that disability must be a tragedy, in that the onset of an impairment marks the start of a story with an inevitably unhappy ending for all those involved.

The inevitability of the tragedy is re-cast by the social model since the social nature of disability is insisted upon, reallocating the responsibility for the negative effects of disability from an individual's bad luck to our shared social attitudes and structures. The deeply felt sense of the tragedy of disability was illustrated by the international interest in the case of a lesbian couple – Sharon Duchesneau and Candace McCullough – who were themselves deaf and who opted to conceive a congenitally deaf child through donor insemination from a deaf man (McLellan, 2002). Whether being deaf constitutes a disability, particularly in a context where sign language is current, is contested among those who associate with a deaf culture (or Deaf Culture). Nonetheless, the wider hearing world found it difficult to see the reproductive choice made by Duchesneau and McCullough in the terms that the women themselves presented it: as a positive and reasonable choice to share their own cultural and linguistic identity with their child. Their narrative of family formation was strongly resisted.

The study of narrative as the central means whereby people rehearse their embodied troubles to renegotiate and make sense of a changed subjectivity in social context has been a central preoccupation of medical sociology. The social model of disability with its 'disembodification' of disability, the desire to avoid hackneyed narratives of tragedy and the growth of disability studies as a specific discipline, have all meant that sociology's focus on narrative has concentrated on narratives of illness rather than disability (although the division between disability and illness is not clear-cut).

Whether a person's impairment arises from infection, accident, chronic disease or deliberate violence, the trauma, pain and suffering in its existential and embodied manifestations provoke questions about the nature of the changes. Why do I suffer? Why do I suffer now? How can this suffering be addressed? Who am I when I suffer? Kleinman has called these questions of order and control, pointing out that medical models are ill equipped to answer them (1988: 29). The general human impulse to tell stories about ourselves and our place in the world is provoked by disruption and difficulty. Kleinman has been a central figure in assessing the storytelling provoked by illness and how the social dimensions of these accounts remake meaning when the social fabric has been disrupted. His body of work has examined the function of illness narratives in clinical settings, as well as their meaning-making at different levels in wider social worlds. Narrative (together with emotion) has been seen as a key means by which the suffering body establishes its social and subjective place: 'It is through narratives and theodicies of illness and pain that people attempt to understand and locate the meaning of their suffering and to effect a realignment between body, self and society' (Bendelow and Williams, 1995: 156). Kleinmann (1988) reminds us that while illness narratives are, at one level, reportage of the experience of an illness, and as such may have a role to play in the education of clinicians, they also perform more sociologically interesting work. Narratives address the moral order, the experience of loss, the causes and the consequences of illness and of pain. Stories about pain and loss describe the experience of 'disordered' embodiment as a process produced by 'the dialectic between cultural category and personal significa-tion on the one side and the brute materiality of disordered processes on the other' (Kleinman, 1988: 55).

Sociological understandings of narratives, while attending to their diversity arising from the circumstances in which they are generated, are alert to cultural patterns that constrain the narratives and give them recognizable forms. Arthur Frank's influential book, which relates his own experience of illness and its medical treatment, describes undergoing treatment for disease as necessitating 'narrative surrender' to medical professionals (1995: 6). Frank sets out a typology of narratives that respond to the disruption of a person's pre-illness narrative and the imposition of a medical narrative. Narratives of 'restitution' (bodies restored to health through compliance with medical regimens), 'chaos' (escape of narrative closure) and 'quest' (illness as a journey) are exemplified by drawing on material from a range of sources. What disease interrupts, narrative can restore, so the 'narrative wreckage' created by disease is addressed and remedied by telling stories (Frank, 1995: 55). The idea that '[o]ut of narrative truths a sense of coherence can be restored' (1995: 61) echoes throughout Frank's book, which uses language with biblical resonance in the demonstration of the redemptive possibility of stories.

This strong sense of narrative as inherently redemptive has been criticized as inadequately sociological. Paul Atkinson characterizes Frank's work as '[n]arrative triumph over illness and over medicine' (1997: 328), saying that it offers an inadequate account of medicine as narrative practice and a romanticized view of the patient, divorced from any social context. Atkinson emphasizes that narrative and other forms of oral performance are central to the culture of medicine, with the clinic involving 'numerous tellings of the patient' and 'telling the case' constituting a powerful mechanism for both the enactment of professional work (1997: 328) and of medical socialization (Bosk, 1979). Atkinson presents Frank and Kleinman's work as over-valorizing narratives of everyday personal experience but ignoring the narratives of medical work (Atkinson, 1997: 339). Atkinson objects to the 'neoromantic construction of the social actor' which he claims is represented as 'a potentially unique site of authenticity' (1997: 330). According to Atkinson, Kleinman's faith in the 'revelatory power of the narrative' as a mode that somehow 'preserves and guarantees the integrity of the life and the experiences of the lifeworld', is not well argued (1997: 332). Kleinman privileges 'narrative self-knowledge and the narrative self-revelation of the patient' as 'inherently more valid and more authentic modes of knowing or experiencing than other modes of interpretation' (Atkinson, 1997: 333).

Its misuse as a means of transcending the realm of analytic methodology risks narrative becoming 'a surrogate form of liberal humanism and a romantic celebration of the individual subject', according to Atkinson (1997: 339). Atkinson accuses Kleinman of being 'at heart a storyteller rather than a story analyst' (1997: 335), looking for the therapeutic rather than the analytic. Atkinson detects a similar longing for redemption through narrative in Frank's work (1995), which he accuses of paying no attention to narratives' formal structures. While admitting that '[t]he modern clinic is a densely narrated environment' (Atkinson, 1997: 340) and that 'illness is, in part, a narrative accomplishment', Atkinson warns that 'the ubiquity of the narrative and its centrality to everyday work are not license to simply privilege these forms' (1997: 341). He urges us to treat narratives as social facts like any other, avoiding any temptation to see stories of personal experience as offering an 'untrammeled access to a realm of hyperauthenticity' (1997: 341), thereby keeping our attention on all forms of action and interaction.

Narratives represent one of various forms of social fact which, as Atkinson asserts, should have no automatic status, least of all as authentic in a positive sense, since narratives have no inherent truth or moral worth. The debate regarding the use of narrative as method and as material for research continues (Thomas, 2010), with a shared conviction of the centrality of narrative as a means (if not the only means) through which humans re-make meaning in the face of suffering and disagreement as to its exact status (Atkinson, 2010; Bochner, 2010; Frank, 2010).

MUTE BODIES

A problem which is not highlighted in the aforementioned debate is that when moral standing is rehearsed and re-made in narrative terms, the mute and inarticulate are, by definition, excluded. Sociological approaches which emphasize the articulation of narrative and so attend to compelling metaphor and arresting simile, thereby reproduce the mainstream exclusion of the taciturn, the incoherent, the silent and the speechless in favour of the fluent and the articulate. Developments in visual sociology notwithstanding, our means of apprehending human experience, including suffering, rely heavily on language – in spoken and written form. As a community of researchers, we remind ourselves to attend to silence and ellipse (Barnard, 2005), but silence, whether voluntary or forced, is very difficult to interpret and we tend to respond more diligently to elegant metaphor and vivid detail. The 'aporia', the gap or missing centre whereby suffering cannot be satisfactorily articulated, notes the impossibility of writing and analysing suffering (Wilkinson, 2005), but does not address bodies whose silence is more mundane. The silence of bodies that not only suffer, but also rejoice, delight and reflect in silence because of their lack of language (or lack of a particular language) attracts less attention than articulate suffering. Despite sociology's sentimental attachment to the underdog (Fox, 1996), there is a preference for the articulate underdog. People with severe disability who overcome impairment to be able to articulate a fictionalized or autobiographical narrative, point up this gap in our approach to human suffering. Christy Brown (1932–1981) and Christy Nolan (1965–2009) both overcame cerebral palsy that prevented speech, and in Nolan's case, almost all voluntary movement. Nolan's writing won prestigious literary prizes, while Brown's autobiography was adapted into an award-winning film. 'Le scaphandre et le papillon', a memoir written by journalist Jean-Dominique Bauby (1952–1997) describing his experience of a stroke which left him speechless and only able to move his left eyelid, became a bestseller in French and English and was adapted into a multi-award-winning film. There is a fascination with apparently silent bodies, able to break their silence and offer a narrative of their condition. But beyond the glamour of best-selling books and film adaptations, this interest does not translate into an interest in bodies that persist in their muted, silent state.

Sociological criticism has pointed to medicine's preference for bodies whose disability or impairment can be fixed or cured through medical methods such that geriatric and rehabilitation medicine have long had low status compared to other specialisms. To some extent, medical sociology has reproduced this reluctance to engage with impaired and inarticulate bodies. The existence of a distinct field of Disability Studies speaks to medical sociology's lack of interest in disability and impairment, as well as the inability of the social model of disability to engage with embodiment and pain. Ageing bodies have come under sociological scrutiny relatively recently (Twigg, 2006; Joyce and Loe, 2010; Twigg et al., 2011) to stake a claim on a fast-developing field, alongside social gerontology, geriatrics and anti-ageing medicine.

Medical sociology has mirrored medicine's preoccupation with fixable bodies and betrays a preference for compelling narrative as both material and method in research. So while pain and suffering have been addressed through narrative and as part of the sociology of emotions, and of embodiment, the suffering of some silent or silenced bodies continues to be ignored. This raises a question as to whether those who cannot describe their own suffering suffer in the same terms as those who can describe it.

META-NARRATIVE AND SUFFERING

Interest in human suffering in the Western world has been persuasively related both to the decline of organized religion as the dominant metaphor for understanding contradictions of human existence and the discovery of the psyche. Organized religion has not disappeared in line with the rationalization of society (as predicted by some watchers of modernity), and strong religious belief coexists as a feature of societies that are otherwise highly secularized.

Theodicy, the justification for a belief in God despite the existence of evil, has been a key theological problem since the term was coined in the eighteenth century. Despite the retreat of religious thought as an organizing principle of social life, the problem remains, although the terms of debate have diversified. What has been called sociodicy – the existential meaning and ethical implications of human affliction and suffering in social life – continues to exercise sociological imaginations (Morgan and Wilkinson, 2001). The decline of strong shared, consensual belief in religious metaphors as the key framework for understanding suffering has allowed an alternative mode for understanding suffering to arise. As Nikolas Rose puts it:

> Over the first sixty years or so of the twentieth century, human beings – at least in the advanced industrial and liberal democratic societies of the West – came to understand themselves as inhabited by a deep interior psychological space. They evaluated and acted upon themselves in terms of this belief. (Rose, 2007: 187–8)

From Rose's perspective, modernity has been associated with humans mapping their thoughts, feelings, emotions, moods, desires, discontents, onto a psychological space, but the rise of neuroscience means that this mapping is now taking place onto the physical body rather than the psyche. While the ongoing development of neuroscience may yet mean that neurological metaphors come to dominate our understanding of our affective state (Rose, 2007), the processes of modernity show a tendency to overlay rather than replace one another. And at least for the time being, psychological discourse is a long way from giving over its dominant influence in structuring human experience and social life and, in particular, understandings of suffering.

Aspects of the body that biomedicine has tended to see as beyond its remit, such as emotions, pain and suffering, have often been ignored by sociology too, as this chapter has considered. There has been an implicit modernist assumption that pain and suffering will dissipate as part of the general moral progress associated with the development of a liberal democracy that will automatically reduce suffering. In highlighting how this implicit assumption has inflected sociological thinking, Morgan and Wilkinson point to an ongoing escalation of violence and exploitation, referring to the twentieth century as 'one of the most disturbed and violent centuries the world has known' (2001: 199). In the light of this ongoing suffering that sociology has tended to ignore, they call for a reassessment of the experience of modernity.

For Eva Illouz, suffering, among other existential problems, is not only ignored, but actually exacerbated as a result of the uncertainty inherent in the condition of modernity. Gender, work and familial roles generate uncertainty through incipient democratic norms and rules in the workplace and in the family, while the multiplicity of social roles assumed by men and women, lead to the 'complexity of a culture riddled with contradictory normative imperatives' (Illouz, 2008: 243).

Illouz argues that these contradictions of modernity are primarily managed through the self and she sees psychology and, more generally, 'psych discourses' as offering the dominant 'techniques to manage those contradictions' (2008: 243). For Illouz, therapeutic psychology is the means of containing the human impossibilities of living in an advanced capitalist economy by providing 'the … emotional "tool kit" for disorganized selves to manage the conduct of their lives' (2008: 241). She contrasts this view of psychology with what she terms the 'standard Foucauldian account': rather than seeing psychology as a biopower that offers a new kind of pleasure through knowing, discovering and exposing, she contends that the psycho-therapeutic narrative 'has actually produced forms of suffering' (Illouz, 2008: 245).

The rise of psychoanalysis in American culture through which Freud's metaphors and narratives were used pragmatically to solve everyday problems has led to the saturation of the institutions of American society with psychology: the state, the family, the corporation, mass media. According to Illouz (2008), psychology has been adopted as the main legitimating discourse of major institutions, with the consumers or patients for psychological services being guided in the 'micro-performance of the therapeutic self' by experts. This construction of the psychological self has further resonated through the media industries of information and entertainment (Illouz, 2008). Sociology can be seen as part of this tendency, with a sociology of emotions interrogating the emotional labour that capitalist systems of exchange impel among employees, while simultaneously reinforcing psychological discourses as a key aspect of modernity. As an aspect of embodiment, suffering has persistently eluded sociological analysis (Wilkinson, 2005), and while emotions and their explication through narrative offer one avenue, it is not one that has yet been sociologically realized. As Illouz argues, suffering and its 'cure' has been the remit of psychological experts, whereas sociology has, at least until recently, had little analytic purchase.

The tendency under high modernity to cope with life's vicissitudes by finding the correct product and expert or professional advice has been one aspect of late modernity's culture of consumption. This emphasis on locating the right support and advice as a means of managing one's failings, has been seen as part of a denial of the vulnerability and limitation of human existence that is an exaggerated feature of American culture (Kleinman, 2006: 7). As part of this process, suffering has become a problem to be managed by experts of the psyche. Clinical psychology has disposed of theodicy (and by extension of sociodicy too) by making misfortune the result of a wounded or mismanaged psyche, thereby explaining, rationalizing and justifying suffering. Illouz sees this as the resuscitation of Weber's description of the fortunate Protestant capitalists wishing to be legitimately fortunate, thereby legitimating the status quo.

> Weber describes the … retrospective explaining and therefore legitimizing of good or bad fortune by hidden virtue or vice. Psychology resuscitates such forms of theodicy … In the therapeutic ethos there is no such thing as senseless suffering and chaos. (Illouz, 2008: 246)

Illouz is concerned that the ubiquity of the practice and language of psychology justifies suffering by blaming it on the individual, thereby giving a bogus reason and a false justification for suffering. Her critique of the excessive influence of psych-discourse in current American society is an implicit call to improve our social understanding and response to human suffering. It also goes some way to showing how the ubiquity and power of psychological discourse, in the USA and beyond, has obscured the embodied nature of suffering from view.

Foucauldian accounts have shown us that people have come to understand their personhood and their bodies in ways that are shaped by the systems of thought of their own historical moment. Illouz (2008) shows how our understandings of ourselves in late modernity are critically formed by psych-discourse, while Rose (2007) points towards neuroscience as the shape of things to come. Our bodies are disciplined by education, by the law and by biomedicine, just as our subjectivity is disciplined by those same systems of knowledge. Sociology is just as much a part of the disciplining knowledge as medicine, in constraining how we view our embodied and pained selves in society. Nick Fox holds sociology responsible for promulgating 'essentialist conceptions of the self' that view selfhood as housed within and interior to the physical body (2002: 352). Fox looks to the work of Deleuze and Guattari for a radical alternative, offering 'the possibility for a subjectivity (and a "health")' unlimited by a body whose meaning is fixed by our current systems of thought. Fox sees the necessity of:

> the dissolution of systems of thought deriving from biomedicine, mind–body dualism (which sees the mind as 'trapped' inside the body), and the interior–exterior conception of subjectivity. The individualizing of pain and suffering by biomedicine (often with the collaboration of the human sciences) territorializes and limits the BwO as organisms or bodies-with-organs, which are then the natural subjects for the expertise of medicine. (Fox, 2002: 353)

Deleuze and Guattari's radical alternative is a metaphorical nomadism, which Fox interprets as 'an aspiration and an alternative philosophy to what they saw as the discursive straitjacket of western thought' to engender 'replacing monolithic definitions of reality with a multiplicity of narratives' (Fox, 2002: 354), thereby resisting the single fixed perspective.

CONCLUSION

In its investigation of suffering, sociology has sought to address the causes of inequality, of injustice and of violence, analysing suffering as a structural problem. Health inequalities structured by gender, class, age and ethnicity are a mainstay of medical sociology, while theories of medicalization have pointed to the ways that biomedical systems create and compound suffering while diagnosing and treating disease (Comaroff and Maguire, 1981). Structural and organizational approaches to suffering have, however, overlooked embodiment and the subjective aspects of illness – the pain and suffering that is experienced emotionally and represented in narrative. An embodied understanding of painful illness has shown the power of psychological discourse to shape our experience and has suggested that the ascendance of neuroscience may reshape our perceptions, as metaphors for suffering move from the psychic to the corporeal. These insights notwithstanding, suffering as an aspect of embodiment has eluded sociological analysis: the process of pain is anti-social, placing a body beyond social bonds, and the process is not easily rendered into language. The inadequacies of verbal and written narrative to capture embodied suffering have been indicated by sociological interventions showing how pain is communicated visually through the study of gestures (Hydén and Peolsson, 2002) and photographic representation (Bell, 2002). Sociological accounts of the vicissitudes of human existence, whether verbal, written, kinaesthetic or photographic, seek to make it meaningful within a rational, or at least an articulate (albeit nomadic) framework.

Studying the narratives of ordinary people's suffering in the face of life's vicissitudes allows, according to Kleinman, the development of an ethics. To avoid the prescriptive morals of religiously guided ethical codes, Kleinman describes narrative ethics as an aspiration to values that transcend the local and that can guide us in living a life (2006: 3). Kleinman urges us to advance an ethical position that transcends local commitments, but that is nonetheless locally applicable and effective at the collective level, that is universal, yet illustrated by the compelling details of individual stories of suffering in the face of adversity (Kleinman, 2006: 21).

Developing an ethical position is not an obviously sociological project. Sociologists have shied away from any prescription of values and have been highly critical of the bioethical project on grounds of its pretensions to universal application (De Vries, 2004). Paul Atkinson's (1997) critique of attributing unwarranted value to narrative, thereby turning sociology into a version of liberal humanism, applies here: looking for ethics in everyday narrative risks over-burdening people's quotidian observations. Iain Wilkinson suggests that working at the edges of what the sociological project can currently encompass is a productive, creative undertaking (2010). Certainly, new lines of critical enquiry can emerge by pushing the boundaries of an intellectual project beyond its existing methodology. Nick Fox's (2002) endorsement of nomadism as a means of disrupting and resisting existing conceptual models and discourses is perhaps a case in point. However, unless nomad-informed research returns to rejuvenate sociological thinking, what looked like a bid to extend the creative possibilities of sociology, might turn out to be a flight from its shortcomings.

The longing to make sense of embodied suffering in the context of an unjust, globalized world is a laudable aspiration. While 'the longing to bend the present world into a different and better future – is often mocked', it is, as John Keane points out, 'a regular feature of the human condition' (2009: ix). What is the appropriate response to such longing and does the response lie in the realms of a current or even a future sociology? An obvious place to look for ways of understanding suffering as an embodied and psychological experience and of responding to it ethically, both as an individual and as a society, is religion. Bryan Turner observes that the sociology of health and illness investigates the meaning of illness and the subjective significance of pain, and this converges with the sociology of religion's focus on suffering, with cultural responses to the problem of theodicy (or sociodicy) representing common ground (Turner, 1996: 101). The intellectual task of making that convergence theoretically systematic and deliberate is, according to him, an important item on the agenda of the contemporary sociology of religion, and of the sociological enterprise as a whole (Turner, 1996: 102). If this intellectual task has been achieved, its ramifications are yet to be felt in medical sociology.

Those in search of the meaning of embodied suffering have regularly turned to the study of narrative, both documentary and fictional. Sociologists and medics alike have used narrative-based methods for their practice, but have also turned to literature in search of a meaningful response to bodies in pain that does not draw on religious or metaphysical metaphors. Iain Bamforth, in his literary tour of the history of medicine and its practitioners, probes how medicine and society have evolved in a close embrace since the end of the eighteenth century (2003). Bamforth insists on the theatricality and the brutality of medicine and shows an abiding interest in how the practice of medicine informs the human condition, highlighting how medicine and society must be understood as working to aid, abet and frustrate one another. As a literary physician, Bamforth takes a sociological starting point to construct a historically and anthropologically inclined collection of writing. The result is engaging and enlightening and offers little prospect that medical sociology might retain any authority as a discipline in the wider medical project, in that the sociological themes that Bamforth introduces are assessed and analysed without further recourse to sociological terms of theory. Perhaps this is the success of sociological approaches to health and medicine: opening up territory which other disciplines can analyse.

In its short history, sociology has been good at offering insights into other disciplines, often having borrowed them from elsewhere. Sociological expertise lies in understanding individuals as part of a wider set of social relations, but medical sociology lacks a specialism with market value akin to the therapeutic claims of psychology and medicine. By studying society, medicine and the processes of health and illness, the sociology of medicine is always in the domain of common knowledge and regularly produces insights that other practitioners and professionals can use. The professional group that has used sociological insights most regularly is medicine, as the limits of its professional and disciplinary project have expanded. Sociology should and doubtless will continue taking insights from beyond its own disciplinary boundaries to grapple with new questions. While this may ensure medical sociology's ongoing usefulness as a mediator of insights from philosophy, psychoanalysis, literary criticism, bioethics and elsewhere for the medical project, a more radical critique, such as Nick Fox's interpolation of nomadism, points to the disappearance of medical sociology as a distinct disciplinary arena.

REFERENCES

Atkinson, P. (1997) 'Narrative turn or blind alley?', *Qualitative Health Research*, 7: 325–44.

Atkinson, P. (2010) 'The contested terrain of narrative analysis – an appreciative response', *Sociology of Health & Illness*, 32(4): 661–2.

Bamforth, I. (2003) 'Introduction', in I. Bamforth (ed.), *The Body in the Library: A Literary Anthology of Modern Medicine*. London: Verso. pp. ix–xxx.

Barnard, M.A. (2005) 'Discomforting research: colliding moralities and looking for "truth" in a study of parental drug problems', *Sociology of Health & Illness*, 27(1): 1–19.

Bell, S.E. (2002) 'Photo images: Jo Spence's narratives of living with illness', *Health*, 6: 5–30.

Bendelow, G. and Williams, S.J. (1995) 'Transcending the dualisms: towards a sociology of pain', *Sociology of Health & Illness*, 17(2): 139–65.

Bochner, A.P. (2010) 'Resisting the mystification of narrative inquiry: unmasking the real conflict between story analysts and storytellers', *Sociology of Health & Illness*, 32(4): 662–5.

Bosk, C. (1979) *Forgive and Remember: Managing Medical Failure*. Chicago: University of Chicago Press.

Boyle, C.M. (1970) 'Difference between patients' and doctors' interpretations of some common medical terms', *British Medical Journal*, 2(5704): 286–9.

Bury, M.R. (1987) 'Social constructionism and the development of medical sociology', *Sociology of Health & Illness*, 8(2): 137–69.

Butler, J. (1993) *Bodies that Matter: On the Discursive Limits of Sex*. London: Routledge.

Carricaburu, D. and Pierret, J. (1995) 'From biographical disruption to biographical rein-
forcement: the case of HIV-positive men', *Sociology of Health & Illness*, 17(1): 65–87.

Clapworthy, G., Kohl, P., Gregerson, H., Thomas, S., Viceconti, M., Hose, D. et al. (2007)
'Digital human modelling: a global vision and a European perspective', in *Digital
Human Modelling: A Global Vision and a European Perspective*. Berlin: Springer.
pp. 549–58.

Comaroff, J. and Maguire, P. (1981) 'Ambiguity and the search for meaning: childhood
leukaemia in the modern clinical context', *Social Science and Medicine*,
15B: 115–23.

Deleuze, G. and Guattari, F. (1972) *Anti-Œdipus* (trans. R. Hurley, M. Seem and
H.R. Lane). London and New York: Continuum, 2004. Vol. 1 of *Capitalism and
Schizophrenia*, 2 vols, 1972–1980. Trans. of *L'Anti-Oedipe*. Paris: Les Editions de Minuit.

Deleuze, G. and Guattari, F. (1980) *A Thousand Plateaus* (trans. B. Massumi). London
and New York: Continuum, 2004. Vol. 2 of *Capitalism and Schizophrenia*, 2 vols,
1972–1980. Trans. of *Mille Plateaux*. Paris: Les Editions de Minuit.

De Vries, R. (2004) 'How can we help? From "sociology in" to "sociology of" bioethics',
Journal of Law, Medicine and Ethics, 32(2): 279–92.

Fleising, U. (2001) 'In search of genohype: a content analysis of biotechnology company
documents', *New Genetics and Society*, 20(3): 239–54.

Foucault, M. (1979) *Discipline and Punish: The Birth of the Prison*. Harmondsworth:
Penguin.

Foucault, M. (1980) *The History of Sexuality. Volume 1: An Introduction*. Harmondsworth:
Penguin.

Fox, K.J. (1996) 'The margins of underdog sociology: implications for the West Coast
Aids Project', *Social Problems*, 46(4): 363–86.

Fox, N.J. (2002) 'Refracting "health": Deleuze, Guattari and body-self', *Health*, 6(3):
347–63.

Frank, A.W. (1995) *The Wounded Storyteller: Body, Illness, and Ethics*. Chicago:
University of Chicago Press.

Frank, A.W. (2010) 'In defence of narrative exceptionalism', *Sociology of Health &
Illness*, 32(4): 665–7.

Hughes, B. and Paterson, K. (1997) 'The social model of disability and the disappearing
body: towards a sociology of impairment', *Disability & Society*, 12(3): 325–40.

Hunt, L.M. and Megyesi, M.S. (2008) 'The ambiguous meanings of the racial/ethnic
categories routinely used in human genetics research', *Social Science and Medicine*,
66(2): 349–61.

Hydén, L-C. and Peolsson, M. (2002) 'Pain gestures: the orchestration of speech and
body gestures', *Health*, 6: 325–45.

Illouz, E. (2008) *Saving the Modern Soul: Therapy, Emotions and the Culture of Self-
help*. Berkeley, CA: University of California Press.

Joyce, K. and Loe, M. (eds) (2010) *Technogenarians: Studying Health and Illness
Through an Ageing, Science, and Technology Lens*. Oxford: Wiley-Blackwell.

Kahn, J. (2006) 'Race, pharmacogenomics and marketing: putting BiDil in context',
American Journal of Bioethics, 6(5): W1–W5.

Keane, J. (2009) *The Life and Death of Democracy*. London: Simon and Schuster.

Kleinman, A. (1988) *The Illness Narratives: Suffering, Healing, and the Human Condition*.
New York: Basic Books.

Kleinman, A. (2006) *What Really Matters: Living a Moral Life Amidst Uncertainty and
Danger*. New York: Oxford University Press.

MacDonald, H. (2006) *Human Remains: Dissection and its Histories.* New Haven: Yale University Press.

McLellan, F. (2002) 'Controversy over deliberate conception of deaf child', *The Lancet*, 359(9314): 1315.

Merleau-Ponty, M. (1962) *Phenomenology of Perception* (trans. C. Smith). London: Routledge.

Morgan, D. and Wilkinson, I. (2001) 'The problem of suffering and the sociological task of theodicy', *European Journal of Social Theory*, 4(2): 199–214.

National Library of Medicine (2008) *The Visible Human Project.* Available at: www.nlm. nih.gov/research/visible/visible_human.html

Nettleton, S. (2010) 'Sociology of the body', in W.C. Cockerham (ed.), *The Blackwell Companion to Medical Sociology.* Malden, MA: Blackwell. pp. 47–68.

Nijhof, G. (1995) 'Parkinson's disease as a problem of shame in public appearance', *Sociology of Health & Illness*, 17(2): 193–205.

Oliver, M. (1990) *The Politics of Disablement.* London: Macmillan.

Petersen, A. (2007) *The Body in Question: A Socio-Cultural Approach.* London and New York: Routledge.

Rose, N. (2007) *The Politics of Life Itself: Biomedicine, Power and Subjectivity in the Twenty-First Century.* Princeton: Princeton University Press.

Shilling, C. (1993) *The Body and Social Theory.* London: Sage.

Thomas, C. (2010) 'Negotiating the contested terrain of narrative methods in illness contexts', *Sociology of Health & Illness*, 32(4): 647–60.

Turner, B. (1984) *The Body and Society.* Oxford: Blackwell.

Turner, B.S. (1992) *Regulating Bodies: Essays in Medical Sociology.* London: Routledge.

Turner, B.S. (1995) *Medical Power and Social Knowledge.* London: Sage.

Turner, B.S. (1996) *The Body and Society*, 2nd edition. London: Sage.

Turner, B. (1997) 'Foreword', in A. Petersen and R. Bunton (eds), *Foucault, Health and Medicine.* London: Routledge. pp. ix–xxi.

Turner, B. (2004) *The New Medical Sociology.* New York: Norton.

Turner, B. and Wainwright, S.P. (2003) 'Corps de Ballet: the case of the injured ballet dancer', *Sociology of Health & Illness*, 25(4): 269–88.

Turner, T. (1994) 'Bodies and anti-bodies: flesh and fetish in contemporary social theory', in T. Csordas (ed.), *Embodiment and Experience: The Existential Ground of Culture and Self.* Cambridge: Cambridge University Press.

Twigg, J. (2006) *The Body in Health and Social Care.* London: Palgrave.

Twigg, J., Wolkowitz, C., Cohen, R. and Nettleton, S. (eds) (2011) 'Bodywork in health and social care: critical themes, future agendas', *Sociology of Health & Illness*, 33(1).

von Lehm, D. (2006) 'The body as interactive display: examining bodies in a public exhibition', *Sociology of Health & Illness*, 28(2): 223–51.

Waldby, C. (2000) *The Visible Human Project: Informatic Bodies and Posthuman Medicine.* London: Routledge.

Walter, T. (2004) 'Plastination for display: a new way to dispose of the dead', *The Journal of the Royal Anthropological Institute*, 10(3): 603–27.

Wilkinson, I. (2005) *Suffering: A Sociological Introduction.* Cambridge: Polity.

Wilkinson, I. (2010) 'Health and suffering', paper presented at the British Sociological Association Annual Meeting, Glasgow, 7 April.

7
THE WORKINGS OF MEDICINE

INTRODUCTION

The sociology of health, illness and medicine has been reluctant to get to grips with health policy, although interested in professional–patient interactions. The study of the day-to-day provision of health services is the preserve of health services research – an area that medical sociology can comfort itself by characterizing as descriptive and atheoretical. This chapter covers sociological approaches to the practice of medicine in the policy environment in which professionals must work. The state plays a central role in the provision of health and social care and in debates about the decline of medical dominance, its regulatory agencies are key. As noted in the prologue, early sociologists did not focus on medicine as an institution that was shaping social relations and so physicians came under sociological scrutiny as exemplars of the rise of the professions in the making of modernist society. The analysis of medicine's contribution to social cohesion through the management of deviance was how medical sociology came of age theoretically (see Chapter 2) and, ever since then, physicians as archetypal professionals and their fate in the changing conditions of modernity have been a focus. Research addressing the extent of physicians' power within the medical division of labour and its penetration into wider society will be considered in this chapter. This research concerns the dominance of physicians as professionals as well as the influence that medical ideas have in defining society's problems and the solutions to those problems.

BACKGROUND

The sociological interest in the professions as an aspect of modernity has frequently used medicine as a special case in seeking to establish whether there is any key quality that distinguishes an occupation from a profession in the social division of labour, and to show the less than altruistic ends which professionals' claims of integrity and trustworthiness serve. In sociological explorations of these questions, medicine (together with law) has come to be seen as a paradigmatic case for examining professions' role in society and the processes at work in maintaining their professional claims. Within the sociology of professions, medicine has been a case study for examining a series of key questions: the role of gender in structuring or re-structuring professions; debates about the role of the public sector in continental Europe compared with the free markets of the USA in the development of autonomous professions; and claims to professional status from occupations associated with medicine, such as nurses, midwives and chiropractors. For medical sociology, charting the rise and fall of medical dominance, and speculation on its future trajectory has involved theories of proletarianization, corporatization and the nature of competition between various medical professions. Professional dominance has been a key idea, which, together with the theory of medicalization, has constituted a critical account of medicine and medical practice, challenging medicine's own account of its linear progress from incoherent speculation to unassailable scientific truth.

MEDICINE'S GOLDEN AGE

The thesis of medical imperialism described medicine's accumulated power as excessive and overweening to show how the social relations of health and illness were distorted as a result. Ever since medical imperialism was posited as a thesis, the decline of medical power has been documented. Accounts of the retreat of medicine's influence imply a golden age (golden for physicians at any rate), now past, when medical professional power and status were less contested than now. The suggestion that medicine had a golden age, the retreat from which medical sociology has described and possibly abetted, is persuasive and upheld by critics within as well as outwith medicine. This golden age was a recent moment in medical history, around the middle of the twentieth century, when the decline of infectious disease, the rise of medical technology and the development of effective antibiotics and vaccination programmes coincided to give medicine a reputation for efficacy, which, together with people's willingness to attend to expert professionals, gave physicians high social, occupational and economic status, as well as cultural capital. Through the course of the twentieth century, a gradual rise in the efficacy of medicine's methods meant that therapeutic intervention slowly caught up with diagnosis. At the start of the twentieth century, physicians were little more than diagnosticians, equipped only with morphine and aspirin, better at diagnosing disease and its course than at offering effective interventions to slow its progress. Despite the weakness of their therapeutic compared to their diagnostic ability, in Northern Europe and the USA, physicians were granted the state monopoly for medical practice, permitting self-regulation and tempering competition from other healing occupations. In Britain, the institution of medicine acquired sovereign control over professional groups that came to be seen as 'allied to medicine'. Chiropodists, midwives, dentists and pharmacists were all subject to medical regulation, especially where they sought to work in orthodox medical settings. The accumulation of institutional influence coincided with the gradual improvement in therapeutics.

While the professional status that physicians had attained at the start of the twentieth century was not justified by therapeutic efficacy, the twentieth century saw a growth in technical competency that apparently justified medicine's professional status and promoted the further accumulation of institutional and professional power. The early decades of the twentieth century saw the development of effective treatment for syphilis, diabetes and a range of bacterial infections. The concentration of medical technology and expertise in hospitals, the mass production of drugs and vaccines, and the development of medical instruments heralded what has been called 'the therapeutic age'. The Second World War promoted these developments by creating opportunities for the development of surgical interventions and industrial processes to mass-produce medical commodities.

While providing the right industrial conditions for therapeutic innovation, the Second World War and its aftermath also constituted the circumstances for organizing social welfare and health services on a national basis. The moral bankruptcy of the Nazi regime (whose leader was, of course, democratically elected) created the need to revivify democracy as a moral and ethical project once hostilities ended. The British state undertook to deliver the basic minimum of health and welfare to all citizens, funded by national taxation as part of the rebuilding of society and the affirmation of a decent standard of living for which people had fought. In this vision of nationalized health, the state is seen as essentially benign and, in partnership with biomedicine, holds out the promise of a rational scientific means of alleviating suffering. The ideal of an honourable partnership between state and profession for the benefit of the patient informed the inception of the National Health Service. In 1948, when the NHS was being established as statutorily funded and free at the point of delivery, hopes for biomedicine rode high. Penicillin and animal insulin were in regular use, the commercial production of cortisone was imminent, the polio vaccination would arrive in the 1950s and synthetic insulin in the 1960s. These therapeutic innovations, with their palpable benefits created hope for, and even an expectation of, magic bullet medicine. Magic medical bullets suggest, not only a pill for every ill, but also that the delivery of the medical therapeutic effect be independent of the affect of the healer: no compassion on the part of the doctor is necessary for inoculation to be effective. In retrospect, the arrival of therapeutic penicillin, insulin, cortisone and the polio vaccination between the 1920s and 1960s may have represented the pinnacle of scientific medical achievement – a golden age even – with a similar surge in benefit to patients yet to be replicated.

The resistance of sections of the medical profession to the establishment of the National Health Service is well documented, as is physicians' successful negotiation of good terms and conditions for the government take-over of hospitals and clinics. As independent contractors paid by the state, General Practitioners (GPs) managed to keep their clinical autonomy largely intact because of the peculiarities of the contract that they negotiated. In the newly established NHS, General Practitioners were paid by the state, but not subject to regulation by statutory agencies, and in this sense experienced a golden age for their practice. In the 1950s and 1960s, General Practitioners had been trained during, and were still associated with, the pre-World War era characterized by deference and paternalism, when the contract between doctor and patient was ethically charged rather than contractually regulated. This was perhaps 'a more innocent time of genuine excitement and decency' (Bamforth, 2003: xxiii) where the doctor was accountable to his patient, rather than to a regu-latory state agency. The same pre-war ethic of deference and paternalism benefitted hospital doctors, for whom the establishment of the NHS facilitated the process of specialization and the increasing use of expensive technology in medical care.

While Bamforth (2003) claims to have met British GPs who report having lived through this medical golden age, McKinlay and Marceau (2002) state that we are too close to events to come to a mature judgement regarding the golden age of doctor-ing (although they go on to explain how it has ended). Porter (1997), in his history of the development of Western medicine, describes the process whereby doctors shifted from being relatively ineffective self-employed providers of bedside services, to the powerful professionals embedded in the medico-industrial complex of the late twentieth century. Porter's history makes clear that medical methods and medical men have long been criticized, but prior to medicine's accumulation of institutional and professional power such criticism lacked bite. Molière, also known as Jean-Baptiste Poquelin (*L'Amour médecin*, 1665) and George Bernard Shaw (*The Doctor's Dilemma*, 1911), attracted paying audiences to laugh at doctors' delusional faith in the efficacy of their own methods and their relevancy to the human condition. Prior to medicine's reputation for therapeutic efficacy, physicians were sometimes good healers, but their ability to alter the course of human suffering was limited and other institutions such as the church were central to understanding the human condition. Lacking any great therapeutic ability or institutional power, physicians could be mocked alongside other professionals such as the clergy and lawyers, and Porter (1997) contends that only when medicine became a key institution for the governance of modern society did the critique of medicine harden.

Whether a golden age really existed in the hiatus between the coalescence of insti-tutional power, therapeutic efficacy and the bite of the critics is unclear, given the subjective nature of what counts as golden. A golden age certainly exists as a herme-neutic in the historical and sociological study of professions and describes the extent of change in terms of contrasts, but in sociological terms what constitutes golden has been implied rather than characterized. Sociology has focused on medical dominance and the question of whether medical dominance constituted a form of medical imperialism. Disentangling the complex inter-meshed interests of corporation, state and professional bodies to assess their mutual and competing interests, has allowed sociologists to describe the rise (and fall) of the medical profession in specific cultural settings (Conrad and Schneider, 2005), but more general theses about medicine are hard to maintain.

Much of the research into medical power has taken place in the USA, where medical care is big business and organized around systems of private insurance and principles of fee-for-service. High levels of specialization among American physi-cians, the magnitude of the US healthcare market and the reach and strength of healthcare corporations have all shaped the terms of the debate. The relationship of medical dominance to the proletarianization or corporatization of the medical pro-fession have been key issues. In Britain, the NHS has been the forum for assessing the role of medicine and the tempering of medical dominance has been through statutory rather than commercial market forces. In US and UK settings, the expan-sion of medicine beyond traditional diagnostic categories and the implications of this expansion for social controls under the aegis of medicine have been studied. Research has addressed the implications of medicine's institutional and professional status for the wider social relations of health and illness and for other professional and occupational groups involved in healthcare.

An important source of physicians' professional power and influence has been the relationship with the patient: medical claims to advocate for the patient, in com-bination with an assertion of superior scientific knowledge, have been central to maintaining medicine's monopoly on orthodox healing practice. However, with trust in experts attenuating, the nature of the doctor–patient relationship has been inter-rogated and other types of formal and informal healthcare relationships have come into analytic view. The rise of health consumerism as part of 'the risk society', the state's investment in individualizing responsibility for health and for illness, which has been echoed in big pharma's direct marketing to individuals, have been highlighted as problematic aspects of medically informed approaches to health, healthcare and health promotion. Meanwhile, sociologists have pointed to the role that medical con-ditions play in identity formation and the informal healthcare economy, as aspects of the social relations of illness that medicine routinely ignores. Relations between doc-tors and other professions involved in medical provision, especially nurses and manag-ers, have been examined as part of an analysis of challenges to medical dominance. These analyses seek signs of cultural shift in the practice of medicine that will suggest the direction of future development and especially whether medical dominance is increasing or decreasing. What regularly gets lost in the hunt for innovative configurations of power and practice is that novel ways of working tend to emerge from and do not entirely replace the context of existing practice. So part of the increasing complexity of medical practice is the diffusion and growth of types of discourse, associated with emergent markets and new regulatory practices that are overlaid on one another and differentially prevalent in differing specialisms and localities. Of course, the expectations of professionals and of patients are not necessarily in tune with the regulatory regime that pertains, having been informed by earlier forms of government.

In the remainder of this chapter, medical power and medical dominance will be described and the relevance of the thesis of medical imperialism considered. The reconfiguration of professional relations around healthcare will be surveyed in terms of the various challenges to medicine and medical power from a range of sources and the implications that these have for the doctor–patient relationship. In the British context, these challenges have increasingly consisted in the regulation of medicine through statutory agencies which structure the context of medical practice, together with the increasing penetration of healthcare by market forces.

MEDICAL POWER

While the relationship between a doctor and his patient became the research object of medical sociology thanks to Talcott Parsons, it was Eliot Freidson who subjected the power of the medical profession to sociological scrutiny. Freidson described medicine's power and its effects, both within the division of medical labour and more broadly in society. In Freidson's view, both the autonomy and the dominance enjoyed by medicine were dimensions of medical power that explained its exalted professional status. His book *Profession of Medicine* (1970) set out a framework for interrogating medicine sociologically both as a profession and as an institution. Analysing medicine as a profession, Freidson described how legitimated autonomy, the high degree of occupational self-control over the terms and conditions of work that medicine enjoyed, were critical for understanding its elevated professional status. The medical profession's autonomy was granted and therefore sanctioned by the state and this legitimated the high level of self-determination, including exemption from external regulation (Freidson, 1970: 72). The significance of this autonomy was that it permitted a doctor control over both the definition of the problems he works on and the way he performs his work. This autonomy is professional and vested in an organized, corporate body but physicians also gain individual autonomy by virtue of their membership of the profession which allows, for instance, clinical freedom in decision making about a patient's treatment. Freidson's analysis of medicine's state-sanctioned professional autonomy pointed to its effects on physicians' position in the division of labour. Medicine operates without competition or regu-lation from other occupations and yet it has been granted the power to regulate and evaluate other occupations, and it is this status that, for Freidson, marked it out as a dominant profession. Medical self-regulation, whereby the profession asserts that its knowledge and practice is so specialist that only other members of the profession can come to judgement on a physician's work, has been crucial to its long-term ability to maintain power. Freidson sees medical dominance as a particular position in the division of labour which can only be maintained as a result of autonomy whereby physicians are immune from regulation by others, together with their dominance over other occupational groups (Freidson, 1970).

MEDICAL IMPERIALISM

The authoritarian power of medicine has led some critics to argue that medicine constitutes an imperial project. This critique was unfolding during the 1960s and 1970s when the end of the golden age of medicine was playing out in parallel with the process of decolonization of Western empires and the legitimacy of political orthodoxies was under interrogation in various political and professional settings. Imperialist tendencies of medicine were identified as part of a more general post-colonial critique that unfolded as imperial political projects were called into doubt. Thus, imperialism in medicine was only referred to in critical terms and not as a legitimate indication of medicine's reach, influence and power structure.

Writing in the 1960s and 1970s, Thomas Sasz, Erving Goffman, R.D. Laing and others established a critique of psychiatry that came to be known as anti-psychiatry (Crossley, 2006). Although covering a range of views, the collective effect was to articulate anti-authoritarian sentiments, characteristic of the liberationist politics of the time, to protest medicine's classification of mental disorder and its means of treatment. Arguing that much mental illness was better seen as a normal response to difficult circumstances, anti-psychiatrists presented a powerful challenge to the legitimacy of the medical profession in its classification of deviant behaviour as illness and its definition of appropriate treatment. Second-wave feminism offered accounts of medicine as a patriarchal project (Ehrenreich and English, 1973), while Marxists showed how medicine worked to support the interests of the ruling classes (Navarro, 1976).

Freidson's work can be seen as part of this anti-imperialist critique, arguing as it does that the medical model of disease was part of the problematically powerful role occupied by medicine (Freidson, 1970). The medical insistence on the objective existence of disease prevented an appreciation of the social nature of illness and so medicine failed to accommodate patients' perspectives on their own suffering, leaving them disempowered.

Crystallizing the countercultural critique of medicine's role as an authoritarian establishment institution in the capitalist and patriarchal order was the focus of the work of Ivan Illich (1926–2002). Illich claimed that medicine represented a major threat to health in terms of the side-effects of surgery and medication and through the negative impact of medicine on the social environment. The claim that medicine not only exaggerated its own utility, but actually did more harm than good was, for Illich, part of a wider critique of modernity. His use of the term 'iatrogenesis' called attention to the damaging effects of medical interventions, seeking to demonstrate that iatrogenic effects such as antibiotic resistance and complications or errors during surgery, actually outweighed any therapeutic effect. What Illich termed 'social iatrogenesis' referred to the medicalization of life events such as birth and death, thereby transforming people into life-long consumers of medical services (1976). Illich argued that medicine prevented people from coping with their own circumstances, and so they became overly dependent on medical services and hence unable to look after themselves or to withstand suffering. He argued that organized medicine had 'undermined the ability of individuals to face their reality, to express their own values, and to accept inevitable and often irremediable pain and impairment, decline and death' (Illich, 1976: 127–8). According to obituaries, Illich embodied his belief in the virtue of self-care by spending his last years with a facial tumour for which he did not seek medical treatment. Illich's work was important in the articulation of a critique of medicine's power, and his work remains widely cited in medical sociology, although not always positively (for instance, Dingwall [1995 [1987]: ix] refers to Illich's 'shortlived nihilism with regard to medicine'). Illich was not a medical sociologist by trade, having a wider critical purview of the processes of modernity.

Another important figure interrogating medical power who did not identify as a sociologist of medicine was Michel Foucault. His work interrogated relationships between psychiatry and modernity to show how subjection to the disciplining gaze of medicine produced the docile body of the patient (Foucault, 1965, 1973). The metaphor of the panoptican for this disciplinary power suggests that Foucault's view of medical power was not along the lines of an imperial power. Rather than a forceful imposition through external methods of social control, Foucault envisaged a force that individuals internalize which shapes their behaviour more insidiously. The locating of disease inside individual bodies was significant in Foucault's assessment of the growing power of the medical profession: the ability to name and locate disease in an individual brought that body under the gaze of the expert doctor (Foucault, 1973). Foucault's account of the power of medicine is convincing in its explanation of how people are complicit in demanding and consuming medical services. The link between the disciplinary power to shape shared perceptions of bodies and disease and the diffuse political power that keeps citizens within their appointed social roles points towards non-imperial forms of power at work in medicine's relationship with society.

Although the thesis of medical imperialism was important at the end of the 1970s (Strong, 1979), it has since been largely refuted, according to Davis (2010), as a result of both empirical and theoretical interrogation; in particular, Foucault's characterization of medical power as dispersed, emergent in sites beyond those of medical encounters and, crucially, involving people's complicity. Models of medical imperialism, especially those positing any direct medical coercion, have retreated, but the issue of medical dominance in terms of professional and occupational divisions of health service labour, medicalization and the influence of the medical model, continue to be part of sociological interrogations of medicine. Through the 1970s and 1980s, sociologists of the professions and of medicine were describing the ways in which physicians' influence was on the wane and their position in the class system being reconfigured by shifts in the cultural and economic systems of late capital.

PROLETARIANIZATION, DEPROFESSIONALIZATION AND CORPORATIZATION

Marxist theories of the development of capitalism suggest that the withdrawal of professional prerogatives such as the ability to set terms and conditions of work meant that professionals such as physicians, lawyers and priests were becoming incorporated into the class of workers who produced surplus value for capital. Proletarianization suggests that eventually all workers, including professionals, will, with the ongoing expansion of capitalism, be absorbed into the mass of workers and be stripped of any control over how their work is conducted, and thereby reduced to proletarian status. Evidence for this occurrence came from the increasing proportion of US physicians over the twentieth century who worked within large corporations, providing medical services, rather than in small independent practices (McKinlay and Arches, 1985). While this move has reduced physicians' ability to set their own levels of renumeration, doctors working for big healthcare organizations cannot easily be characterized as wage slaves. While physicians' move from self-employed to employee status is an important aspect of the wider economic and cultural shifts in late capitalism, the changing class location of professionals cannot be read as proletarianization simply as a result of employee status.

Other commentators see professionals maintaining their professional power and privilege despite employee status, since capital needs professional expertise as a productive resource, while medicine, in the absence of a nationalized system, needs capital to fund its research and clinical activities (Derber et al., 1990). In this scenario, even in the American private healthcare market, proper proletarianization is an unlikely outcome for doctors.

Deprofessionalization theory constitutes another description of the waning of medical power. First formulated in the 1970s, it focused on professionals' loss of their monopoly over medical knowledge and of authority over clients (Haug, 1973). This loss stemmed both from the widening access to knowledge through information technology and increasing levels of education, transforming patients into knowledgeable consumers, and the massive knowledge explosion which meant that physicians found it impossible to stay abreast of expanding medical knowledge. These twin processes mean that physicians, like other professionals, potentially fail to stay one step ahead of their patients (or clients).

Following deprofessionalization came the description of corporatization (Starr, 1982), whereby third parties organize and fund healthcare, sidelining the physician in the process of commissioning care. In the USA, the expansion of commercial healthcare corporations that buy health services on behalf of patients, represent the interests of capital at the heart of the medical enterprise. The trend for ever larger commercial institutions (health maintenance organizations or HMOs) that own and control the healthcare industry has been a key political concern, linked as it is with the concentration of ownership and the role of profit-making in an industry with high inflationary costs. These debates have not been so central to the UK, where healthcare is funded through central taxation. Despite the lack of health insurance corporations, private capital is nonetheless present in the NHS, with some key services provided by commercial organizations and, from the 1990s, the financing of major hospital building projects through private finance initiatives. Private finance initiatives are a neo-liberal means of raising capital from corporations that the taxpayer must reimburse over a long period of time and at considerable additional expense. However, corporatization, in the way it is used to describe North American healthcare, has not been a central debate in the British context.

Descriptions of changes to the medical profession from the 1970s on were prescient in their anticipation of dramatic changes that have since taken place. Proletarianization was, it is largely agreed, an overstatement of events, while corporatization and deprofessionalization represent important aspects of ongoing changes to the medical profession, but neither theory is adequate alone. Since the 1980s, the debate has been framed in terms of challenges to medicine, and assessing those challenges from and the implications for the various parties involved: the state, corporate and commercial interests, professional and occupational interests, and those of patients, unskilled healthcare workers and informal carers.

CHALLENGING MEDICINE: EFFICACY, EFFICIENCY, ACCESSIBILITY

Challenges to medicine's power and influence are seen as having eroded its autonomy, and as diminishing its dominance over other occupational groups and patients. The complexity of medical power as an internalized force dispersed across institutions and complicit individuals means that any loss of power to physicians does not imply a simple gain to a rival agent such as patients or managers or nurses. Rather, each challenge to medical power has to be examined for its particular implications, including medicine's response, which can consolidate institutional influence, even as individual physicians lose autonomy. Medicine's state-sponsored monopoly as provider of orthodox medical services, its regulatory role over other professions allied with medicine and claims for the special nature of the doctor–patient relationship all pertain now, as at the start of the twentieth century. However, the complexity of the context in which physicians practise has increased enormously, in terms of the variety of statutory, commercial and professional institutions involved in the delivery of healthcare. When Mari Haug was writing about deprofession-alization in the 1970s, she identified consumerism as a serious threat to the medical profession in its relations with patients (Haug, 1973). What was harder to see then was how patients as consumers of healthcare services and users of medical knowledge would reconfigure some of the ways that medicine is practised, without causing an absolute disjunct from existing practice. In the following account, the challenges to medicine are considered in terms of the structural changes primarily in the British context to establish the framework for medical practice, before turning to the smaller scale effects on the relationship between clinician and patient.

EFFICACY, EQUITY AND EFFICIENCY

Interrogation of the value and efficacy of medical methods and the sovereign power of medical practitioners has been part of a wider interrogation of medical practice and its effects. The autonomy of medical practitioners, key to their status and ways of working with other occupational groups, has come under scrutiny from various quarters: academic, clinical, legal and managerial. In the British context, changes to the organization of the NHS are key to understanding physicians' status and autonomy.

The general willingness to question authority and expert knowledge that characterized industrialized society from the 1960s onwards was a tendency from which medicine was not exempt, as we have seen. Some of the most powerful challenges to medicine's legitimacy and authority came from within the institution itself, from physicians who did not see themselves as part of a counter-cultural movement. Medicine's claim for the efficacy of its methods and their unbounded potential to benefit humankind has been critical to its development as a powerful institution: hence the questioning of this efficacy has been a significant calling to account of medicine's institutional and professional standing. While Illich queried from outwith the profession, Thomas McKeown (1912–1988), physician and professor of social medicine, did so from within. McKeown was interested in why human populations had increased over time, with a key question being whether medicine was influential in this growth. While his work is often grouped with that of counter-cultural critics of medicine working at the same time, McKeown's research was 'situated firmly within the medical establishment and its traditions' (Bynum, 2008: 645) and he is regarded as a founder of social medicine. He questioned the efficacy of medicine's methods by suggesting that medical claims to have improved human health had been overplayed since declines in mortality could be attributed to improvements in nutrition and hygiene, rather than medical advances (McKeown, 1976). McKeown's interrogation of the usefulness of medicine in improving population health was radical, particularly given that his answer was that medicine's therapeutic effect had been minimal, a line of analysis that suggested devoting resources to medical technology represented a poor investment in human health (McKeown, 1979). McKeown's methods have been criticized by clinicians, historians and demographers in terms of the construction and interpretation of the data on which his appraisal of the minimal therapeutic effect of medical care on declining mortality was made. Fellow physicians have characterized his work as 'therapeutic nihilism' (Tudor Hart, 2000) and alternative analyses have shown how medical care has, in fact, contributed to improvements in life expectancy (Bunker et al., 1994).

Nonetheless, McKeown's work was an important plank in the critique of medicine in exposing the weakness of medical claims of efficacy. McKeown's criticism has met with a range of medical responses, from the accusation of nihilism cited above, to the development of the field of social medicine, which examines the social, economic and political causes of ill health. Although established since the Second World War, through the second half of the twentieth century, social medicine has been part of the rise of 'lifestyle medicine' in which patients' individual behaviours and habits are understood as key modifiable variables in the control of disease (Porter, 2006). Debate around the role of socio-economic and political factors in rates of morbidity and mortality has extended medicine's boundaries to include these factors as part of its own already broad remit. Medicine's continued ability to adapt to and accommodate challenges is part of what justifies sociology's continuing critical interest.

MANAGERS, MANAGERIALISM AND MARKETS

The corporatized and bureaucratized aspects of the healthcare organizations within which physicians work, are a crucial part of understanding medicine's influence on healthcare. Ideally, the system which delivers healthcare should be accessible, efficient and equitable, particularly in a nationalized system, dependent on funding from central taxation. Ensuring that healthcare is delivered in the most efficient manner possible has become ever more important over the last 50 years, as it becomes clear that the demand for healthcare is elastic rather than finite. Although it seems astonishingly naive now, the NHS was established with an expectation that once unmet healthcare needs had been addressed, demand for services would fall. It now seems that the delivery of healthcare services tends to create further need, both by deferring death and by raising expectations of freedom from morbidity and disability among doctors and their patients.

The efficiency of the NHS has been on every political party's agenda since the economic recession of the early 1970s. Given the public's attachment to the NHS, for obvious reasons of service provision, but also as an icon of Britishness, no party seeking election can propose to dismantle it, nor even to reduce its level of resource, judging by twenty-first-century elections, but only to improve its efficiency. In looking for a means of controlling the cost of healthcare and the rise of NHS-specific inflation, the exertion of 'managerial pressure to the NHS' has, historically, been a preferred option for government (Appleby, 1999). The need for reform in the 1970s was predicated on a view of the NHS as a highly inefficient and inflexible bureaucracy structured around the needs of medical professionals. This view was part and parcel of the transformation in economic forms, whereby industrial models of production were giving way to a flexible economy focused on knowledge and information production rather than material goods. Successive governments have sought to modernize the NHS with the introduction of centralized initiatives in terms of funding structures, management schemes and other regulatory administration, often in the wake of a consultation exercise or an expert report. The speed with which NHS management has changed and redefined its goals and techniques, and the quickening tempo of structural reorganization as the twentieth century gave way to the twenty-first, has provoked cynicism among healthcare staff who complain of constant revolution in the NHS for the last 40 years. Both structurally and culturally, reform has altered the NHS as a place in which to practise medicine since the early days of its inception.

The maintenance of medical power was a condition for the cooperation of physicians with the establishment of the NHS, and the preservation of clinical autonomy meant that consultants retained enormous influence. For three decades from 1948, there was no mechanism to restrict clinicians' use of resources, which were disbursed according to their individual estimation of clinical need. The 1970s saw a Labour government introduce consensus management as part of a reorganization which introduced Area Health Authorities. This system of management was designed to support a multidisciplinary NHS by allowing every occupational group to have a voice in decisions, but given the differentials of power and influence between the various groups, it left medical dominance largely untouched.

In 1983, under a Conservative government, Sir Roy Griffiths wrote a report on NHS management, or rather its dearth. Griffiths expressed the problematic lack of accountability in the NHS in a memorable phrase that continues to be quoted: 'If Florence Nightingale were carrying her lamp through the corridors of the NHS today, she would almost certainly be searching for the people in charge' (Griffiths, 1983: 12).

In the wake of the Griffiths report, consensus management was disbanded and those who had administrated the consensus were replaced by managers with decision-making power, some drawn from doctors' and nurses' ranks. The replacement of consensus management with general management meant that every tier of the organization had a single identifiable figure in charge. At the same time, clinical budgets and cost improvement programmes were introduced. It was expected that such management-led pressure would be an effective mechanism to control NHS costs and/or to improve efficiency, but retrospective analysis suggests that any such effect was slight (Appleby, 1999). The post-1974 period has been characterized as one of excessive managerialism without any great gain in the internal coherence or efficiency of the health service (Berridge, 1999). Furthermore, general managers seem to have had little effect on physicians or on other ward staff, and, perhaps more surprisingly, seem to have had little expectation that they would have any such influence (Harrison et al., 1992). Thus, the autonomous medical power that had been identified as a hindrance to reform in the 1970s, remained largely intact by the end of the 1980s and hence a new round of new initiatives to rationalize NHS processes began.

The next phase of management reform was an attempt to introduce marketplace competition in the provision of secondary and tertiary healthcare services in order to drive down 'unnecessary' costs. 'Internal' or 'quasi' markets were engineered by designating GPs to be the purchasers of services, and therefore distinct and separate from the role of hospital-based providers of services, despite both of these roles being located within a single health authority. General Practitioners have long been gate-keepers for more expensive hospital treatments, but their rationing role had been informal and unregulated, driven by individual assessments of clinical need, without any formal mechanism to temper individual idiosyncrasy. Economists borrowing ideas from commercial settings, proposed that competition between providers of services should result in 'efficiency savings' as well as improving performance in public services. General Practices who came forward for the scheme to be designated fund-holders were able to decide between providers when referring their patients for secondary and tertiary services. The assumption was that by introducing competition, hospitals would become more responsive to General Practices in an effort to secure their referrals and, it was hoped, General Practices would become more responsive to their patients' needs. By controlling their own budget, a General Practice could, in theory, influence the quality of care and represent patients' needs to the providers of hospital services.

In retrospect, any effects of the quasi-markets were highly attenuated by the ongoing force of central directives, for instance to reduce waiting times, as well as constraints placed on the operation of market forces to prevent economic competition from disrupting the status quo. The creation of a division between purchaser and provider in healthcare was a matter of free market dogma, rather than a reflection of how good healthcare systems actually tend to work in response to patients' needs.

One lasting impact of the drive to make healthcare subject to market forces has been a shift in the balance of power away from hospital providers, towards General Practitioners and, to a lesser extent, in favour of healthcare managers. Another impact, and one that was not predicted by the architects of these reforms, was the extra administrative and management cost incurred by new requirements for audit information and the need to negotiate contracts in the newly created internal market.

CHALLENGING EQUITY

The need for audit as a management tool not only created extra work, but also created information that exposed systematic inequities. The publication of various measures of the quality of healthcare, such as frequency of intervention, length of stay, type of intervention available and drug prescription, exposed marked variations in the system that came to be known as a postcode lottery. The rationing of resources which clinicians had performed implicitly on an individual basis, came under scrutiny with the production of new information required for management systems. One easily grasped aspect of the inequitable distribution was the variation in rates of surgical intervention that showed divergence over time (Black, 1984), across national boundaries, across smaller areas and across social groups (Coulter et al., 1988). While rates of surgical intervention are relatively straightforward variables to construct from administrative and audit data, the meaning of the variable is not, as the following description, referring to surgery for glue ear, makes clear:

> The rate of surgery is the last step in a sequence that includes the morbidity of the condition; the rate of referral from general practitioners to specialists; and, finally, the

rate of operation of the surgeons. Each rate may be affected by a host of factors, some of which relate to the characteristics and behaviour of patients and some to the availability and organisation of health services. (Black, 1985: 1963)

Drastic variation in rates of surgery suggested that criteria other than the interpretation of clinical signs to assess clinical need were at work. Some of the reasons suggested for the lower rates of hysterectomy in Britain compared with other nations included the provision of: 'fewer health care resources (hospital beds, surgeons); much less fee-for-service medicine; differences in the attitudes of surgeons; differences in health care organisation, in particular the gatekeeping role of general practitioners; and differences in patients' expectations' (Coulter et al., 1988: 987).

The variation in rates of hysterectomy and surgery for glue ear was not surprising given that since the inception of the NHS, services had grown up haphazardly without central planning or monitoring. Over four decades, individual hospitals and clinics and subsequently health authorities, influenced by those medical consultants who wielded most power, had made local decisions on the availability of treatments and drugs. These variations were exacerbated with the introduction of the 'internal markets' and the implementation of fund-holding for General Practices. Patients of a budget-holding GP tended to have better access to hospital treatment than patients of non-fund-holding practices, which raised fears of the emergence of a two-tier health system (BMJ, 1994).

Around the same time that research was revealing the extent of the disparities in rates of surgery, other initiatives were making it possible to interrogate medical practice through systematic survey methods. Established in 1993, the Cochrane Collaboration was named after a British epidemiologist, Archie Cochrane (1909–1988), who advocated the use of randomized controlled trials as a means of reliably informing healthcare practice (Cochrane, 1972). The Collaboration currently describes itself as 'an international, independent, not-for-profit organisation of over 27,000 contributors from more than 100 countries, dedicated to making up-to-date, accurate information about the effects of health care readily available worldwide' (www.cochrane.org/). The Collaboration makes available systematic assessments of healthcare interventions by publishing them online in The Cochrane Library. These reviews: 'are intended to help providers, practitioners and patients make informed decisions about health care, and are the most comprehensive, reliable and relevant source of evidence on which to base these decisions' (www.cochrane.org/).

The Cochrane Collaboration's publication of systematic reviews facilitated and coincided with the rise of evidence-based medicine. Evidence-based medicine is:

the conscientious, explicit, and judicious use of current best evidence in making decisions about the care of individual patients. The practice of evidence based medicine means integrating individual clinical expertise with the best available external clinical evidence from systematic research. (Sackett et al., 1996)

The concept of evidence-based medicine was taken up with the arrival of a new Labour administration in 1997, determined to tackle the variations in access to and use of services, treatments and drugs that had become increasingly apparent over the previous decade. A new system of governance was established over Labour's early years in office. The need for consistency and regulation in the availability and quality of services across geographical areas was addressed by the establishment of the National Institute for Clinical Excellence in April 1999 (subsequently renamed the National Institute for Health and Clinical Excellence, but retaining the acronym NICE). This public body makes available evidence on the effectiveness and cost-effectiveness of treatments and interventions, with guidance on suitability for use within the NHS in England and Wales (www.nice.org.uk/aboutnice/whoweare/who_we_are.jsp).

NICE makes economic assessments using a cost-utility approach whereby the cost per quality adjusted life year is calculated to advise health professionals on providing their NHS patients with appropriate standards of clinical care. This allows judgements about cost-effectiveness to be made in order to balance the tensions between efficiency and equity across a nationalized service (Rawlins and Culyer, 2004). The watchdog for NICE guidelines, with a statutory duty to assess the performance of healthcare organizations, is the Healthcare Commission (formerly known as Commission for Healthcare Audit and Inspection or CHAI which, in turn, took over from the Commission for Health Improvement or CHI). Among other duties, the Healthcare Commission seeks to ensure that healthcare trusts, including Primary Care Trusts, have implemented 'clinical governance', which refers to the ongoing improvement of clinical services at an individual and professional level.

In seeking to establish and monitor equality of access and equitable standards of care across the UK, various national service frameworks have been introduced. For the first time in the UK, nationwide standards of care have been set for particular conditions and diseases such as mental illness and heart disease. The introduction of the frameworks has often been associated with the appointment of a 'Tsar' for the field in question, such as cancer, emergency care or addiction. NICE and the Healthcare Commission have national remits for advice and regulation, which are potentially in tension with more recent moves to make NHS Trusts and Foundation Trusts both locally accountable and autonomous from central government management.

In 1999, the Labour government introduced Primary Care Groups to replace fund-holding General Practices. These were essentially sub-committees of Health Authorities that introduced General Practitioners to the corporate world and had complex organizational functions, including the provision and commissioning of care. Primary Care Groups, like the Primary Care Trusts which were their successors, were given the responsibility of managing the budget for the healthcare of their registered populations, while also improving the quality of care and integrating services through closer partnerships with other institutions.

Legislation to permit the creation of NHS Foundation Trusts was passed at the end of 2003. Foundation Trusts differ from existing NHS Trusts in terms of both their accountability to the local population, who can be members and governors of that Foundation, and their autonomy from regulation by central government. Supporters see local accountability and responsibility as key to making services patient-centred and improving quality, whereas critics see Foundations as back-door privatization that unravels the principles of equity and universality, resulting in a two-tier system.

HAS THE NHS IMPROVED?

Attempts to reform the National Health Service, one of the world's largest employers, have been compared to trying to change the direction of a super-tanker: any change of direction takes a long time and building up speed in the new direction takes even longer (Appleby, 1992). Furthermore, attempts to alter the direction of the NHS super-tanker have been frequent. Rudolf Klein (2008) characterizes the past 60 years of policy in the NHS in terms of 'flux and conflict' and predicts that this is likely to continue into the future. In Klein's view, 'heroic policy initiatives' cannot resolve the tensions that are inherent in any healthcare system, including the NHS, because they arise from the impossibility of keeping in play values that are in conflict with one another. For instance, the NHS is widely criticized for being excessively centralized – for instance, with prescription decisions subject to NICE guidelines, regardless of individual circumstances. The development of Foundation Trusts would devolve decision making to the local level and yet what is sometimes called 'postcode rationing', whereby the availability of different treatments varies by locality, is also unacceptable. So, as Klein (2008) asks, how 'are uniform national standards to be brought about without central direction?'.

After three terms of office, the Labour administration lost the general election in May 2010, ceding power to an alliance between the other two main political parties in Westminster – the Conservatives and Liberal Democrats. While the flux and conflict of NHS policy and the near constant pace of reform make it difficult to evaluate effects of specific policies, the end of 13 years of Labour government provided a convenient moment at which to draw up a balance sheet.

Just before the general election of May 2010, The King's Fund (an independent charity) published an investigation of how far the investment and accompanying reforms since 1997 had transformed the NHS in England into 'a high-performing health system'. The report notes that the creation of NICE represented an important development in:

> delivering evidence-based and consistent guidance to the NHS on what drugs and treatments are clinically effective and cost effective. Uptake of approved drugs has improved consistency of service across the NHS but variations in access to drugs have not been eliminated. (Thorlby and Maybin, 2010: 1)

Elsewhere, NICE has been described as 'one of the most admired NHS organisations internationally' (Appleby, 2010) and, together with the National Service Frameworks, it is judged to have 'substantially increased the availability of evidence-based standards' (Thorlby and Maybin, 2010: 3). The King's Fund report goes on to state that: 'Waiting times for hospital care have been reduced, and access to primary care has been improved. There has been progress in making the NHS more accountable and transparent to government and taxpayers' (Thorlby and Maybin, 2010: 5).

A report from the Nuffield Trust confirms that the NHS has made progress in providing evidence-based care as well as in: reducing death rates for major disease groups (especially cardiovascular diseases); reducing waiting times for hospital, outpatient, and cancer care; increasing provision of staff and technology; and in some places providing better community-based mental healthcare; and reducing rates of hospital infection (Leatherman and Sutherland, 2008). The King's Fund report commends the progress made, but suggests that work remains to be done in addressing:

> unwarranted variations in access, utilisation and quality of care even where national guidelines exist; ensuring that patients' experiences have a real impact on the quality of care locally; and, above all, ensuring there is adequate investment and energy in tackling the preventable causes of ill health and better support and care for those living with chronic conditions. (Thorlby and Maybin, 2010: 5)

The NHS context, in which doctors undertake most of their medical work in the UK, is judged as having improved over the late 1990s and first decade of the twenty-first century in terms of being an efficacious and equitable health service. The establishment of NICE, National Service Frameworks and the Healthcare Commission has changed the nature of medical power with its (further) withdrawal from individual practitioners and dispersion in corporate and bureaucratic bodies. The King's Fund report makes clear that there are particular problems that remain to be addressed in terms of equity, the application of national guidelines, health inequalities and the patient-centredness of healthcare. But, overall, the effectiveness of the system has, apparently, improved. However, whether this continues under a new government that is focused on reducing the public deficit is another matter.

At the end of 2010, the health secretary announced that NICE would be divested of its power to make recommendations on the use of new medical technologies in the NHS, although it would continue to provide guidelines. The change is proposed in order to devolve decisions about the use of drugs back down to individual clinicians who will respond to patients' needs. However, particularly with the increased economic power of General Practices, removing NICE's power to establish which drugs and other therapies should be used, raises the prospect of the re-emergence of the 'postcode lottery' or area-based inequality in access to treatment which NICE was designed to prevent. Promoting clinicans' and patients' choice in drug prescription is diametrically opposed to the aspiration to have an equitable national health system. Clinical safety and excellence (the professional aspiration), efficient and economic use of resources (the managerial imperative), and local accessibility (the public preference) are all worthy goals, but they are not necessarily and invariably consistent with each other (Klein, 2008).

THE DOCTOR–PATIENT RELATIONSHIP IN A REGULATORY FRAMEWORK

NICE and National Service Frameworks regulate some aspects of healthcare provision, but they do not go to the heart of the encounter of the doctor–patient relationship. Despite the enormous changes in health policy and governance over the last 60 years, some aspects show a remarkable continuity. A King's Fund report on efforts to introduce patient choice around hospital provision found that patients valued the friendliness of healthcare staff and the quality of care that they received over and above other dimensions of healthcare, such as the distance to travel to receive care or being able to choose to see a particular consultant (Dixon et al., 2010). Despite efforts to introduce information-led consumer choice to NHS patients through the publication of league tables comparing healthcare providers and the online 'choose and book' system, in real healthcare choices, people tended to rely on past experience and their GP's advice (Dixon et al., 2010). Despite the rise in managerialism, and the corporatization and informatization of healthcare provision, the relationship between doctor and patient remains key to patients' medical encounters and their journey through the health services.

Since medical influence stems, in part, from physicians' claim to advocate for patients' best interests as trusted experts, patients' positive evaluation of the friendliness and the quality of care over and above other aspects of medical treatment is no trivial matter (Dixon et al., 2010). The characterization of the physician's role as straightforwardly beneficent has been a long-standing justification for medicine's lack of outside regulation. The real dangers of the relative absence of regulation or oversight of the doctor–patient relationship were made dreadfully clear in two cases of medical maleficence in the 1990s. Official inquiries into Harold Shipman's work as a General Practitioner and the practice of surgeons at the Bristol Royal Infirmary showed how a reliance on benign expertise and professional self-regulation can dramatically fail to regulate the conduct of physicians who ignore patients' interests.

The centrality of the doctor–patient relationship for physicians' professional status was illustrated by an editorial in the *British Medical Journal*, published after Harold Shipman's conviction for murdering 15 of his patients, which stated: 'Serial killers in health care like Shipman … are particularly shocking because they damage the trust that exists between clinicians and their patients' (O'Neill, 2000: 329). This comment was notable because there were so many other aspects of the Shipman case that might have been considered more shocking than the damage to the doctor–patient relationship.

The independent inquiry into paediatric cardiologists' practice in Bristol in 1999 found that professional rather than patient interests were paramount. Poor decision making was exposed at the Bristol Infirmary during the early 1990s, when babies' heart conditions were aggressively treated and their organs posthumously retained. Treatment of hopeless cases and the retention of organs without permission served medical interests at the expense of patients and families and underlined the need for clinical governance and outside regulation.

Harold Shipman (1946–2004) was a General Practitioner who was found guilty of murdering 15 of his patients in January 2000, but was probably responsible for more than 200 deaths over the course of his working life. Dame Janet Smith, a high court judge, chaired an investigation into the case of Harold Shipman after the court hearing (www.shipman-inquiry.org.uk/). She reported that the General Medical Council (GMC, the regulatory body for physicians) had failed in its duty towards patients, tending to protect its own professional interests in preference to considering the public's safety or best interests (Smith, 2005), echoing earlier sociological work that had emphasized the GMC's preoccupation with the profession's interests (Stacey, 1992). The recommendations from the Shipman inquiry, together with evidence of other cases of malpractice that were heard at the GMC, gave impetus to establishing a means of overseeing the work of qualified doctors through a system of outside scrutiny and professional revalidation. However, the speed of progress towards establishing such a system has been slow. Within the NHS: 'Professional regulation has also been overhauled, with the aim of making the professions more responsive to public rather than professional interests, but many of the changes are still very recent' (Thorlby and Maybin, 2010: 5).

One of the areas where medicine betrays its self-interest is in its unwillingness to report on its own mistakes. Despite long-standing recognition of the need to

acknowledge medical error (Hilfiker, 1984), individual physicians who break professional ranks to become 'whistle-blowers' often have their allegations dismissed and
obtaining employment subsequently can be difficult. As was shown in classic sociological studies, the discussion of medical errors tends to remain within the profession,
withheld from patients and the wider public: being privy to the discussion is part of
the process of becoming a doctor (Bosk, 1979). Colleagues' unwillingness to report
on fellow physicians may have played a role in facilitating the maleficence of Harold
Shipman and paediatric heart surgeons at Bristol Infirmary.

Since the recent overhaul of professional regulation, evidence suggests that the
proportion of medical errors reported from hospital settings has risen, but that a
similar rise has not been seen in the reporting of errors in General Practice which
has not been subject to the same level of scrutiny (Hayes, 2010). Proposals for
physicians to be periodically revalidated from the GMC would partially address
this lack of scrutiny. Such proposals had been in development for 10 years before
arriving at the point in 2010 where a detailed plan could be released for consultation. The British Medical Association immediately called for these plans to be
scrapped, describing them as 'threatening and disproportionate' (Wilkins, 2010). The
British Medical Association's objections are not to the principle of revalidation but
to the workings of the system being proposed. In principle, the idea of revalidation
has been accepted: all doctors should be annually appraised and these appraisals,
together with testimony from patients and evidence of any further training or
qualifications, should go to the GMC every five years to demonstrate a doctor's
professional competence.

A decade after the seriously poor judgement of the Bristol Infirmary's paediatric
heart surgeons and of Shipman's medical colleagues in failing to notice his murderous
practice came to light, there is still no system of checks on a working doctor. Once
training has been completed and a doctor is certified qualified and registered with the
General Medical Council, under the system at the time of writing, no checks need
ever be done on their competence or skills again. The lack of operational revalidation
procedures is perhaps testament to the ongoing power of the medical profession and
confirms physicians' dominant place in the medical division of labour.

THE LEGAL CHALLENGE

Medical dominance means that the legal profession is the only non-medical profession that arbitrates on medical matters when disputes go through the courts, or are
subject to formal inquiry. One theme of the medical reaction to Dame Janet Smith's
reports on the aftermath of the Harold Shipman case was that without medical
training, lawyers could not understand the nuanced complexity of the clinical process

and without an appropriate appreciation of medicine could not and should not regulate medicine. Nonetheless, patients' families do resort to the courts in order to influence clinical judgements being taken for very ill babies. The parents of young children with complex medical problems for which the therapeutic benefit is marginal or uncertain are sometimes using legal means to force physicians to continue treatment.

In three cases of very ill babies, their parents have resorted to legal action when agreement with doctors over appropriate treatment for their child proved impossible to achieve: parents wanted more aggressive treatment or resuscitation than doctors felt was warranted. The parents of Charlotte Wyatt, Babies OT and MB (whose anonymity has been lawfully protected) did not agree with the assessment made by doctors who were treating their children. In Charlotte Wyatt's case, the judge imposed a 'Do Not Resuscitate' (DNR) order, in line with doctors' views, although it was subsequently lifted when the child survived longer than had been expected. Doctors wanted to withdraw life-sustaining treatment from Baby MB on the grounds that he was suffering intolerably, but the judge ruled in favour of the parents, who argued that their son's life was worth living. In the case of Baby OT, the judge upheld the doctors' decision to turn off life-support machines on the grounds that the child was suffering.

The complexity and emotionally fraught nature of these cases turns on defining what is in the sick child's best interests and whether the child has a life that is worth living. The ethical dilemmas surrounding the treatment of very premature and/or very impaired newborns are directly related to the recent development of technology and treatment that sustains premature or difficult births. The cases of Charlotte Wyatt, Babies OT and MB came to public attention in the aftermath of the public inquiry into the Bristol Infirmary paediatric cardiac surgeons. Where the surgeons were condemned for excessive intervention that did not benefit the babies under their care, the parents of Babies OT, MB and Charlotte Wyatt sought more aggressive medical intervention, even though physicians expressed concern that it would cause the child to suffer. The role played by so-called pro-life religious organizations in campaigning around these British cases is unclear in the press coverage available.

Such cases do not often end up in the courts in the UK, and, when they do, lawyers are providing something akin to a mediation service, rather than behaving as a regulatory body. This contrasts with the situation in the USA where clinicians know that many of the interventions given to neonates are not for the child's benefit, but are given as a defensive manoeuvre against potential legal challenge (Mesman, 2008).

Although it seems unlikely that the NHS will become as driven by the threat of litigation, compared with the healthcare system in the USA, there has nonetheless been a marked increase in patients' willingness to make formal complaints and to pursue legal cases when treatment fails. The willingness to complain and to pursue a complaint varies considerably by medical specialism and locality (Mulcahy, 2003). For the period 2009–10, the NHS information centre reported a 13.4 per cent rise in written complaints, which was the largest year-on-year increase since the first report was published in 1997–98 (www.ic.nhs.uk/pubs/nhscomplaints0910). The NHS information centre points out that over a similar time period, hospital admissions had increased by 28 per cent (1998–99 to 2008–09) and GP consultations had increased by an estimated 44 per cent (1998 and 2008), and, furthermore, work had been undertaken to streamline the process of making a complaint. The reasons behind the upturn in numbers of complaints notwithstanding, the increased willingness to complain can be seen as part of the process of medical care being suffused by a consumerist ethic.

CONSUMERISM IN MEDICINE

The NHS represents, or perhaps more accurately, represented, a collectivist ideal whereby the redistribution of wealth through central taxation ensured that everyone, regardless of the ability to pay, had access to healthcare at the time they needed it. This remains a hugely powerful ideal, but one that is often at odds with the ethic of consumption of late capitalism. The manifestation of consumerism in healthcare and medicine, like the wider process of fragmenting markets reconfiguring to attend to (and create) customers' demands, has used the rhetoric of consumer power. In 1991 the Patient's Charter was published, outlining the rights of NHS patients, a document that was subsequently revised twice. The emphasis on patients' rights in the 1990s was criticized both for being too weak in upholding patients' rights and for failing to outline their responsibilities. The charter did not offer patients any real rights and failed to emphasize patients' responsibilities towards providers of healthcare, so making working conditions for staff worse than before. Under the new Labour government, the charter was replaced in 2001 by 'Your guide to the NHS: getting the most from your National Health Service' which was itself replaced in 2005 by 'Your guide to local health services'. In 2008, a change in policy resulted in the publication of 'Best practice guidance for your guide to local health services', which Primary Care Trusts had to follow when writing an annual guide for the public outlining local health services available and the best way to use them. This guide has moved away from discussing rights, in favour of a balance of the responsibilities that patients have as well as what they can expect in terms of standards of care, and is locally rather than nationally configured.

The relationship that Talcott Parsons analysed as involving reciprocal, consensual roles with a benign expert professional seeking the patients' best interests in a privatized setting is a long way from the contractual nature of the healthcare consumer's expectations of his or her healthcare corporation. The tendency for patients to see themselves as consumers of services has been supported by the proliferation of providers of healthcare services (allopathic and otherwise) and of sources of information regarding healthcare and medical conditions. The nineteenth-century state-sponsored medical monopoly prevented alternative healing professions competing with medicine on the same footing, and the establishment of the NHS, making biomedically-informed care available without fees, reduced the market for complementary medicine. Nevertheless, alternatives to biomedicine have never disappeared and medical pluralism – patients consulting alternative sources of expertise – has long been the norm. Patients' uptake both of alternative therapies and sources of medical information (for example, telephone health lines such as NHS 24 and NHS Direct, internet health sites and self-help books and programmes) is strong. The ongoing specialization of medicine, together with the enormous public appetite for a range of therapies, including biomedical care for an ever-expanding range of new conditions, means that the doctor–patient relationship has become less and less exclusive and less like the idealized Parsonian closed bond of trust.

SPECIALIZATION

The range of divisions within medicine has grown with the knowledge explosion of the late twentieth century. Specialist doctors now have hugely detailed knowledge of specific conditions and parts of the body, but despite common early medical training, practitioners from different specialisms can have very little common knowledge or shared practice. The specialization of physicians is accompanied by greater specialization in associated professions, such as nursing – nurse practitioners, specialist clinical nurses and anaesthetic practitioners – who take on work that was formerly undertaken by doctors. In the USA, physician assistants and medical assistants work with different levels of supervision from a physician. Medical specialization in clinical care has brought indisputable benefit, for instance the replacement of ageing hip joints has become an efficient and highly effective routine intervention. But the high degree of specialization that allows orthopaedic surgeons to perfect joint replacement also introduces organizational, institutional and cultural barriers to holistic patient care. As discussed in Chapter 6, the failure of medicine to care for the whole patient can compound suffering, rather than alleviate it.

ALTERNATIVE MEDICAL PRACTITIONERS

The trend for increasing specialization, together with the routinization and bureau-cratization of medicine, have been suggested as reasons why patients seek alternative services. The enormous growth in so-called 'complementary and alternative medicine' (CAM) has been taken as an indication of patient dissatisfaction with biomedical provision and potentially as a threat to physicians as the main gateway to further care. Cant and Sharma (1999) date the burgeoning of complementary medicine to the late 1960s and ask whether such evidence of medical pluralism undermines medical dominance. The threat to medical power of people paying for acupuncture and aromatherapy services seems minimal, given that the services tend to be used as a complement to orthodox medicine rather than as an alternative. Indeed, in the NHS, complementary therapies are, in some cases, being commissioned in Primary Care Trusts, as a cost-effective means of responding to patients' non-medical needs for care. The commissioning of alterative therapies under the auspices of biomedicine is open to interpretation as a shoring up of medical dominance rather than the emergence of a new medical pluralism.

MEDICAL TOURISM

Another example of patients flexing their consumer power beyond the medical monopoly is medical tourism, whereby patients travel beyond their usual locality to get healthcare, potentially disrupting medical power, at least in a national setting. Of course, travelling to obtain expert medical advice and treatment is a strategy that a global elite have long made use of. The falling cost of air travel means that a larger proportion of the population may choose to circumvent the expense, or the inconvenient waiting time of getting treatment in their own country through travel. Travelling abroad for procedures unavailable on the NHS, such as cosmetic plastic surgery or fertility treatment, has been a means of patients getting access to the latest treatment options before a professional and social consensus to fund them has developed at home. Travelling to meet a physician to administer the drugs for an assisted suicide, which is illegal in most countries, has been the subject of intense discussion as euthanasia proponents seek legal reform in national settings. Buying hip operations in Germany or plastic surgery in South Africa could, potentially, relieve the pressure on healthcare resources at home. But surgery which fails to heal properly and the occurrence of medical error abroad, creates extra work for the medical tourist's local physicians and disrupts the sense that a doctor and patient have an exclusive relationship. So-called suicide tourism offers a profound challenge to medicine in testing the boundaries of what doctors can or should do for their patients.

Medical tourism and patients with a greater preparedness to complain and use the courts to assert their will are interpreted as signs of a growing commodification of health as a market-style consumer good. Consumerism invites us to appraise healthcare using ideas of choice and competition and to compare our experience of healthcare with other service industries. The rise of competition between service providers and patient choice as recurring motifs for the NHS suggests a break with the ideals of collectivism and solidarity with which the organization caught the world's imagination (Hunter, 2008).

MEDICALIZATION IN A DIGITAL ERA

From its idealistic inception, the NHS had discontents designed into its fabric: the insoluble tension of a service that seeks to be comprehensive, universally accessible, free and paid for out of restricted funds. Patients' dissatisfaction with the limitations and inaccessibility of services has, to some extent, been contained by their relationship with a General Practitioner: the GP has long been a gatekeeper to tertiary services, and, as a community-based physician, has been the focus of communication between medicine and the patient. In the post-Second World War period at the outset of the NHS, the chances of a patient being grateful for the newly nationalized service while retaining some deference to a professional who may have lived in the same neighbourhood as his patients, were probably higher than they are now. As patients have become less dependent on their family physician for information and access to services and care, the discontents have become more manifest, more vocal.

Sociologists of the 1960s and 1970s paid attention to the medical power entrenched in modern systems of health and social care, with some seeing medicine's intent to enlarge its system of influence through medicalization (Zola, 1972) and the subordination of other divisions of healthcare labour (Freidson, 1970), as ruthless. A dominant medical profession depends on the idea of 'a docile lay populace, in thrall to expansionist medicine' (Ballard and Elston, 2005: 228). If this was ever an appropriate sketch of NHS patients, the post-modern consumer of healthcare demonstrably plays a more active role in bringing about or resisting medicalization. In linking medicalization to modernity and the rise of rationalism and science, Ballard and Elston (2005) suggest that with the passing of modernity a decrease in medicalization might be expected. In any case, they advocate abandoning a uni-linear model of medicalization, linked to imperialist doctors. If modernity is a tendency to increasingly subsume social life within spheres of bureaucracy, calculability, administration and control, then successive attempts to reform the NHS have certainly facilitated this process and doctors as autonomous individual practitioners have ceded influence. Nurses' and midwives' drives for professional autonomy during the 1990s, at a time when physicians were becoming increasingly subject to regulation, have left them increasingly personally accountable for their actions (Annandale et al., 2004). For example, midwives have sought greater continuity of care with pregnant women which has made their work more demanding and contributed to record numbers leaving midwifery as a result of burnout (Sandall, 1998).

The organizational and structural reforms to promote patients' rights to an equable, equitable and dignified health service over the last 20 years have had the effect of withdrawing autonomy from healthcare personnel, including physicians, in favour of those who oversee the organizational frameworks and manage the information systems. Since physicians play such a range of different roles across a healthcare service – managers, chief executives, policy advisers, researchers in commercial and public bodies – the institutional power of the medical profession may have shifted away from practising clinicians, but has not necessarily dissipated overall. Professionals working in the twenty-first century are less able to wield sovereign power than the doctors in the early years of the NHS, yet medicalization remains a feature of society nonetheless. The ubiquity of medicalization in the absence of imperialist medics is partly due to the evolution of a corporate elite in medical institutions who are not only or necessarily physicians and are certainly not frontline clinical workers (Lewis and Considine, 1999).

While medicalization is not necessarily led by imperialist clinicians, it is certainly driven by a broader range of social forces, including the market and management classes, as well as consumers of health informatics and health services (Furedi, 2006: 15). Furedi cites the pressure to diagnose conditions such as dyslexia, ADHD and other learning difficulties in children that comes from parents, teachers and the educational marketplace. Having a child's behaviour or learning difficulties labelled as a disorder and, potentially medicated, can offer educational advantages. While psychiatrists have played an important role in the medicalization of children and adolescents' behavioural, educational and emotional problems, as seen, for example in the rates of diagnosis of ADHD, they have not been the only players. Foucault's description of the diffuse nature of medical power, operating with the complicity of patients, is pertinent here.

Despite various challenges to medicine's autonomy and dominance, 'a strong desire for biomedical solutions to human suffering persists', as shown by the public interest in 'claims for the potential benefits of new genetic, neurological and pharmacological medical developments' (Nettleton, 2006: 5), as well as the boom in ADHD diagnosis. In revisiting medicalization in an era of health informatics and consumer culture, sociologists must attend to professionals' use of the discourse of medicine as well as the responses of sceptical consumers seeking the best treatment available from a range of advisers and practitioners. Sociology sees the boundaries of medicine as an outcome of socio-economic and political processes, and the processes that determine what counts as legitimate medical knowledge and practice have, in turn, transformed the object of medicine's attentions. The digital era has altered some of these processes, not least by making medical information readily available beyond the profession.

Medicine as a practice is constituted through the flow of information. Paul Atkinson shows how medical talk *is* medical work in the sense that a case is dislocated from the patient's bedside and physical form, being constituted though the presentation of the case at a conference or review. The narration of the patient's case is how 'diverse types and sources of knowledge and actions derived from different time frames are brought together under the auspices of a single discursive organisation and made available for the collective gaze of medical colleagues' (Atkinson, 1995: 149). This narration is also 'a potent device for the reproduction of medical knowledge' (Atkinson, 1995: 149). Despite the fact that the 'processes of knowledge production and opinion formation are dispersed in time, space and personnel' and that the narrative construction of patient cases is open to challenge and negotiation, medical knowledge and practice is not characterized as uncertain (Atkinson, 1995: 151). Although scientific medicine often claims to be shaped by the natural objects of which the profession has an accurate knowledge, such as bodies and pathogens, the socially negotiated nature of its practice and knowledge can no longer be located simply with an imperialist doctor wielding his clinical gaze at the prone patient's bedside. Rather, the negotiations are located across the laboratory and other technologies of modern medicine within the increasingly complex healthcare organization of personnel, material infrastructure, and, increasingly, the digital world. Atkinson insists that a sociology of the clinic must attend 'to the distribution of knowledge and expertise within this complex social and technical division of labour' (1995: 148).

For Nettleton and Burrows (2003), digital technology is not only a new medium through which the social relations of disease are negotiated and performed in the clinic, but is altering the location and practice of medicine by taking it beyond the formal institutions of the medical establishment. They coin the term 'e-scaped medicine' to describe how networked computer systems as the dominant technological form give rise to a new medical cosmology by mediating and rendering diffuse the spaces, sites and locations of the production of medical knowledge. The dual role of ill people as both consumers of medical technology, including health informatics, as well as producers of medical knowledge, particularly since the inception of web 2.0 applications, is key to how this reshaping of the social relations of medicine could play out (Nettleton, 2009). The internet has the potential to facilitate the rise of the 'new medical pluralism' (Cant and Sharma, 1999) in addition to the 'reskilling' of lay people in their engagement with, and definition and management of, health and illness (Giddens, 1991). In undoing some of the social iatrogenesis to which Illich (1976) referred, the internet aficionado 'expert patient' may challenge the power of the physician (Hardey, 1999). Patients and carers contribute knowledge, information and experience on the web via peer-to-peer chat rooms, blogs and information exchange forums, as well as being consumers of services and products through sophisticated marketing techniques deployed by the pharmaceutical, biotechnology and healthcare industries (Nettleton and Burrows, 2003).

The role of big pharma in promoting so-called 'prosumers' who are both producers and consumers in the new medical markets, through web-based networks that support patients in advocating for wider access to particular drugs, remains less prominent than the discourse of the 'brave battling patient'. In the case of Herceptin, an expensive drug used for particular types of breast cancer, two women went to court in order receive it on the NHS, thereby over-turning a NICE protocol (*Times Online*, 2009). The broadening of the category of cancer patient that could benefit from Herceptin generated considerable publicity that may have benefitted Roche, the manufacturers of the drug, but it also posed critical questions regarding the effectiveness and high price of the drug (List, 2006). However, the transformative role of digital informatics goes beyond their role as new tools for existing players that might shift power relations in the social relations of health and illness such that the networked digital world offers new metaphors and models for medicine as practice and as discipline.

Andrew Webster tells us that, increasingly, medicine is not just being sped up or enhanced by informatics, but in fact information is what it consists in:

> The rapid spread of both genetics and health informatics within clinical science and medicine, as well as their deployment for health management purposes (as in DNA registers, or in health information management systems such as the electronic patient record [EPR]), suggest that the contemporary medical portfolio is becoming increasingly 'informaticized'. (Webster, 2002: 451)

This is a development of Atkinson's call to look at the distribution of information, to attend to how medical practice is infused not only by technical information, but saturated by the systems that manage that information. The delivery and management systems used by medicine are becoming increasingly information-based, while 'diagnosis, clinical decision making and practitioner–patient communication are being affected by the nature of information that derives from assessments of medical interventions and/or assessments of risk of various sorts' (Nettleton, 2004: 666). For Nettleton (2004), clinical decision making and clinical activities have come to depend not only on the results of tests within the laboratory, but also upon the systematic reviews of research undertaken by information scientists. She uses the phrase bodies 'over the wire' to describe how patients' bodies might escape from the boundaries of the clinic or the hospital (Nettleton, 2004: 669), for example through the

PATSy system, a web-based multimedia database that makes 'virtual patients' available to students of neuroscience, clinical science, medicine and related fields (www. patsy.ac.uk/). While the PATSy system is supported by the Nuffield Foundation and hosted by Edinburgh University, other systems of healthcare informatics represent an interpenetration of the public and the private – for instance, Dr Foster, a commercial provider of healthcare information, that works in partnership with the Department of Health to publish various guides on the use of the NHS. Dr Foster Holdings owns and maintains websites that offer products and services to health professionals and consumers of health services, which, in the company's own words, seek to:

> improve the quality and efficiency of health and social care through better use of information. We will make it easier for professionals and the public to access health and social care information through a range of innovative products and services. (www.drfosterintelligence.co.uk/about-us/)

The company publishes comparative data on hospitals' rates of procedure, scores on patient safety, clinical effectiveness and patient experience, as well as a national listing of consultants and of complementary therapists, promoting the idea of the patient as an informed consumer who will choose where to give birth or have a surgical procedure based on quantitative assessments. The website for professionals offers statistics for commissioners and providers of services as well as 'mental health solutions' and research services to, for instance, 'tackle health inequalities'. Dr Foster represents a blurring of boundaries that have traditionally existed between the public and private sectors as it employs the techniques of commerce such as 'social marketing' to define and target people and sell health messages where the old-style public sector has failed. And it is professionals as well as patients who are the potential customers for the providers of such services. Thus, patients' digitized, informatized bodies have escaped the clinic and dispersed into the marketplace, a market that is nonetheless embedded in the agencies of the state.

Andrew Webster sees new health technologies, operating in an era of reflexive risk evaluation, as bringing about a new negotiation between patients and professionals over the meaning and utility of clinical intervention and techniques (2002: 452). For Webster, medical diagnosis is taking on a greater provisionality which, together with the emphasis on the negotiation of 'risk allocation between health practitioners, counsellors and those consulting them', has proliferated the number and type of sites where health information, treatment and care can be accessed. This is significant because it means that (private) professional self-regulation is giving way to publicly accountable forms of clinical governance, in particular 'debates over the meaning of "informed consent" to treatment by a medical technology' (Webster, 2002: 452).

CONCLUSION

The informatization and marketization of the social relations of health have fundamentally altered the medical cosmology. Talcott Parsons' idealized dyad of doctor and the patient captured the imagination of his own and subsequent generations of sociologists and his identification of a desire for authoritative biomedical care for our human ailments persists. Criticism framed in terms of professional dominance and medicalization crystallized an ongoing scepticism of legitimized professional authority, even while demand for medical services grew. The enormous complexity of pressures on the medical consultation and its location in a nexus of informatics, and interpenetrated statutory and market forces means that medicalization has to be seen as a dispersed, diffuse phenomenon that encompasses contradictory forces. The complexity of current medical systems implies more than these systems just being complicated: 'theories of complexity indicate that systems interact in ways that heavily influence the probabilities of later events, such that they are irreducible to elementary laws or simple processes' (Urry, 2005: 3). Complexity has emerged as a key idea in biomedical sciences, but is not a motif that can easily be translated into clinical settings.

One stable feature in a changing world is humanity's appetite for scientifically-informed medical solutions to a wide range of problems. Humanity's fear of pathogenic threat (HIV; swine or bird flu; *Staphylococcus aureus* and *Clostridium difficile*) and the urgent demand for solutions from big pharma persist, despite knowledge of the appalling errors that have occurred. Even after the effects of thalidomide (the supposedly safe sedative subsequently associated with birth defects) and of a synthetic oestrogen associated with cancer, we want to believe in the beneficial possibilities of technologically advanced biomedicine. This desire to believe was in evidence in patients' cooperation with the early operations that led to the development of organ transplantation techniques that are now routine. Even though no medical intervention since penicillin and vaccination has measured up in terms of being straightforwardly beneficial, as a society we fund medical research and participate in trials. We have demonstrated a willingness to believe the potential of the new genetics which in retrospect has been termed 'genohype' (Fleising, 2001) and, while this potential is yet to be realized, we nonetheless look to the next technological development with high expectations. For instance, medical applications of nanotechnology have been hyped as offering a whole new means of managing disease which would render current surgical procedures such as organ transplants obsolete. And yet, the lack of tangible benefits from nanotechnological research prompted an editorial stressing the 'strong need for more success stories' to demonstrate the field's viability (*Nature Materials*, 2006).

Hyperbolic claims regarding the genetic management of disease are put into context by a *British Medical Journal* editorial on the new genetics as follows:

As we watched the growing excitement and hype around the human genome project, we at the BMJ had a vision of the Oscar ceremonies. The scientists are in their tuxedos and sparkling dresses, slapping each other on the back, slurping champagne, and making extravagant, tearful speeches. Our readers are like the silent army of cleaners waiting outside: once the scientists have moved on to the next (postgenomic) party, they'll come in and start cleaning. (*BMJ*, 2001)

Medicine is absolutely at the heart of modernism and, as such, is subject to the processes of bureaucratization and reconfiguration in line with calculable risks that characterize modernity. Medicine – both its practice and the expectations that surround its potential – has played an important role in fuelling the juggernaut-like momentum of modernity towards late- or post-modernity, and the accompanying new medical cosmology. The question is whether the new cosmology will actually contain the same old problems.

REFERENCES

Annandale, E., Elston, M.A. and Prior, L. (eds) (2004) *Medical Work, Medical Knowledge and Health Care*. Oxford: Blackwell Publishing.

Appleby, J. (1992) *Financing Health Care in the 1990s*. Buckingham: Open University Press.

Appleby, J. (1999) 'Government funding of the UK National Health Service: what does the historical record reveal?', *Journal of Health Services Research and Policy*, 4(2): 79–89.

Appleby, J. (2010) 'Come off it, Dr Cameron', *Guardian*, 4 January. Available at: www.guardian.co.uk/commentisfree/2010/jan/04/cameron-changes-nhs-happened-already

Atkinson, P. (1995) *Medical Talk and Medical Work*. London: Sage.

Ballard, K. and Elston, M.A. (2005) 'Medicalisation: a multi-dimensional concept', *Social Theory & Health*, 3: 228–41.

Bamforth, I. (2003) 'Introduction', in I. Bamforth (ed.), *The Body in the Library: A Literary Anthology of Modern Medicine*. London: Verso. pp. ix–xxx.

Berridge, V. (1999) *Health and Society in Britain since 1939*. New Studies in Economic History. Cambridge: The Economic History Society and Cambridge University Press.

Black, N. (1984) 'Surgery for glue ear: a modern epidemic', *The Lancet*, 323(8381): 835–7.

Black, N. (1985) 'Glue ear: the new dyslexia?', *British Medical Journal (Clinical Research Edition)*, 290(6486): 1963–5.

BMJ (1994) 'Fundholders' patients are treated quicker says BMA', *British Medical Journal*, 308: 11.

BMJ (2001) 'Editorial', *British Medical Journal*, 305: 322.

Bosk, C. (1979) *Forgive and Remember: Managing Medical Failure*. Chicago: University of Chicago Press.

Bunker, J.P., Frazier, H.S. and Mosteller, F. (1994) 'Improving health: measuring effects of medical care', *The Milbank Quarterly*, 72(2): 225–58.

Bynum, B. (2008) 'The McKeown thesis', *The Lancet*, 371(9613): 644–5.

Cant, S. and Sharma, U. (1999) *A New Medical Pluralism: Complementary Medicine, Doctors, Patients and the State*. London: Taylor and Francis.

Cochrane, A.L. (1972) *Effectiveness and Efficiency: Random Reflections on Health Services*. London: Nuffield Provincial Hospitals Trust.

Conrad, P. and Schneider, J.W. (2005) 'Professionalization, monopoly and the structure of medical practice', in P. Conrad (ed.), *The Sociology of Health and Illness*, 7th edition. New York: Worth. pp. 170–88.

Coulter, A., McPherson, K. and Vessey, M. (1988) 'Do British women undergo too many or too few hysterectomies?', *Social Science & Medicine*, 27(9): 987–94.

Crossley, N. (2006) *Contesting Psychiatry: Social Movements in Mental Health*. London: Routledge.

Davis, J.E. (2010) 'Medicalization, social control and the relief of suffering', in W.C. Cockerham (ed.), *The New Blackwell Companion to Medical Sociology*. Malden, MA: Blackwell. pp. 211–41.

Derber, C., Schwartz, W. and Magrass, Y. (1990) *Power in the Highest Degree*. Oxford: Oxford University Press.

Dingwall, R. (1995 [1987]) *Aspects of Illness*. Aldershot: Ashgate.

Dixon, A., Robertson, R., Appleby, J., Burge, P., Devlin, N. and Magee H. (2010) *Patient Choice: How Patients Choose and How Providers Respond*. London: King's Fund.

Ehrenreich, B. and English, D. (1973) *Witches, Midwives, and Nurses: A History of Women Healers*. New York: Feminist Press.

Fleising, U. (2001) 'In search of genohype: a content analysis of biotechnology company documents', *New Genetics and Society*, 20(3): 239–54.

Foucault, M. (1965) *Madness and Civilization: A History of Insanity in the Age of Reason*. New York: Pantheon Books.

Foucault, M. (1973) *The Birth of the Clinic: An Archaeology of Medical Perception*. London: Tavistock.

Freidson, E. (1970) *Profession of Medicine*. Chicago: University of Chicago Press.

Furedi, F. (2006) 'The end of professional dominance', *Society*, 43(6): 14–18.

Giddens, A. (1991) *Modernity and Self-Identity: Self and Society in the Late Modern Age*. Cambridge: Polity.

Griffiths, R. (1983) *Griffiths Report: NHS Management Inquiry Report*. London: DHSS.

Harrison, S., Hunter, D., Marnoch, G. and Pollitt, C. (1992) *Just Managing: Power and Culture in the National Health Service*. London: Macmillan.

Hardey, M. (1999) 'Doctor in the house: the internet as a source of lay health knowledge and the challenge to expertise', *Sociology of Health & Illness*, 21(6): 820–35.

Haug, M. (1973) 'Deprofessionalization: an alternative hypothesis for the future', *Sociological Review Monograph*, 2: 195–211.

Hayes, J. (2010) '"Fear of reprisals and loss of reputation" stops GPs reporting medical errors', *British Medical Journal*, 340: c2936.

Hilfiker, D. (1984) 'Facing our mistakes', *The New England Journal of Medicine*, 310(2): 118–22.

Hunter, D.J. (2008) *The Health Debate*. Bristol: Policy Press.

Illich, I. (1976) *The Limits to Medicine*. London: Boyars.

Klein, R. (2008) 'Editorial: What does the future hold for the NHS at 60?', *British Medical Journal*, 337: a549.

Leatherman, S. and Sutherland, K. (2008) *The Quest for Quality in the NHS*. London: Nuffield Trust.

Lewis, J.M. and Considine, M. (1999) 'Medicine, economics and agenda-setting', *Social Science & Medicine*, 48(3): 393–405.

List, K. (2006) 'Will Herceptin media blitz help or harm patients?', *Scoop*, 14 February. Available at: www.scoop.co.nz/stories/HL0602/S00144.htm

McKeown, T. (1976) *The Modern Rise of Population*. London: Edward Arnold.

McKeown, T. (1979) *The Role of Medicine: Dream, Mirage or Nemesis*. Oxford: Blackwell Publishing.

McKinlay, J.B. and Arches, J. (1985) 'Toward the proletarianization of physicians', *International Journal of Health Services*, 15(2): 161–95.

McKinlay, J.B. and Marceau, L.D. (2002) 'The end of the golden age of doctoring', *International Journal of Health Services*, 32(2): 379–416.

Mesman, J. (2008) *Uncertainty in Medical Innovation: Experienced Pioneers in Neonatal Care*. Basingstoke: Palgrave.

Mulcahy, L. (2003) *Disputing Doctors: The Socio-Legal Dynamics of Complaints about Doctors*. Buckingham: Open University Press.

Nature Materials (2006) 'Editorial. Nanomedicine: a matter of rhetoric?', *Nature Materials*, 5: 243.

Navarro, V. (1976) *Medicine Under Capitalism*. London: Croom Helm.

Nettleton, S. (2004) 'The emergence of e-scaped medicine?', *Sociology*, 38: 661–79.

Nettleton, S. (2006) *The Sociology of Health and Illness*, 2nd edition. London: Polity.

Nettleton, S. (2009) 'Commentary: the appearance of new medical cosmologies and the re-appearance of sick and healthy men and women: a comment on the merits of social theorizing', *International Journal of Epidemiology*, 38(3): 633–6.

Nettleton, S. and Burrows, R. (2003) 'E-scaped medicine? Information, reflexivity and health', *Critical Social Policy*, 23(2): 165–85.

O'Neill, B. (2000) 'Doctor as murderer', *British Medical Journal*, 320: 329–30.

Porter, D. (2006) 'How did social medicine evolve, and where is it heading?', *PLoS Med* 3(10): e399.

Porter, R. (1997) *The Greatest Benefit to Mankind: A Medical History of Humanity from Antiquity to the Present*. London: Harper Collins.

Rawlins, M. and Culyer, A.J. (2004) 'Education and debate: National Institute for Clinical Excellence and its value judgments', *British Medical Journal*, 329: 224–7.

Sackett, D.L., William, M.C., Rosenberg, J.A., Muir Gray, R., Haynes, B. and Scott Richardson, W. (1996) 'Editorial. Evidence based medicine: what it is and what it isn't', *British Medical Journal*, 312: 71–2.

Sandall, J. (1998) 'Occupational burnout in midwives: new ways of working and the relationship between organizational factors and psychological health and wellbeing', *Risk, Decision and Policy*, 3(3): 213–32.

Smith, Dame Janet (2005) *Fifth Report of the Shipman Enquiry*. Available at: www.shipman-inquiry.org.uk/fifthreport.asp

Stacey, M. (1992) *Regulating British Medicine*. London: Wiley.

Starr, P. (1982) *The Social Transformation of American Medicine*. New York: Basic Books.

Strong, P.M. (1979) 'Sociological imperialism and the profession of medicine: a critical examination of the thesis of medical imperialism', *Social Science & Medicine*, 13A: 199–215.

Thorlby, R. and Maybin, J. (eds) (2010) *A High-performing NHS? A Review of Progress 1997–2010*. London: The King's Fund.

Times Online (2009) 'Ann Marie Rogers, Herceptin campaigner, dies of cancer', 5 March. Available at: www.timesonline.co.uk/tol/news/uk/health/article5853302.ece

Tudor Hart, J. (2000) 'Commentary: three decades of the inverse care law', *British Medical Journal*, 320(7226): 18–19.

Urry, J. (2005) 'The complexity turn', *Theory, Culture & Society*, 22(5): 1–14.

Webster, A. (2002) 'Innovative health technologies and the social: redefining health, medicine and the body', *Current Sociology*, 50: 443–57.

Wilkins, R. (2010) 'BMA criticises latest plans for revalidation', *British Medical Journal*, 340: c2850.

Zola, I. (1972) 'Medicine as an institution of social control', *Sociological Review*, 4: 487–504.

8
CONCLUSION

INTRODUCTION

The survey of sociological approaches to health and medicine presented in the preceding chapters has, of course, omitted as much as it has included. And exclusions, whether deliberate or through oversight, create a story as much as what is included. Omissions notwithstanding, this book has discussed a range of work, interrogating the social relations of health in terms of the interests of labour, capital, the professions and the state, which employs a range of methods and theoretical interests. What counts as sociology goes all the way from the social end of epidemiology to the philosophical leanings of social theory, and the breadth of this range is part of a persistent uncertainty as to whether sociology (let alone a sociology of health and medicine) constitutes a coherent discipline (see Prologue). While sociological work ranges in scale from the minutiae of conversation analysis to the global interests of big pharma, there is a common commitment to questioning received wisdom of what is natural, inevitable and best. Sociology's critical perspective has shown how the apparently self-evident truths of both medicine and capital can work against the interests of citizens, workers, patients and carers. An appreciation of gender, class, ethnicity and other characteristics which are simultaneously matters of structure and of identity, together with a willingness to embrace complexity and contingency, mark out a sociological approach.

This final chapter will make an assessment of what constitutes sociology's main contributions to a critical understanding of health and medicine and consider the lines of ongoing development in the discipline. Researching the doctor–patient relationship remains a central part of the sociological critique of medicine and the effects of recent developments in biotechnology in reconfiguring the nature of medical expertise, patient-hood and suffering are a key area of continuing interest.

Understanding the globalized interconnectedness of healthcare systems that continue to be constructed as nationally bounded, remains an unfinished sociological project. Sociology's attention to the flexible adaptation of the interests of corporate capitalism in healthcare organization has to keep track of biotechnological developments and the globalized structures, as well as the ways that statutory and bureaucratic interests cooperate with those of capital.

THE PRACTICE OF MEDICINE

A critical appraisal of the doctor–patient relationship suggests that even with the ongoing evolution of the medical model, physicians continue to deal with problems located in individuals that are biomedical in nature and only amenable to individual therapy. Sociological criticism of medicine has, of course, been closely bound up with biomedical advances: feminist criticism of the brutality of childbirth was facilitated by the reduction in perinatal and maternal mortality rates. With the retreat of infectious disease, the long-term study of the interactions of health professionals and patients has had one (but not the only) outcome: an assertion of the patient's view into proceedings. This emergence of the life-worlds of patients as independent of medical personnel has given us a 'broader more humane view of rationality' (Charmaz and Olesen, 1997: 484). Criticism of medicine's imperial tendencies, arising from the patient's perspective, has led to efforts to de-medicalize the clinic and offer patients more holistic, joined-up care. Maintaining a critical view, sociology has described how the arrival of social, community or advocacy workers as key liaison staff for medical case management has permitted a closer interrogation and more total surveillance of the patient and, in particular, an ever widening range of psychological states has been subject to the medical gaze.

One of sociology's strengths in assessing the development of patients' relationships with health professionals has been the combination of empirical methods and theoretical models. The struggles of both professionals and the people that they care for, to maintain ethical, rational and humane behaviour in the increasingly intricate and complex healthcare process involving highly sophisticated technology, requires that sociologists 'go beyond the effects of societal reactions and focus on what actually takes place at the interface of diagnosis and prognosis, of actors and technology, of medical facts and moral concerns' (Mesman, 2008: 3).

Jessica Mesman's ethnography of two neo-natal intensive care units shows how innovations in medical care practice play out in the care of very sick newborns as she seeks to document what actually happens when the processes of diagnosing and prognostication meet the need to establish facts and values for professionals and parents. Mesman describes the world of the neo-natal intensive care unit as one of state-of-the-art technology and cutting-edge medicine, where very ill children regularly and suddenly collapse, leading to uneasy parents and frustrated staff (2008: 47). Although the staff that Mesman observes are all expert, they are not all equally experienced and have disciplinary differences in their training in neonatology or cardiology intensive monitoring. This dual disciplinary approach, aimed at ruling out uncertainty in the condition of the neonate, becomes, paradoxically, a source of uncertainty for both nursing and medical staff because not all of the most experienced staff in both disciplines can be available on the unit throughout every shift (Mesman, 2008: 96).

Mesman's account of the paradoxes and contradictions of medical work shows that uncertainty will always feature because of the nature of sick children and the drive to 'break new ground' (2008: 194) that is characteristic of neonatology, among other medical specialties. She also shows the role that technological intervention and the expectant hopes of parents and staff play in infants' suffering through the case of Tom, a child subject to 'maximal intervention'. Tom was very sick at birth and, in order to arrive at the right course of medical action, a detailed picture of his condition had to be assembled, implying 'a sheer endless series of interventions in the form of checks and tests' (Mesman, 2008: 172). Later, a non-intervention decision was made and the child was left alone. Mesman notes that Tom benefits by sleeping well and being 'less panicky … very active, clear and eats well' (Mesman, 2008: 172). The improvement in Tom's condition painfully revealed how the previous regimen of interventions as part of 'the treatment trajectory' had contributed to his deteriorating condition. Despite this period of improvement, Tom eventually dies aged six months, in his mother's arms. Mesman makes the point that the ultimate outcome of the treatment, such as Tom's death, puts pressure on the moral correctness of the initial decision to intervene on a small sick baby. She refers to the correctness of any such decision as 'fragile', since effects, unforeseen risks and contingent events may turn a decision in unanticipated directions such that the final qualification of a decision to intervene as correct at the end of the treatment trajectory involves a certain amount of 'moral luck' (Mesman, 2008: 186).

Mesman's work picks out two key figures of sociological interest: first, the suffering patient, in this case the neonate – a fragile scrap of humanity bearing a heavy freight of adult hope, expectation and fear; second, the professional medic – doctors and nurses – faced with finely balanced decisions where good intentions do not guarantee good outcomes. Crucially, both of these players interact with a variety of medical technology, and this process constitutes and reconstitutes the players and the technology itself. Sociology's interest has remained focused on the two sides of the medical encounter, with ongoing research into the education and socialization of physicians and their use of technology, as well as an interrogation of how illness is experienced within the medical system and, crucially, beyond it.

MEDICAL ENCOUNTERS

The critique that physicians are all too often inadequately trained to function in the complex organizational and social systems that characterize modern practice has led to suggestions that physicians should be trained in the social sciences as well as in biomedicine (Sales and Schlaff, 2010). Yet, even though social and behavioural sciences are mandatorily included on medical curricula to a historically unprecedented extent, practising physicians continue to have highly individualistic views about the role of class, gender and racism, such that socio-demographic variables are seen as largely irrelevant to physician–patient interactions (Beagan, 2000). The individualistic and sociologically problematic approach of physicians has been attributed to the ongoing dominance of the medical profession by the White middle classes (Robb et al., 2007). Where medical students do reflect a local population's diversity, a strong homogenizing effect of medical education has been held responsible for the profession's characteristically individualistic approach to illness (Beagan, 2000). The divide between the physician and patient often comes into focus around issues of suffering and can be analysed post-hoc after a death: a death casts evaluative light back on previous decisions to intervene, whereas averting death is an achievement that can retrospectively justify considerable suffering.

The role of trust in the medical encounter looks set to remain an important sociological focus, particularly in the midst of the collapse of trust in experts generally and especially in global economic markets. Patients' views or stereotypes about their physicians can have significant effects on their interactions with health services. For instance, individuals who hold more negative views about physicians in one American study, sought care less often when they were sick, were less satisfied with the care that they did obtain, and were less likely to adhere to physician recommendations for treatment (Bogart et al., 2004). These findings were racialized in the sense that African-Americans (but not Whites), with more positive stereotypes reported better adherence and were more satisfied with their care (Bogart et al., 2004). The racialized dimension of trust between physician and patient in the USA is further illustrated by analysis of nationally representative survey data to show that White patients treated by White physicians have 33 per cent lower odds of reporting medical errors than White patients treated by non-White physicians (Stepanikova, 2006). By contrast, there was no effect noted for the report of medical errors by non-White patients (Stepanikova, 2006). It has become commonplace to note the racialized mistrust in medical science in the USA arising from the notorious 1970s study of untreated syphilis in Macon County (the Tuskegee syphilis experiment [Wailoo, 2001]). However, attributing racialized mistrust in medicine as explicable with reference to a single (albeit appallingly misconceived) study, thereby isolating it from the general structure of the medical encounter, perpetuates a racialized divide that sociology should be interrogating. A sociology of expectations might place racialized encounters alongside the more generally applicable individualistic failure of medicine to appreciate or even notice patients' world view. Clinical management systems operate to eliminate uncertainty from the process of diagnosis and treatment where possible, to the extent of ignoring significant aspects of experience, including suffering and identity. Clinical practice exacerbates rather than alleviates suffering where uncertainty, pain and existential anxiety as aspects of the experience of illness, are ignored. Sociology has persistently raised doubts about professional definitions of health and whether clinical interventions pursue this version of health in a way that benefits patients more than they are harmed.

Medical educators have been criticized for teaching students to strive for an unrealistically error-free practice (Mulacahy, 2003). Being taught to cope with error and uncertainty as part of clinical reasoning might help physicians to take patients' experiential and biographic evidence on their own illness more seriously. A better tolerance of uncertainty in clinical communication would also benefit patients from minority cultures (Gerrish et al., 1996): rushing to a diagnosis based on misunderstood or missing patient evidence may give the impression of certainty, but in fact covers up that which remains unknown. Allowing some queries to ride from consultation to consultation may, in some cases, be a professional and appropriate response to issues that cannot be rapidly or satisfactorily resolved. In some cases, uncertainty is not tolerated by patients and so the professional's sense of maintaining the patient's trust is crucial to the style of clinical practice that is appropriate.

An initiative that attends to the cultural complexities of the medical consultation termed 'social poetics', claims to provide a 'cultural go-between' to mediate between doctor and patient in diagnostic interviews (Katz and Shotter, 1996). The go-between's task is to 'be open to being "arrested", or "moved" by, certain fleeting, momentary occurrences in what patients do or say', thereby giving a sense of their 'inner world of pain and suffering', that is a 'boundary crossing' stance that creates comparisons useful in relating what patients say to the rest of their lives (Katz and Shotter, 1996: 919). Schemes of advocacy and cultural interpretation in the areas of mental health, pregnancy and child health have regularly attempted to address the lack of communication between medical staff and minority ethnic group patients. These schemes have often emphasized that the non-communication between staff and minority ethnic group patients goes beyond the need for linguistic translation and turns upon a fundamentally different world view, which requires cultural interpretation. The need for a cultural go-between or a patient advocate implies that medical professionals cannot apprehend the world of the patient and his or her expectations and needs – surely a fundamental flaw in the doctor–patient relationship. The 'social poetics' initiative suggests that communication difficulties that have been attributed to the education, or linguistic or cultural deficit of minority ethnic groups are actually a more general problem. This suggests that minority ethnic patients' needs should be considered in the same frame of reference as the majority population so that the professional–patient encounter remains the object of socio-logical critique.

The need to 'research up' in the sociology of health and medicine has never been stronger, but so is the need to research out, since although medicine clearly retains institutional power, it does not necessarily lie with all medical professionals to the same extent. While Phil Strong (1979) saw part of sociology's mission as chucking rocks at medicine, one difficulty is to identify whereabouts to aim the rock, given the ever-more institutionally complex structure of medicine. Concerns regarding the fragmentation of the medical profession and even its wholesale proletarianization, have been attempts to describe the complex patterns of stratification that have accompanied medicine's professional and disciplinary expansion. The corporate elite of medicine remains a powerful group and in an international policy context, with its general trends towards globalization and an emphasis on neo-liberal economics, the imperative towards cost containment and cost reduction is strong (Lewis and Considine, 1999). While the corporate elite of the profession is influential, the front-line service providers are not necessarily, since influential individuals tend to be located in large and prestigious organizations and are increasingly likely to have an economics training, with experience as health bureaucrats rather than as medical professionals (Lewis and Considine, 1999). The bureaucratic context in which the interests of the state and of capital are pursued under the auspices of medicine is a key concern for a sociological view.

BIOTECHNOLOGY

Alongside the health professional and the patient, another player in the medical encounter is the technology that has increasingly become an integral part of the practice of medicine and that can be seen as servicing the interests of capital, state and citizen. Advances in pharmacogenetic medicine, nanotechnology, stem cell research and brain imaging are key sociological topics (Blaxter, 2000: 1140), and sociology has been responsible for describing biotechnology's record of broken promises. Innovative technological approaches have promised, not only to address our pain and suffering in the rich world, but also to assuage the institutional violence of global health inequalities through the prevention of major diseases and the remote provision of medical expertise to a wider range of the population. The potential of technology such as smart phones – so enthusiastically adopted by consumers – to, for instance, monitor heart conditions (Shim et al., 2009), is extraordinary: complex medical images on everyday phones represents the e-scape of medicine posited by Nettleton and Burrows (2003) (see Chapter 7). But lest we be dazzled by the potential of the new technology, we should remember that it is the old technology of the combustion engine that is, for instance, providing crucial services in remote areas of Zambia, where robust motorbikes are compensating for the lack of transport infrastructure by getting patient samples to laboratories for timely diagnoses and hence appropriate treatment of malaria, TB and HIV (Morris, 2010). Notwithstanding the assertion that the washing machine changed the world more than digital technology (Chang, 2010), what has sociology offered by way of critique for the breathless claims of the limitless potential of technological medical innovation?

Perhaps the key sociological insight has been to point out that technological developments create, not only new therapeutic possibilities, but also new dilemmas and new forms of suffering. The shifts that are brought about by new technology are not limited to laboratories or hospital wards but extend to include regulatory bodies, insurance practices and family life (Mesman, 2008: 2). Technology's role in society is not in any sense neutral, and, for instance, devices that measure blood sugar do much more than simply accumulate data (Mol, 2000). Rather, through the measurement of a patient's blood sugar levels, the technology confers ontological status on the patient's state of health by translating the subjective experience into an object.

Pascale Lehoux (2008) follows this reasoning in her investigation of the role of technological innovation in the constitution of chronic illness. Measurement of the fluctuations of a chronic illness ('an inconclusive, boundless process unfolding over a lifetime' [Lehoux, 2008: 88]) requires that the expected and unexpected variations be interpreted and responded to by clinical intervention. Interventions such as a change in drug, dietary or exercise regimen, imply further monitoring of the ongoing fluctuations in the patient's state, thus drawing on the example of remote patient monitoring: '[c]hronic illness and technology thereby become part of a circular relationship, wherein one entails the existence of the other' (Lehoux, 2008: 88). In noting the development of numerous tele-health applications which permit patients to be monitored from afar, Lehoux points out that distance monitoring has been a widely promoted innovation for managing conditions as various as cardiovascular problems, high-risk pregnancies and diabetes. However, she warns that, as a society, we have lost sight of the ways in which health technology design is embedded in 'broad socio-political practices that can be examined, called into question, and modified through appropriate policy initiatives' (Lehoux, 2008: 96). Crucially, technology operates in the context of global marketplaces, so, despite claims that telemedicine is simply a new approach to delivering healthcare more effectively, it can also be understood as a method of configuring communities of healthcare (users and providers) to match the demands of a global health economy (Cartwright, 2000).

Telemedicine has, in theory, offered a hugely progressive means of extending healthcare to the poorest communities in the world, thereby undoing some global inequalities is health and healthcare. But telemedicine is not simply a new approach to delivering healthcare more effectively and to more people, and the technology involved is not neutrally beneficial. As Lisa Cartwright argues, it is a 'method of reordering geography and identity through new styles of health management that involve[s] new configurations of population and different ways of imagining what global health is and will be' (Cartwright, 2000: 347).

If place is linked to identity, then distance medicine and the ways that it reorganizes geography will also alter experiences of identity. In other words, telemedicine, as an actuarial set of techniques and practices, offers:

> new and relatively benign ways to organize, assess, compare, and rank bodies in the form of client pools, catchment regions, or populations. These intersecting claims converge in the general argument that telemedicine is a set of techniques in the broader health and communications apparatus that is gearing up for the management of health care capital, labor, markets, and knowledge for the 21st century. (Cartwright, 2000: 348)

Monitoring how technological innovations reconfigure the social and medical context in which they operate, including in the marketplace, is an ongoing sociological agenda.

ETHICS AND EXPECTATIONS OF BIOTECHNOLOGICAL INNOVATION

A key sociological concern has been the ethical regulation of biotechnological innovation and the ways in which patients' rights are safeguarded in the face of other imperatives. The touchstone of ethical regulation of medical practice, regardless of its technological content, has long been informed choice for patients. But with the gathering pace of technological change, the enormous challenge of giving patients appropriate information to make such a choice, has become apparent. In their interviews with medical staff who managed or implemented hospital prenatal screening policies, Williams et al. (2002) found a widespread recognition of the centrality of informed choice for ethical prenatal screening, alongside doubts as to whether it could actually be achieved. Most of those interviewed regarded the expansion of screening, which would likely further compromise informed choice, as an inevitable and inexorable process over which they had little, if any, control. The reported sense that the expansion of medical technologies was inexorable and beyond individuals' control was notable, since these were the people who were managing the expansion itself, and illustrates how technology and society co-configure one another (Williams et al., 2002).

The expectations of the social actors involved in the implementation of technological interventions is highly influential, as Kitzinger and Williams point out with regard to the rhetorical strategies used in reporting embryo stem cell science: 'The real battleground is about the plausibility of diverse visions of utopia and dystopia and about who can claim the authority (in terms of both morality and expertise) to produce a credible version of the future' (Kitzinger and Williams, 2005: 739). Successful rhetorical strategies in reporting stem cell science, unsurprisingly, were those that created an association 'with the right sort of people and values' (Kitzinger and Williams, 2005: 739), rather than simply reporting the correct scientific facts. Kitzinger and Williams (2005) suggest that health and science journalists are often predisposed to accept an optimistic scientific agenda while the financial interest that scientists have in promoting their own technology may be seen as un-newsworthy by journalists familiar with entrepreneurial scientists' working methods. The idea of biomedical progress driven by selfless scientists striving to create technological and pharmacological solutions for our suffering persists in various forms, despite decades of critique. Journalists and their audience may be predisposed to accept the most optimistic version of the possibilities that new science can offer, but the leap from scientific innovation to clinical application also depends on the expectations of both scientists and clinicians.

Stem cell research has held out huge promise for therapeutic innovation, including around the treatment for major chronic diseases such as diabetes. Wainwright et al. examine the discourses surrounding the prospects for stem cell research becoming clinically applied to note the 'performative nature of the discourses of expectations' (2006: 2062). In discussing institutional and scientific barriers to developing therapeutic applications of stem cell science, scientists framed their work in the context of others' expectations, such as research-funding institutions, as part of a means of distancing themselves from excessively hyped expectations (Wainwright et al., 2006). The relationship between scientific research and clinical application cannot be adequately understood as taking discoveries from the lab to the bedside, since there are also periods 'characterized by a clinically driven shift from the imagined possibilities of the clinic back into exploratory fundamental research' (Martin et al., 2008: 33). The relationship between expectations of research's potential and the success of the research or the clinical application is not straightforward. The long-term variations in the expectations of fields such as stem cell research is characteristic of the biosciences, in its successive cycles of disappointment and then re-investment. According to Martin and colleagues (2008: 34), claims of the future potential of a technology can peak shortly before a dramatic downturn in expectations, as key stakeholders invest extra effort in shoring up a vision that is under threat. An emergent sociology of expectations seeks to show how the various social actors' hopes and imagined futures are enmeshed in the processes that link biotech ideas and their clinical application.

THE CULTURE OF BIOETHICS

Alongside the rapid rise of technologically sophisticated biomedical research, has been the development of bioethics as the key discipline and practice that regulates the risk economy of such research. Sociologists have made it their business to subject bioethics, by definition a normative practice, to scrutiny (de Vries et al., 2007). Bioethics has been criticized for its aspiration to universalism, deemed 'at best an illusion' (Kalekin-Fishman, 1996: 818), which, together with its 'essentially western-ized' nature, means that models of ethics are inevitably the products of specific cultural settings (Kalekin-Fishman, 1996: 819). Kristina Orfali (2004) contrasts the role that parents play in medical decision making in French and American neonatal intensive care units to show the cultural variation in how decisions are conceptualized as ethical dilemmas. While Orfali sees the ongoing medical authority within ethics as a threat to patients' interests, other critics see the possibility of developing an international ethics with a goal of discovering 'the kinds of ethical choices which are possible and indispensable ... There must be a dialogue between researchers and researched throughout the world in order to achieve as clear an understanding of diversity and unity in morality as possible' (Kalekin-Fishman, 1996: 819).

Others point towards the impossibility of an even-handed bioethics 'amidst eco-nomic inequalities and contrasting socio-cultural worlds' (Fairhead et al., 2006). The case that illustrates such impossibility is a pneumococcal vaccine trial conducted by Medical Research Council (MRC) Laboratories in The Gambia jointly with the Gambian government and presented as an exemplar of international best practice in trial communication and informed consent procedures. Despite exemplary practice, the study's actual and potential study subjects' views on participation were shaped not by trial specificities, but by broader, historically shaped views and expe-riences of the MRC as an institution (Fairhead et al., 2006). Gambian parents held a pervasive view that the MRC offered good, free medication to participants, along-side a view that it 'stole blood'. Widespread concerns with blood-stealing emerge from a local understanding of an 'economy of blood' in which blood is treated as a tradable good but also one that accumulates or is depleted during bodily processes. Transactions in blood can, for Gambian parents, be more or less reasonably con-ducted. According to Fairhead and colleagues, understandings of the tradeable nature of blood should not be dismissed as based on rumour and the occult, as has happened in the past, but rather 'require serious attention and need to inform open dialogues between scientists and the public if medical research in resource-poor settings is to continue to be sustainable and politically legitimate' (Fairhead et al., 2006: 1109). Bioethical questions are rooted in their own cultural context. The centrality of informed consent as the iconic safeguard against abuse using biotechnology has been called into doubt in Western settings (Williams et al., 2002). However, where the assumption that informed consent can be managed at the level of the individual child and his or her parents is unwarranted, the usefulness of informed consent looks even more doubtful.

In terms of substantive areas, the need for a sociological critique of the ongoing development of biotechnologically sophisticated medicine and its application as both threat to and safeguard for human health is central. A less developed, but nonetheless important, area is the threat to human health of global instability in the physical environment in terms of climate change and consequent commodity shortages, as well as in the economic environment whereby trading in commodities such as food, fuel and other minerals entrenches inequalities and precipitates (or follows on from) violent unrest.

GLOBAL HEALTH

International evidence on health and social stratification across European countries (see Chapter 3) and beyond has long been an aspect of sociology's interrogation of the social relations of health. International documentation of the gap between official claims of universal and equal access to statutory healthcare and the measurable disparities by social division of access has been undertaken from Iceland (Vilhjalmsson, 2005) to Nigeria (Alubo, 1987), and compared across countries (such as India and China [Leslie, 1985]). These examples notwithstanding, American and British sociology of health and medicine has generally shown 'low levels of interest' in engaging with macro-structural concerns, including the global and the international (Seale, 2008: 692). This absence is striking given that sociology has been at the forefront of describing and theorizing the diverse processes of social change in an era of globalization (Walby, 2009). As Seale comments: 'the topics of globalisation, internationalism in health care and social systems-level analysis appear to have been neglected by medical sociologists in the pages of their leading journals' (Seale, 2008: 693).

Sociology has tended to confine its analyses to national settings, rather than to consider medicine and healthcare as global and globalized systems (Pescosolido et al., 2000). An emphasis on the influence of political, economic, civil rights and general citizenship policies on global health (Clair et al., 2007: 257) would increase the international relevance of sociological approaches, and perhaps 'help the sub-discipline relate more actively to the concerns of the parent discipline of sociology' (Seale, 2008: 694). Beyond the documentation of inequality, international dimensions of health research have been neglected, despite themes such as migration offering so many connections with work in cognate disciplines (Nettleton, 2007; Seale, 2008). The next section considers the emergent sociological agenda around medical migration, its connections with suffering and globalization, and the reasons for its neglect hitherto.

MEDICAL MIGRATION

As skilled workers with knowledge that is claimed as universally applicable, medical personnel have been key players in the rise of global migration. The global dominance of English as a language of education and science has promoted the migration of nurses, doctors, pharmacologists and other health personnel from former British colonial protectorates and possessions to the wider Anglophone world. The immigration of physicians and nurses to the UK has been an important feature of the development of the National Health Service through the twentieth century. With the emigration of British doctors to Canada, the USA and Australia, in search of a standard of living better than post-war Britain could offer, along with the expansion of medical services, immigrant labour – both skilled and unskilled – was crucial to the maintenance and development of the health service. Medical migration to the UK of students and workers followed historical patterns, largely based on colonial links, and has been much less studied than skilled migration associated with, for instance, the financial sectors (Raghuram and Kofman, 2002).

Medical immigration has been regulated by wealthy nations to make up shortfalls in their medical labour force: British general practice (Taylor and Esmail, 1999) and inner-city emergency wards have depended on such labour. Specialist areas such as geriatrics would not have been able to develop without immigrant physicians from South Asia (Raghuram et al., 2011). Neo-liberal approaches to economic globalization assumed that the poor nations sending medical migrants to wealthy states would benefit in terms of remittances and the reduction of skilled unemployment. Freedom of movement as a human right and the lack of specialist training places for physicians in poorer nations, as well as an ideological commitment to the removal of trade and migration barriers, favoured international medical migration. However, the entrenching of inequalities between rich and poor countries of which medical migration forms a part, has become hard to ignore. At the turn of the twenty-first century, it was clear that HIV infection and AIDS had become major public health issues for the world's poorest countries, in an era when the absence of the most basic sanitation and immunization is still responsible for high child mortality rates.

Expressions of concern regarding this reliance on global migrants in the UK (Buchan and Dovlo, 2004), Canada, Australia and the USA (Mullan, 2005), can be seen as part of the growing disenchantment with the neo-liberal model of economic development which has assumed that free markets will distribute resources (in this case people) according to both need and some equitable principle. Africa as a continent bears 24 per cent of the global burden of disease with only 3 per cent of the healthcare workforce and 1 per cent of the world's financial resources (WHO, 2006). Of 57 countries identified as suffering from a severe shortage of healthcare workers, 36 of these were in sub-Saharan Africa (WHO, 2006). For instance, in Malawi, there are an estimated two doctors for every 100,000 people (WHO, 2006: 194). Estimates suggest that with 'just 600,000 doctors, nurses, and mid-wives for 600 million people, African countries need the equivalent of at least 1 million additional workers in order to offer basic services consistent with the United Nations Millennium Development Goals' (Chen and Boufford, 2005: 1851).

In the light of the severe shortages of medical personnel in the poorest countries, the substantial transfer of physicians to the USA, the UK, Canada and Australia has been criticized as a 'brain drain' that weakens 'the physician work-forces of many poor nations and limits the ability of those nations to respond to HIV infection, AIDS, and other pressing needs' (Mullan, 2005: 1817). Describing the problem in more emotive terms, African countries are said to be:

> moving backward, with the hemorrhaging of clinical and professional leaders crippling the already fragile health care systems. These failures have been characterized as 'fatal flows', because poor people are left vulnerable to devastating diseases and avoidable death. The exodus also constitutes a silent theft from the poorest countries through the loss of public subsidies for medical education, estimated at $500 million annually for all emigrating skilled workers from Africa. (Chen and Boufford, 2005: 1851)

Optimistic analyses suggest that increased investments in domestic medical education of the poor nations from the rich nations receiving medical migrants might reduce the flow of doctors out of poor countries, helping 'lower-income nations to retain physicians and focus training on national needs rather than on the international physician market' (Mullan, 2005: 1817). However, a more detailed analysis of WHO data suggests that in 10 out of 12 of the sub-Saharan African countries studied, the numbers of healthcare staff currently being trained are inadequate, even if medical migration were not reducing their numbers further: even if staff numbers in these 10 countries were only dropping because of 'involuntary factors such as premature mortality', with current workforce training patterns it would take 36 years for physicians and 29 years for nurses and midwives to reach WHO's recent target of 2.28 professionals per 1000 population for the countries taken as a whole and some countries would never reach it. (Kinfu et al., 2009: 225)

From the point of view of the migrants themselves, the decision to migrate is often for economic reasons and health careers are attractive because they offer the prospects for migration (Connell et al., 2007). As well as the 'pull factor' of an improved standard of living, there are considerable pressures associated with working in poorly funded healthcare systems, including working on crowded wards where death rates are high, with few drugs and little essential equipment, thus inducing feelings of helplessness among staff. African health workers cite low salaries, limited opportunities for promotion or development and a general feeling of being undervalued as reasons for leaving their home countries, where they trained (VSO, 2010: 4). Doctors who migrated from South Africa to Canada describe their preference for working in a socialized health insurance environment that offers wider accessibility rather than the two-tiered system favouring a privileged few that has developed in their homeland (Joudrey and Robson, 2010). The devastating effect of the emigration of Malawi's nursing staff is described by Dorothy Ngoma, the Executive Director of the National Organisation of Nurses and Midwives of Malawi:

We lost the majority of registered nurses at their prime. In a country with about 1000 registered nurses, we lost about 600 of them. I believe those who left were the most assertive ones, the ambitious ones, those who would have made really good mentors and strong leaders ... that just weakened our system and our profession very much and I would say we have not recovered from that. It's not just the numbers – it removed a whole strong group of professional capable people. If you find them [health workers] now, you will find that they are very young, very junior, they are alone, confused, they haven't had strong mentors. They are not as good as those who left, because there haven't been strong people to lead them and support them. (VSO, 2010: 9)

Medical migrants very rarely return to their home countries and, when they do, they tend to eschew the public health system in favour of private practice (VSO, 2010). The long-term damage being caused and exacerbated by medical migration is not in doubt, and is reflected in the considerable economic cost for the countries sending migrants in terms of their own education and health systems through depleting workforces, diminishing the effectiveness of healthcare delivery and reducing the morale of the remaining workforce (Connell et al., 2007). What is less clear is what can be done to manage migration, mitigate its harmful impacts and strengthen African healthcare systems.

The WHO has developed a 'Global Code of Practice on the International Recruitment of Health Personnel', aiming to achieve an equitable balance of the interests of health workers, source countries and destination countries (WHO, 2010). While some commentators have discussed civil society working towards monitoring global compliance (Buchan, 2010), since this is a *code* and not a *treaty*, compliance is voluntary and, while it can be used as 'a tool to remind or even shame countries into action' (Pearson, 2010: 26), it cannot be enforced. However, given the inequitable state of global health, the very notion of establishing recruitment practices that are ethical has been called into question (Macintosh et al., 2006). In the absence of constructive forms of compensation or technology transfer to the countries sending their medical personnel, migration is only set to increase, hence exacerbating existing inequalities in access to adequate healthcare (Connell et al., 2007).

A report on medical migration from VSO (Voluntary Service Overseas), an international development charity, suggests that rather than seeking to prevent emigration from African counties, circular migration should be promoted. The report is entitled *Brain Gain*, playing against the more usual 'brain drain', and emphasizes that medical migrants often wish to return to their homeland and to ameliorate the health system in which they trained (VSO, 2010). However, the bureaucratic and legal difficulties of moving, for instance, between the UK and African countries, and of practising medicine in more than one setting, make this almost impossible.

> [P]olicy makers should implement measures that will promote circular migration, the legal and recurring movement of people between countries. Circular migration should facilitate the mutual gain of skills and knowledge, at the same time ensuring migrants are not exploited. Barriers to returning home, such as rigid citizenship pathways, should also be reduced for those migrants choosing to go back to their country of origin temporarily or permanently. (VSO, 2010: 5)

Medical migration is, as others have pointed out, ripe for sociological investigation, but so far this has been undertaken to a limited extent with regard to physicians (Joudrey and Robson, 2010) and nurses (Bourgeault and Wrede, 2008). The initiative in researching this field has been taken by geographers and migration specialists (Connell, 2008) as well as clinical specialists (see the special issue of the *Journal of Clinical Nursing* in 2007). Furthermore, the focus has been on the implications of medical migration for the countries of immigration, in terms of integration and discrimination with the local workforce and the gendered status of nursing work (Culley and Dyson, 2001; Bourgeault and Wrede, 2008), rather than the implications for the countries of emigration. The neglect of medical migration as a research topic of global importance is all the more striking given that the ethical dimensions were implicit in health economics from the early 1970s (Wright et al., 2008).

GLOBAL SUFFERING AND SOCIOLOGY

One of the solutions touted for the global disparities in access to healthcare lies in developing biotechnological solutions. The potential of technology to resolve health-care problems has powerful promoters in corporations seeking commercial gain through provision and servicing of technological commodities and in statutory agencies seeking solutions for an ever-growing burden of care. Considerable effort is being put into anti-malarial vaccines, which, once effective, would go some way to easing the shocking child mortality figures of the global south, and would represent a considerable commercial asset. However, the promotion of remote surgical intervention via fibre optic cables and computer-assisted distance diagnosis for rural areas cannot make good the shortage of workers and is no substitute for trained local medical staff. The relentless promotion of technological solutions seems impervious to sociology's documentation of technology's history of broken promises. The reiteration of technology's future promise, despite previous disappointment, is more powerful than sociologists' less optimistic, albeit more realistic, message. Communicating the unpredictability of the mutual reconfiguration of technology and society in ways that heavily influence the probabilities of later events, such that they are complex but not chaotic (Urry, 2005), is less compelling material than 'things are going to get better!'.

Biotechnology and bioethics are twinned industries in a global marketplace in which public and private spheres are interpenetrated and characterized by inequalities. While inequalities pertain across a range of resources, including access to healthcare and protection from the risks of clinical trials, they are related to one another in complex systems that compound disadvantage to the global poor. As described in the previous section, the maintenance of healthcare systems in the 'over-developed' world through the recruitment of migrant medics has impeded healthcare provision in the countries of emigration. Global medical migration has enhanced medicine as a career for aspirant migrants and the flow of migrants has facilitated the growth of medicine as a discipline and a profession. A reluctance to include those whose interests were harmed in analysing the global medical migration of the twentieth century, facilitated the unregulated 'theft' of medical expertise from countries least able to afford it (Macintosh et al., 2006).

The global marketplace for developing, testing and promoting pharmaceuticals and biotechnology further illustrates why sociology has to see through socially and politically constructed national boundaries. As big pharma searches for products to address global chronic health problems such as diabetes, obesity and depression, it also needs populations that are not already using pharmaceuticals for chronic disease. These populations tend to be far from the metropolitan centres and so inaccessible to the sociologist and the agencies of bioethical regulation, alike. While social anthro-pology values fieldwork in remote areas as central to its disciplinary character, it might be more likely to be represented in a remote 'field', but have less interest in understanding people's experience of drug trials alongside the interests of corporation, capital and profession (although exceptions abound). Sociology's problem is its willingness to ignore the effects of capitalism beyond the industrialized and post-industrialized world, and the connections that globalized systems imply. Another way of saying this is that sociology is willing to ignore the suffering of people remote from the over-developed world's metropolitan centres and, at least in this respect, is insensible to the effects of globalization.

The urgency of the international, global research agenda could also have far-reaching implications for the disciplinary configuration of the sociology of health and medicine. For instance, widening a sociological critique of biomedicine to consider inequalities in health and well-being on a global scale takes in disciplinary territory currently occupied by public health, medical anthropology, science and technology studies, social geography and development studies. Research that takes informatics and technology seriously in a global setting could revitalize the sociological agenda on health and medicine or it could dissolve disciplinary distinctions to the extent that our sub-discipline disappears. The persistence of a distinctly sociological view may depend on keeping suffering, as well as equity, in our intellectual purview, alongside historical as well as biographical processes.

Sociology should be in a position to comment on the most pressing global threats to health: security of resources including food and water, global warming, the threat of new epidemics and the resurgence of old pathogens and their connections to war and other conflict. While the over-developed world has felt the fear of new viral threats and of reduced access to oil accentuated by conflict in the Arab world, for the most part the suffering associated with global financial, commercial, socio-economic and meteorological systems has stayed in the poor world. In the rich world, we tend to experience problems of chaotic weather, food shortages and violent struggle through news reporting, and yet as sociologists we should see such global troubles as our concern. Rees Jones has pointed out, with respect to war, that if modernity, the key research object of sociology, 'is seen as a tendency to increasingly subsume forms of life within spheres of bureaucracy, calculability, administration and control, then war should be seen as a key catalyst for this tendency' (Rees Jones, 2003: 132). Sociology's reticence to describe the threats to health from global conflicts for resources is curious given that the reduction of inequalities in health status by social classes and locality remains a key goal for policy and research in national settings (Marmot et al., 2010), across Europe.

While sociology has found it difficult to grasp the global interconnectedness of systematic inequality in health, we have also struggled with how to represent suffering and the encounter with disease and illness at the individual level. Despite the centrality of the representation of health beyond its binary with illness as a key theme, examples of work which successfully combine the subjectivity of individual or familial suffering with sociological analysis are rare (Weitz, 1999; Blaxter, 2009). Grasping for an understanding of health beyond its binary opposition to illness has taken some commentators beyond the realms of social sciences as conventionally configured (Radley et al., 2006).

In order to explore the relationship between the world of illness and the world of health, Radley (2009) argues that pictures, photography, narrative and poetry need to be considered because they go beyond first person or personal illness narratives in their validation, authentication and illumination of suffering. Radley wants to get beyond the 'merely descriptive or confessional' and exclude sentimentality, to find a way of talking about illness that encompasses an aesthetic dimension. Noting that medical sociology currently has no place for aesthetics, Radley suggests that the discipline should address how pictures and stories do their work, how artefacts make meaning and, thereby, potentially, organize social action (2009). Sociological representations of suffering, disconnected from an aesthetic dimension, perhaps risk a routinization and dehumanization that has been criticized in bureaucracies, statutory welfare systems and institutionalized medicine.

CONCLUSION

Sociology is a powerful means of making sense of the world and the critical qualities that it offers are crucial at a time of complexity, uncertainty and information overload. Sociology is good at asking awkward critical questions and exposing vested interests, and, in the process of deconstructing experts' spurious claims and vested institutional interests, has built up and defended its own expertise. Sociology has been constructively chucking rocks at medicine for decades, and has maintained its critical gaze so as to note the ways that medicine has adapted to the rocks in reconfiguring its practice and knowledge claims. The sociological approach to health and medicine is a compelling means of interpreting the social world that has informed major changes in the ways that medicine is practised, regulated and remunerated. Critical sociological perspectives continue to assess medicine in an effort to re-imagine its practice along humane and creative lines. In the wider social relations of health, sociological work has changed the terms of the argument about equity of opportunity and outcome in health and had profound effects in social representations of illness as well as health. Aiming a critical gaze at globalized, and not just nationally bounded, settings while bearing in mind the vision of suffering humanity that is at stake in the social relations of health and medicine, perhaps sums up the contradictions of our work as compassionate rock-chuckers.

REFERENCES

Alubo, S.O. (1987) 'Power and privileges in medical care: an analysis of medical services in post-colonial Nigeria', *Social Science & Medicine*, 24(5): 453–62.

Beagan, B.L. (2000) 'Neutralizing differences: producing neutral doctors for (almost) neutral patients', *Social Science & Medicine*, 51(8): 1253–65.

Blaxter, M. (2000) 'Editorial: Medical sociology at the start of the new millennium', *Social Science & Medicine*, 51: 1139–42.

Blaxter, M. (2009) 'The case of the vanishing patient? Image and experience', *Sociology of Health & Illness*, 31(5): 762–78.

Bogart, L.M., Thorburn Bird, S., Walt, L.C., Delahanty, D.L. and Figler J.L. (2004) 'Association of stereotypes about physicians to health care satisfaction, help-seeking behavior, and adherence to treatment', *Social Science & Medicine*, 58(6): 1049–58.

Bourgeault, I. and Wrede, S. (2008) 'Caring *Beyond Borders*: comparing the relationship between work and migration patterns in Canada and Finland', *Revue Canadienne de Santé Publique*, 99(Supplément 2): S22–S26.

Buchan, J. (2010) 'Challenges for WHO code on international recruitment', *British Medical Journal*, 340: c1486.

Buchan, J. and Dovlo, D. (2004) *International Recruitment of Health Workers to the UK: A Report for DFID*. London: DFID Health Systems Resource Centre. Available at: www.dfidhealthrc.org/publications/country_information/int-rec-main.pdf

Cartwright, L. (2000) 'Reach out and heal someone: telemedicine and the globalization of health care', *Health*, 4: 347–77.

Chang, H-J. (2010) *23 Things They Don't Tell You About Capitalism*. London: Allen Lane.

Charmaz, K. and Olesen, V. (1997) 'Ethnographic research in medical sociology: its foci and distinctive contributions', *Sociological Methods & Research*, 25: 452–94.

Chen, L.C. and Boufford, J.I. (2005) 'Fatal flows: doctors on the move', *New England Journal of Medicine*, 353: 1850–2.

Clair, J.M., Clark, C., Hinote, B.P., Robinson, O., Caroline, A. and Wasserman, J. (2007) 'Developing, integrating, and perpetuating new ways of applying sociology to health, medicine, policy, and everyday life', *Social Science & Medicine*, 64: 248–58.

Connell, J. (ed.) (2008) *The International Migration of Health Workers: A Global Health System?* London: Routledge.

Connell, J., Zurn, P., Stilwell, B., Awases, M. and Braichet, J.M. (2007) 'Sub-Saharan Africa: beyond the health worker migration crisis?', *Social Science & Medicine*, 64(9): 1876–91.

Culley, L. and Dyson, S. (eds) (2001) *Ethnicity and Nursing Practice*. Houndmills: Palgrave.

de Vries, R., Turner, L., Orfali, C. and Bosk, C. (2007) 'Social science and bioethics: the way forward', in R. De Vries, L. Turner, C. Orfali and C. Bosk (eds) *The View from Here: Bioethics and Social Sciences*. Oxford: Blackwell Publishing. pp. 1–12.

Fairhead, J., Leach, M. and Small, M. (2006) 'Where techno-science meets poverty: medical research and the economy of blood in The Gambia', *West Africa Social Science & Medicine*, 63(4): 1109–20.

Gerrish, K., Husband, C. and MacKenzie, J. (1996) *Nursing for a Multi-ethnic Society*. Buckingham: Open University Press.

Joudrey, R. and Robson, K. (2010) 'Practising medicine in two countries: South African physicians in Canada', *Sociology of Health & Illness*, 32(4): 528–44.

Kalekin-Fishman, D. (1996) 'The impact of globalization on the determination and management of ethical choices in the health arena', *Social Science and Medicine*, 43(5): 809–22.

Katz, A.M. and Shotter, J. (1996) 'Hearing the patient's "voice": toward a social poetics in diagnostic interviews', *Social Science & Medicine*, 43(6): 919–31.

Kinfu, Y., Dal Poz, M.R., Mercer, H. and Evans, D.B. (2009) 'The health worker shortage in Africa: are enough physicians and nurses being trained?', *Bulletin of the World*

Health Organization, 87(3): 225–30. Available at: www.who.int/bulletin/volumes/87/3/08-051599.pdf

Kitzinger, J. and Williams, C. (2005) 'Forecasting science futures: legitimising hope and calming fears in the embryo stem cell debate', *Social Science & Medicine*, 61: 731–40.

Lehoux, P. (2008) 'The duality of health technology in chronic illness: how designers envision our future', *Chronic Illness*, 4: 85–97.

Leslie, C. (1985) 'What caused India's massive community health workers scheme: a sociology of knowledge', *Social Science & Medicine*, 21(8): 923–30.

Lewis, J.M. and Considine, M. (1999) 'Medicine, economics and agenda-setting', *Social Science & Medicine*, 48(3): 393–405.

Macintosh, M., Raghuram, P. and Henry, L. (2006) 'A perverse subsidy: African trained nurses and doctors in the NHS', *Soundings*, 34(9): 103–13.

Marmot, M., Allen, J. and Goldblatt, P. (2010) 'A social movement, based on evidence, to reduce inequalities in health', *Social Science & Medicine*, 71: 1254–8.

Martin, P., Brown, N. and Kraft, A. (2008) 'From bedside to bench? Communities of promise, translational research and the making of blood stem cells', *Science as Culture*, 17(1): 29–41.

Mesman, J. (2008) *Uncertainty in Medical Innovation: Experienced Pioneers in Neonatal Care*. Basingstoke: Palgrave.

Mol, A. (2000) 'What diagnostic devices do: the case of blood sugar measurement', *Theoretical Medical Bioethics*, 21: 9–22.

Morris, A. (2010) 'Motorbike boost to Zambia's health hopes', BBC World News, Zambia. Available at: http://news.bbc.co.uk/2/hi/business/8504921.stm

Mulacahy, L. (2003) *Disputing Doctors: The Socio-legal Dynamics of Complaints about Medical Care*. Maidenhead: Open University Press.

Mullan, F. (2005) 'The metrics of the physician brain drain', *New England Journal of Medicine*, 353: 1810–18.

Nettleton, S. (2007) 'Editorial: Retaining the sociology in medical sociology', *Social Science & Medicine*, 65: 2409–12.

Nettleton, S. and Burrows, R. (2003) 'E-scaped medicine? Information, reflexivity and health', *Critical Social Policy*, 23(2): 165–85.

Orfali, K. (2004) 'Parental role in medical decision-making: fact or fiction? A comparative study of ethical dilemmas in French and American neonatal intensive care units', *Social Science & Medicine*, 58: 2009–22.

Pearson, B. (2010) 'International health migration: landscape changes as ethical recruitment policies adopted', *Africa Health*, July: 24–6.

Pescosolido, B., McLeod, J. and Alegria, M. (2000) 'Confronting the second social contract: the place of medical sociology in research and policy for the 21st century', in C. Bird et al. (eds), *Handbook of Medical Sociology*. Englewood Cliffs, NJ: Prentice-Hall. pp. 411–26.

Radley, A. (2009) *Works of Illness: Narrative, Picturing and the Social Response to Serious Disease*. Ashby-de-la-Zouche: InkerMen Press.

Radley, A., Cheek, J. and Ritter, C. (2006) 'The making of health: a reflection on the first 10 years in the life of a journal', *Health*, 10: 389–400.

Raghuram, P. and Kofman, E. (2002) 'The state, skilled labour markets, and immigration: the case of doctors in England', *Environment and Planning A*, 34: 2071–89.

Raghuram, P., Bornat, J. and Henry, L. (2011) 'The co-marking of aged bodies and migrant bodies: migrant workers' contribution to geriatric medicine in the UK', *Sociology of Health and Illness*, 33(1): 321–35.

Rees Jones, I. (2003) 'Power, present and past: for a historical sociology of health and illness', *Social Theory & Health*, 1(2): 130–48.

Robb, N., Dunkley, L., Boynton, P. and Greenhalgh, T. (2007) 'Looking for a better future: identity construction in socio-economically deprived 16-year olds considering a career in medicine', *Social Science & Medicine*, 65(4): 738–54.

Sales, C.S. and Schlaff, A.L. (2010) 'Reforming medical education: a review and synthesis of five critiques of medical practice', *Social Science & Medicine*, 70: 1665–8.

Seale, C. (2008) 'Mapping the field of medical sociology: a comparative analysis of journals', *Sociology of Health & Illness*, 30(5): 677–95.

Shim, H., Lee, J.H., Hwang, S.O., Yoon H.R. and Yoon Y.R. (2009) 'Development of heart rate monitoring for mobile telemedicine using smartphone', *13th International Conference on Biomedical Engineering IFMBE Proceedings*, Volume 23, Track 3, 1116–19.

Stepanikova, I. (2006) 'Patient–physician racial and ethnic concordance and perceived medical errors', *Social Science & Medicine*, 63 (12): 3060–6.

Strong, P.M. (1979) 'Sociological imperialism and the profession of medicine: a critical examination of the thesis of medical imperialism', *Social Science & Medicine*, 13A: 199–215.

Taylor, D.H. and Esmail, A. (1999) 'Retrospective analysis of census data on general practitioners who qualified in South Asia: who will replace them as they retire?', *British Medical Journal*, 318(7179): 306–10.

Vilhjalmsson, R. (2005) 'Failure to seek needed medical care: results from a national health survey of Icelanders', *Social Science & Medicine*, 61: 1320–30.

VSO (2010) *Brain Gain: Making Health Worker Migration Work for Rich and Poor Countries. VSO briefing: The Perspective from Africa*. London: VSO. Available at: www.vso.org.uk/Images/Brain%20Gain%20Report_FINAL%20lores1_tcm79-28845.pdf

Urry, J. (2005) 'The complexity turn', *Theory, Culture and Society*, 22(5): 1–14.

Wailoo, K. (2001) *Dying in the City of the Blues: Sickle Cell Anemia and the Politics of Race and Health*. Chapel Hill, NC: University of North Carolina Press.

Wainwright, S.P., Williams, C., Michael, M., Farsides, B. and Cribb, A. (2006) 'From bench to bedside? Biomedical scientists' expectations of stem cell science as a future therapy for diabetes', *Social Science & Medicine*, 63: 2052–64.

Walby, S. (2009) *Globalization and Inequalities: Complexity and Contested Modernities*. London: Sage.

Weitz, R. (1999) 'Watching Brian die: the rhetoric and reality of informed consent', *Health*, 3: 209–27.

Williams, C., Alderson, P. and Farsides, B. (2002) 'Too many choices? Hospital and community staff reflect on the future of prenatal screening', *Social Science & Medicine*, 55: 743–53.

World Health Organization (WHO) (2006) *Working Together for Health: The World Health Report 2006*. Available at: www.who.int/whr/2006/whr06_en.pdf

World Health Organization (WHO) (2010) 'WHO Global Code of Practice on the international recruitment of health personnel', WHA63.16 Agenda item 11.5, Sixty-third World Health Assembly, 21 May. Available at: http://apps.who.int/gb/ebwha/pdf_files/WHA63/A63_R16-en.pdf

Wright, D., Flis, N. and Gupta, M. (2008) 'The "brain drain" of physicians: historical antecedents to an ethical debate, c. 1960–79', *Philosophy, Ethics, and Humanities in Medicine*, 3: 24. Available at: www.peh-med.com/content/3/1/24

GLOSSARY OF TERMS

Actor network theory – an analysis of relationships that are simultaneously conceptual and material which originated with Science and Technology Studies. The theory insists on the performed and contingent nature of social relations and has engendered controversy over the agency of non-human actors within networks.

Biomedicine – refers to scientifically informed medicine which employs chemistry, biology and physics to develop new diagnostic and therapeutic approaches to disease. Associated with a reductionist and individualizing approach that focuses on pathology and ignores the social context in which the ill person lives and thereby limits therapeutic possibilities.

Capitalism – an economic system associated with industrialized society, whereby the means of production is in private ownership and operated as a profit-making concern by manipulating wages and commodity prices. Karl Marx's critique of capitalism and those who have built on his work, remain central to sociological analyses of modernity.

Class system – a hierarchy of classes of the populace from the powerless and disenfranchised through to the powerful elite. A Marxist definition of class depends on a group's relationship to the means of production, whereas Weberian approaches emphasize differentials in status and prestige as well as wealth and income.

Corporatization – public services, including healthcare, are taken over by commercial corporations and organized to maximize profit, rather than following professional or humanitarian values.

Cultural capital – associated with Pierre Bourdieu's description of assets such as education and skills that are distinct from economic assets (wealth, income) and social assets deriving from networks of influence and support.

Cyborg – a being with organic and artificial (electronic or mechanical) components used as a metaphor for the reconfiguration of gender and ethnicity in late modernity and associated with Donna Harraway's description of humanity's altered status in a technologically sophisticated society.

Deprofessionalization – the loss of status and authority of professionals where a population's high levels of education and of access to information mean that knowledge is no longer restricted to a particular group, such as doctors.

Determinism – generally a doctrine that attributes the cause of events, including human behaviour, to external causes, rather than individual will. Sociologically, its use implies a social feature that is taken to be an inevitable corollary of a biological trait or economic character such that, for instance, all women are assumed to be caring and all poor people to be uneducable.

Disability – a physical, sensory, cognitive or developmental impairment that differentiates a person from the group norm and limits individual activities and/or social participation. Impairments do not necessarily amount to a disability since the latter is a social as well as an embodied process.

Discourse – a set of communicative activities, whether written, spoken, broadcast or enacted, that address a particular topic such as 'women's health problems' or 'migrants'.

Embodied – to be a reflective, spiritual being whose body takes part in the social and psychological processes involved with living in society, including negotiating health and illness.

Embodiment – the social and cultural processes by which we construct reality, which involve the interplay of both conceptual and bodily aspects.

Empiricism – a theory of knowledge in which observations from the natural world, and especially those derived from experiments, are seen as necessarily more valid and reliable than any other.

Enlightenment – a historical period where reason became valued as the main source of authority, over and above religion, custom or tradition. This rise of rationality and scientific reasoning paved the way for modernity and the industrial revolution.

Equality – a state of parity between two groups or classes of people on a measurable variable or observable trait.

Equity – parity between two groups or classes of people that reflects processes of fairness and social justice.

Essentialism – a view that certain specific traits are always associated with a particular class of people, independent of context.

Ethnicity – the characteristic commonality around which ethnic groups identify, usually composed of a common and specific culture often identified in terms of language, religion, marriage patterns and origins. Ethnicity is both a voluntaristic self-identification as well as a negotiation with what minority and majority groups permit.

Ethnic group – a group of people who identify as sharing a common ancestry and culture, often including a religion, and who identify with a common future. Ethnic identification may depend on a common language (or idealized language) or an ideal or actual homeland, and may involve an idea of biological as well as social reproduction.

Feminism – a practice and a theory that looks at how gendered inequality affects women's social and economic standing and seeks the means of promoting women's rights, opportunities and status. Liberal feminism seeks to promote women's participation in existing social and economic institutions whereas radical feminism seeks to reconfigure those institutions along feminist principles, variously defined.

GDP (Gross Domestic Product) – a macroeconomic measure that is a summation of the value of one country's production of goods and services over a limited period and used as an indicator of standard of living.

Gender – the social attribution of feminine and masculine qualities which may be justified by recourse to biological indicators of sex.

Globalization – international economic trade has increased the volume and rate of flows of commodities, information, investment, ideas, people and pathogens between formerly distinct national settings. Effects of this flow include a greater international connectedness (at least for some classes), a homogenization of culture and language, and, more controversially, an increased demand for democracy, and increased militarization.

Healthy migrant effect – a theory that only people with good health and vitality will volunteer for, and be able to withstand, the exigencies of migration; and therefore when they arrive in a new society, this section of the population should have better health on average than the local, non-migrant population.

Iatrogenesis – damage as a direct result of medical intervention intended to be therapeutic and that may occur to individual bodies or to social groups.

Identity – refers to a person's self-image in every-day language, whereas sociological usage implies the constraints that social attitudes and structures place on the identities an individual can claim. Identities around gender, sexuality, ethnicity, class and age are negotiated between the subjectivity of the individual and the range of what is bureaucratically and culturally permitted.

Impairment – a loss or absence of a bodily structure or function or psychological ability that would normally be expected to be present. The result of this loss or absence may be disabling. An impairment does not necessarily amount to a disability since the latter is a social as well as an embodied process.

Individualism – an ideology that values the individual as sovereign and emphasizes individual choice as the key locus for social action, thereby individualizing social problems and denying the possibility of collectivism and solidarity.

Inequality – an observed or measurable difference that exists between two groups or classes of people.

Inequity – a difference between two groups or classes of people that is unfair and unjust.

Informatization – the process whereby information technology and health informatics has infused service provision to the extent that these activities have been reconfigured to consist in the flow and exchange of digitized information.

Interactionism – a view of the self as a reflexive social product arising from inter-actions with, and responses from, others, largely mediated through language.

Marketization – formerly publically funded services are deregulated and replaced with commercial structures in pursuit of profit, as a means of reducing statutory costs and responsibilities.

Marxian – refers to a rather looser connection to Marxist models and is often used in contrast to Weberian (see below).

Marxist – the scholarship of Karl Marx himself, describing the class structure of capitalist society and the possibilities for revolutionary change to abolish class divisions, was developed by others during his own lifetime and over the subsequent 130 years. The term Marxist tends to indicate a view of society as structured in socio-economic terms with a commitment to the possibility of progressive change towards socialism.

Materialism – an analysis that places the material necessities of food, shelter and clothing, and the human activity around economic production to fulfil these needs, at the centre of the system of social relations. A materialist approach to health inequalities focuses on levels of income, standards of housing, schools, libraries and access to benefits before less tangible status-related aspects of social life, including relative poverty.

Medical dominance – the authority and autonomy of medicine, including its regulation of other occupations involved in healthcare provision, that together confer a status that extends beyond the institution of medicine.

Medicalization – a process whereby conditions formerly seen as non-medical (i.e. having social, economic or chance causes) come to be defined and treated as medical problems.

Modernity – a historical period that follows the enlightenment and accompanies industrialization and the process of rationalization and secularization, whereby the certainties of religion and custom are lost, to be replaced by ideology that tends to be oriented to the future rather than the past. Post-modernity or high modernity follow modernity and imply a rise of uncertainty and an assertion that any truth serves a vested interest. The idea of multiple or alternative modernities sidesteps the ethnocentricity of the global North as offering the only model for socio-economic development.

Morbidity rate – a measurement of the occurrence of symptoms or disease in a population over a fixed period of time.

Mortality rate – a measurement of the occurrence of death in a population, usually expressed as a standardized mortality rate or SMR that sums the number of deaths per 1,000 population, standardized for age.

Naturalist essentialism – the view that certain specific traits are always associated with a particular class of people, independent of context, and that also depends on an idea of naturally occurring characteristics with a timeless, universal, unalterable quality.

Phenomenology – the experiential construction of meaning through the routine negotiation and resistance that constitutes interaction and speech.

Positivism – a belief that only knowledge affirmed through scientific methods is credible and authentic.

Poverty – in the absolute sense, poverty implies a lack of basic human needs such as food, shelter, education and clothing. In a stratified society, the people with fewest resources live in relative poverty, even if their basic needs are met.

Power – the capacity to effect one's will which may be individually or collectively organized and exercised, and derives from economic, political and social resources and influence.

Proletarianization – a proposed effect of capitalist expansion whereby all workers, regardless of their professional status, are eventually stripped of their autonomy and lose control over their conditions of work to become proletarian.

Racism – prejudiced beliefs, attitudes and behaviour about people who are differentiated from oneself in essentialist ethnic or cultural terms.

Reductionism – a means of understanding a complex system, such as a human body or a society, by reducing it to smaller constituent parts and ignoring interactions between the constituent parts.

Reflexivity – a means of gaining some perspective on our and others' subjectivity by considering values and beliefs alongside our assessments and analysis in an effort to offer a full account from a particular point of view without claiming neutral or superior status for that knowledge.

Sexuality – sexual desires and practices are understood to be socially constructed, in terms of their relationship with gender, age, queerness or straightness. Medicine has played an important role in determining deviant sexuality and its governance.

Social capital – associated with Pierre Bourdieu's description of the assets deriving from networks of influence and support and distinct from cultural capital (education and skills) and economic assets (wealth, income).

Social cohesion – the extent to which a social group is mutually and reciprocally supportive in their economic, political and social relationships.

Social constructionism – normalized knowledge or practice can be understood as a result of the particular power relations pertaining in that historical and social context such that there is no 'neutral knowledge' since every representation of the way the world works serves some party's interests.

Social stratification – the hierarchy of classes, defined by social and economic indicators, that runs from the lower class that is least privileged and least powerful to the upper class or elite that enjoys most privilege and exercises most power.

Sociodicy – the existential meaning and ethical implications of human affliction and suffering as part of social life.

Socio-economic class – a description of the systematic hierarchy of strata in society that uses both social and economic indicators of status.

Structural functionalism – a theory that society operates as a stable and cohesive system due to norms, customs, traditions and institutions playing their constituent parts.

Subjectivity – in opposition to objectivity, subjectivity refers to people's way of thinking and being that includes beliefs and values as well as the effects of social and demographic characteristics. An assessment of another group or person inevitably includes the effects of our own beliefs and values.

Theodicy – the existential meaning and ethical implications of human affliction and suffering in religious thought and particularly the question of how human suffering affects our view of God.

Weberian – relating to Max Weber's theories and, in particular, the way that his work on social status modified Marxist theories which emphasize economic social structures.

INDEX

Lightning Source UK Ltd.
Milton Keynes UK
UKHW01f1049221018
330972UK00003B/394/P

Bradby offers insightful analysis as well as synthesis in areas such as inequalities, gender and ethnicity, where she is a leading expert. Throughout the book, Bradby's command of her material is impressive, and expressed in an approachable and lively style. Highly commended – a key work for all students of medical sociology.

Mike Bury, Professor Emeritus of Royal Holloway College

Sharp, bold and engaging, this book provides a contemporary account of why medicine and health matters in our modern society.

Combining theoretical and empirical perspectives, and applying the pragmatic demands of policy, the book explores society's response to key issues such as race, gender and identity to explain the relationship between sociology, medicine and medical sociology.

Each chapter includes an authoritative introduction to pertinent areas of debate, a clear summary of key issues and themes and dedicated bibliography.

Chapters include:
• Social theory and medical sociology
• Health inequalities
• Bodies, pain and suffering
• Personal, local and global

Brimming with fresh interpretations and critical insights this book will contribute to illuminating the practical realities of medical sociology.

This exciting text will be of interest to students of sociology of health and illness, medical sociology, and sociology of the body.

Hannah Bradby has a visiting fellowship at the Department of Primary Care and Health Sciences, King's College London. She is monograph series editor for the journal *Sociology of Health and Illness* and co-edits the multi-disciplinary journal *Ethnicity and Health*.

Cover image from iStockphoto

www.sagepublications.com
Los Angeles • London • New Delhi • Singapore • Washington DC

ISBN-13: 978-1-4129-2074-2